P9-DVF-945

Justice

OLIVER
WENDELL
HOLMES

&

Utilitarian Jurisprudence

Justice

OLIVER
WENDELL
HOLMES

&

Utilitarian Jurisprudence

H. L. Pohlman

Harvard University Press
Cambridge, Massachusetts, and London, England
1984

Copyright © 1984 by the President and Fellows of Harvard College
All rights reserved
Printed in the United States of America
10 9 8 7 6 5 4 3 2 1

Publication of this book has been aided by a grant from the Andrew W. Mellon
Foundation.

This book is printed on acid-free paper, and its binding materials have been chosen
for strength and durability.

Library of Congress Cataloging in Publication Data
Pohlman, H. L., 1952–
   Justice Oliver Wendell Holmes and utilitarian jurisprudence.

   Bibliography: p.
   Includes index.
   1. Holmes, Oliver Wendell, 1841–1935. 2. Juris-
prudence. I. Title.
KF8745.H6P63   1984   347.73′2634 [B]   84-6570
                         347.3073534 [B]
ISBN 0-674-49615-9 (lib. bdg. : alk. paper)

To my mother, Agnes Pohlman,
and in memory of my father, Otto Pohlman

ACKNOWLEDGMENTS

I am glad of this opportunity to thank the teachers who have done so much for me and the schools I attended. During my undergraduate years at the University of Dayton, I was fortunate to have studied under W. K. Howard, Gerald Kerns, John Quinn, and David Ritchards. They introduced me to the intellectual world and were largely responsible for my choice of an academic career and for my pursuit of specific interests in analytical philosophy and political-legal theory. Columbia University generously gave me a President's Fellowship and later a Preceptorship. My teachers at Columbia have helped me immeasurably. Herbert Deane and Julian Franklin have read and criticized my academic work for the last ten years and their comments have saved me from many mistakes. More generally, Deane and Franklin taught me the significance of history and gave me, through conversation and their own writings, a sense of the standards of the profession. I would also like to thank Kent Greenawalt of Columbia Law School. The discussions we had concerning criminal responsibility and the nature of a legal system were very helpful. And I especially want to thank my friend Robert Amdur for all his advice and encouragement over the years. His patience with an academic novice and his friendly interest are warmly appreciated.

For the typing that has gone into this study, I wish to thank Victoria Kuhn, the irreplaceable secretary of the Political Science Department at Dickinson College, who helped finish the final manuscript. But my wife deserves special recognition. Patricia (always with a smile) has not only, until very recently, edited and typed everything that I have written, but she has also financed much of my education. Without her help, I would never have finished this book.

H. L. Pohlman
Dickinson College

CONTENTS

IV

JUDICIAL IDENTIFICATION, INTERPRETATION, AND LEGISLATION

V

REALITY, IDEAS, AND LANGUAGE

VI

CONCLUSIONS AND COMMENTARY

NOTES

PRIMARY SOURCES

INDEX

Justice

OLIVER
WENDELL
HOLMES

Utilitarian Jurisprudence

I

THE PROBLEM WITH HOLMESIAN SCHOLARSHIP

The legal philosophy of Mr. Justice Holmes has often and not inaccurately been described as the foundation of the school of legal realism that once flourished in American jurisprudence. Moreover, though legal realists have been especially vocal, many twentieth-century legal commentators have proclaimed themselves followers of Holmes and appeal to his authority to resolve contemporary issues of legal philosophy. Indeed, intellectual battles have raged for his *imprimatur*. Though the apotheosis of this "Yankee from Olympus" is at first puzzling, familiarity with the content and style of Holmes's legal writings renders the phenomenon understandable, if not entirely admirable. Its effect upon our understanding of Holmes's legal ideas, however, has been very unfortunate. The preeminence of his position in American jurisprudence has encouraged polemical distortions of his legal philosophy and a biographical attitude too appreciative of its subject matter. These cycles of intellectual anachronisms, panegyrics, and condemnations have produced a strained, inadequate appreciation of the subtlety, complexity, and unity of Holmes's legal philosophy. By treating Holmes's ideas primarily as answers to questions that currently perplex us, twentieth-century reviewers have oversimplified his thoughts, reducing them to a bundle of aphorisms that can be easily distorted and thereby even more easily condemned or extolled.[1]

However, not all reviewers have ignored Holmes's intellectual antecedents. For example, Mark DeWolfe Howe has certainly considered Holmes's intellectual predecessors. On the one hand,

1

Howe claimed that "there can be no doubt" that Sir Henry Maine's book *Ancient Law* "was a major influence in guiding Holmes's inquiries into the history of the common law."

Surely it was not mere coincidence that Maine's chapters on Delict and Crime, Contracts, Property, and Succession in the ancient law of Rome were matched by Holmes's lecture on Tort, Crime, Contracts, Possession, and Succession in the common law of England. It would not, I think, be a great exaggeration to say that Holmes borrowed from Maine the spectacles which the Englishman had used for observing the law of ancient Rome and looked through them at the common law of England.[2]

However, after making this rather abstract claim about Holmes's debt to Maine, Howe failed to describe any specific similarities. Indeed, when he turned to the specific doctrines of Holmes's jurisprudence, Howe argued that Holmes's definition of the law as "the prophecies of what the courts will do in fact," his view of duty as "involving something more than a tax on conduct," and his understanding of liability "as not requiring moral fault" were all consciously formulated by Holmes in opposition to the ideas of John Austin.[3] Howe went on to speculate that Holmes became interested in history to expose Austin's theory of legal liability as a historical anomaly.[4] Consequently, he seems to have believed that Holmes's legal philosophy is best understood by noting the ways in which it departed from (not the ways in which it coincided with) earlier traditions of thought, especially utilitarian jurisprudence. Maine's influence in fact plays a negligible role in Howe's elucidation of Holmes's ideas.

Morton White reached similar conclusions. In his book on American social thought, White groups Holmes with John Dewey, Charles A. Beard, James Harvey Robinson, and Thorstein Veblen.[5] These prominent American intellectuals (White informs us) were in "revolt against formalism." They opposed their predecessors and initiated an intellectual revolution; in their respective fields, these theorists refined a peculiarly American outlook that later flowered into pragmatism. Holmes was thus not significantly indebted to utilitarian jurisprudence or to any other tradition of thought. He was an intellectual rebel, a founder of a scientific school of legal philosophy that evolved into pragmatic legal realism.[6] Indebted to no one, his legal philosophy is therefore not explicable upon utilitarian grounds.

More recently, Martin P. Golding has briefly but insightfully analyzed certain traditions of thought to which Holmes responded.[7] They were the Austinian tradition of analytical jurisprudence, the Kantian and Hegelian-inspired continental jurisprudence, and C. C. Langdell's conception of legal development. In reaction to the first, Holmes fashioned his definitions of law and duty; against the second, he constructed his external and objective theory of legal liability; and against the third, he formulated his policy-oriented theory of judicial decision-making. But in each case, no important similarities between Holmes's legal philosophy and those of his predecessors or contemporaries are mentioned or examined. Though Golding occasionally hints that Holmes's conclusions may not have been altogether un-Austinian,[8] his entire approach again encourages us to understand Holmes's legal philosophy by its distinctiveness, by noting how different it was from previous theories. Thus, Holmes reacted against, but was not indebted to, utilitarian analytical jurisprudence.

This is the predominant theme of Holmesian literature:[9] Holmes's legal philosophy was so innovative and unique that little is gained by examining its historical origins. Not only the anachronistic expositions of Holmes's legal theory and the appreciative biographies, but also studies that purport to describe Holmes's intellectual context or antecedents express this point of view. If the traditions of thought are considered at all, they are considered only as foils for Holmes's critical theories. The purpose of this book is to qualify, if not correct, this narrow attitude. The assumption is that the necessary though missing ingredient in our understanding of Holmes's legal philosophy is an appreciation for the historical traditions to which he was indebted. Only when we place Holmes in the right century, only when we understand his legal philosophy as a product of nineteenth-century traditions of thought, will we avoid the problems of anachronisms, eulogies, and obloquies. I hope to show the advantages of a historical approach to Holmes's legal theory, and if I am successful, the end result will be a better sense of the subtlety, complexity, and unity of Holmes's jurisprudence.

Of course it is impossible to consider thoroughly every tradition to which Holmes was possibly indebted. Space alone justifies limiting the inquiry to one tradition of thought. But the choice of the analytical school of English utilitarianism may seem paradoxical, in view of Mark DeWolfe Howe's suggestion that Sir Henry

Maine and the English and German historical schools of jurisprudence are more plausible sources of Holmes's ideas. However, the obvious here is not true. First, Holmes understood Maine as a *vulgarisateur* of German legal philosophy, detested his unquestioning admiration of the Roman law, and doubted that he would leave much of a mark on jurisprudence.[10] Consequently, though no doubt Holmes adhered to a historical method, it was not to Maine's. Furthermore, Holmes's historical orientation does not explain the important substantive doctrines of his jurisprudence. It cannot explain Holmes's external theory of legal responsibility, his definitions of sovereignty, law, and duty, or his policy-oriented theory of judicial decision-making by the fact that Holmes was a historian. No doubt Holmes's relationship to the historical school of jurisprudence, especially to the more original German branch,[11] is a worthwhile subject. But the essentials of Holmes's substantive jurisprudence must be derived from other traditions of thought. I believe that we will more clearly understand these essentials only by uncovering Holmes's relationship to the analytical utilitarian school. My thesis is that the central core of Holmes's substantive jurisprudence and philosophical methodology arose from the premises of utilitarian legal philosophy.

Moreover, the utilitarian analytical school of jurisprudence deserves consideration in any exploration of the historical origins of Holmes's legal philosophy because of its status in the nineteenth century. It was the orthodoxy of its day. Though it came under heavy fire late in the century, during the 1860s few questioned its validity. In spite of a few Savigny-inspired objections that Maine made, utilitarian jurisprudence reigned supreme well into the 1870s, even in America. John Chipman Gray has claimed that Anglo-American jurists were busy formulating Austinian analytical classifications of law up until Maine's publication of *Early History of Institutions* in 1874.[12] Holmes, who received his legal education during the 1860s, was immersed in this intellectual milieu. His first article, "Codes, and the Arrangement of the Law,"[13] expressed these Austinian assumptions and goals; he sketched an analytical classification of the common law based upon duties. Consequently, it seems probable that Holmes breathed more Austinian air than even he realized. Of course Holmes considered himself a critic of Austin and Bentham. But we cannot grant Holmes the privilege of writing his own intellectual biography. As he himself has admitted, history shows us to what degree the past

4

rules over the present despite ourselves.[14] I believe this same historical assumption holds with Holmes's legal philosophy. To understand his ideas completely, we must examine to what degree utilitarian ways of thought seeped into Holmes's jurisprudence without his acknowledgment.

But Holmes was not so antagonistic to the utilitarian jurists as the above might suggest. He credited them with insights deserving study and attention. "One of the courses to be pursued is the anatomy of legal ideas worked out by the English school of jurisprudence; another is the embryology of the same conceptions to be found in history as the Germans have taught it to the world."[15] Holmes admitted that this historical work required a working knowledge of Roman law to explain "the origin and anomalies of our own system. But for the philosophy of law," he insisted, "the 'Fragment on Government' and Austin's lecture are worth the whole *corpus*"[16] of Roman law. Consequently, a scholar or a historian needed to study Roman law thoroughly, but not a practitioner. For his more practical needs, Holmes thought that "a young man who has understood John Austin's tedious and often mistaken book has taken a real step forward."[17] I hold that the attitudes expressed in these quotes symbolize Holmes's actual relationship to the utilitarian jurists. Holmes certainly neither accepted every conclusion of the utilitarian school nor derived every one of his doctrines from a utilitarian source. However, one need not prove that the utilitarians were always right or that Holmes was unoriginal to show his debt to utilitarian jurisprudence. The issue is not black or white, but gray. Of course the precise shade of gray is the question at hand. I believe that the number and significance of the similarities between Holmes's legal philosophy and the utilitarians' will justify my approach; we shall understand more deeply the core of Holmes's thought by noting its historical relationship to utilitarian jurisprudence.

Perhaps a couple of examples will indicate in what sense Holmes was indebted to his utilitarian predecessors. The standard view is that the historically oriented Holmes opposed codification and criticized utilitarian jurists upon this ground.[18] But is it not anomalous that Holmes throughout his life admired a philosophically arranged *corpus* of law?

We are inclined to believe that the most considerable advantage which might be reaped from a code is this: that being executed at the expense of government and not at the risk of the writer, and the whole work being under the control of one head, it will make a philosophically arranged *corpus juris* possible ... The importance of it [the code], if it could be obtained, cannot be overrated ... A well-arranged body of the law would not only train the mind of the student to a sound legal habit of thought, but would remove obstacles from his path which he now only overcomes after years of experience and reflection.[19]

Moreover, this ideal of a philosophically arranged system of law was not a childish infatuation that Holmes quickly outgrew. In Holmes's view, the chief end of man was to generalize.[20] When he was sixty years old and a mature judge reflecting upon the thousand cases that he had decided, Holmes regretted the incomplete nature of his work.

A thousand cases, when one would have liked to study to the bottom and to say his say on every question which the law ever has presented, and then to go on and invent new problems which should be the test of doctrine, and then to generalize it all and write it in continuous, logical, philosophic exposition, setting forth the whole *corpus* with its roots in history and its justifications of expedience real or supposed.[21]

According to Holmes, jurisprudence meant "simply the broadest generalization of the principles and the deepest analysis of the ideas at the bottom of an actual system."[22] He offered his objective and external theory of legal liability as an example of such jurisprudence. It generalized and set forth the necessary and sufficient conditions of legal liability in all areas of the common law. Likewise, Holmes approvingly quoted T. E. Holland's opinion that the "old-fashioned English lawyer's idea of a satisfactory body of law was a chaos with a full index."[23] Clearly, Holmes accepted the utilitarian ideal of a philosophically arranged body of law.

But what then was Holmes's objection to a code? Since it reduced the legal chaos to a logical order, it would seem that his principles would lead him to support codification. However, Holmes distinguished a philosophic exposition of the law from a code.

The periodical codification of statutes is now a matter of course in the United States, but to codify the law eliminated from judicial decisions seems to us far from equally desirable. We go so far as to say that the very qualities of certainty and accuracy, which are the reputed advantages of a code, are those in which it would prove inferior to the materials used in its construction. The best draughtsman that ever lived can

6

feel a ground of decision more accurately than he can state it. Suppose he succeeds in stating a rule that would have sufficed for the correct decision of all past cases, it is in the highest degree probable that some future case will require some more refined discrimination not allowed by the words of the code. Yet, if the code is law, the wrong decision must be given; for the moment the judges are allowed to look at the decisions from which the code rule was made up, and to construe it in any way consistent with them, or otherwise than according to the literal significance of the words, the code ceases to be law, what ever it may be called . . . For, we repeat, that if more than that is allowed, the code is nothing but a text-book.[24]

This quote indicates the *verbal* nature of Holmes's objection to Austin's plan of codification. Though he opposed codification "eliminated from judicial decisions," he supported codification in conjunction with judicial decisions. Though Bentham's position was more extreme, Austin also never believed that a code should be made independent of judicial decisions, or that judges should be prohibited from referring back to previous decisions, or that judges should not supplement the code with judicial legislation. Holmes himself saw that his basic objection to codes "might be obviated by a law commission, with authority somewhat similar to that attributed by Austin to the Prussian. Then, if the courts should find themselves required by the letter of the code to decide a case contrary to principle, the letter might be at once amended so as to express the principle more accurately thereafter."[25] The easiest solution was to give courts the power to correct the code.[26] Holmes concluded that if the court was "at liberty to decide *ex ratione legis,*—that is if it may take into account that the code is only intended to declare the judicial rule, and has done so defectively, and may then go on and supply the defect,—the code is not law, but a mere text-book recommended by the government."[27] But whether it was called a code or a textbook, Austin and Holmes supported an official philosophical exposition of the law. According to both, its importance could not be overrated. Their only objection was to a code that prevented the common law from developing in its traditional manner of "successive approximations."[28] Therefore, Austin and Holmes not only permitted codes that still allowed judicial legislation, but strongly encouraged them.

However, the apparent differences between Holmes's ideas and the utilitarians' are not all so easily dismissed. But some of these

7

are differences outside our topic of jurisprudence and therefore have little significance. For example, Holmes dismissed as a fiction the view that the standard of utility was an objective moral principle. On the other hand, Holmes admired the classical utilitarian economists, especially "St. Malthus," who (in Holmes's opinion) had destroyed many a "humbug."[29] But our topic is confined to legal philosophy; how did Holmes's legal ideas resemble or diverge from those of the utilitarians? From this perspective, two important differences were Holmes's distrust of "universal jurisprudence" and Austin's talk of legal rights, especially his distinction between "primary" and "sanctioning" rights.

Sir James Stephen is not the only writer whose attempts to analyze legal ideas have been confused by striving for a useless quintessence of all systems, instead of an accurate anatomy of one. The trouble with Austin was that he did not know enough English law. But still it is a practical advantage to master Austin, and his predecessors, Hobbes and Bentham.[30]

Holmes doubted whether legal concepts were necessarily found in all legal systems. Hence, notwithstanding the practical usefulness of his writings, Holmes believed that Austin's fundamental goal was illusory. Austin's concept of right and his distinction between "primary" and "sanctioning" rights are examples of ideas that he believed could be found in every modern legal system. A sanctioning right was a right to initiate sanctions against a person who had violated a more basic primary right.[31] For example, upon a favorable judgment, a landlord has a right to a public eviction of a tenant who had violated his lease. But Holmes had become "less and less inclined to make much use of the distinction between primary rights duties and consequences or sanctioning rights . . . The primary duty is little more than a convenient index to, or mode of predicting the point of incidence of the public force."[32] Holmes's reason for his disdain for Austin's distinction was that he had become dissatisfied with the term "legal right" in general. He wanted to replace all of Austin's talk of rights with the concept of prophecy: "But for legal purposes a right is only the hypostasis of a prophecy—the imagination of a substance supporting the fact that the public force will be brought to bear upon those who do things said to contravene it—just as we talk of the force of gravitation accounting for the conduct of bodies in space."[33] Any kind of right was "merely the hypostasis of the prophesied fact and an empty phrase. So we get up the empty substratum, a *right,* to pretend to account for the fact that the courts will act in a certain way."[34] But Holmes had no use for empty phrases or fictional explanations. Consequently, far from thinking it a necessary legal concept, Holmes advised throwing the term "right" out of the law.[35] Indeed, Holmes preferred to eliminate all "morally tainted words" because they "have caused a great deal of confused thinking."[36] The philosophy of law could not only eliminate the distinction between sanctioning and primary rights, but also abandon all talk of rights with no loss to clear thinking. Indeed, Holmes thought it would help.

These Holmesian criticisms of Austin express indisputably serious differences of opinion. There are also other small disagreements between Holmes and the utilitarians, some of which will be noted along the way, others ignored. But the fact that Holmes's ideas at times diverged from the utilitarians does not end the matter; it is necessary to compare the differences to any similarities of method and substance that may exist, at least if we wish to arrive at a balanced judgment of Holmes's debt to utilitarian jurisprudence. The areas under scrutiny will include Holmes's theory of legal liability, his conception of a legal system and theory of legal obligation, and his theory of judicial decision-making. I believe that together these form the core of Holmes's legal philosophy and that they are best understood as refinements of utilitarian jurisprudence.

Since so many commentators have written so much on Holmes's jurisprudence already, it seems hard to justify yet another study. Nevertheless, I hold to my conviction that an exploration of Holmes's legal philosophy from a historical perspective will improve our understanding of Holmes's thought. In the last chapter I explain the value of my approach by criticizing the major alternative interpretations of Holmes's legal philosophy. However, there is another important reason for taking a fresh look at Holmes. Contemporary legal philosophy is increasingly becoming more academic, abstract, and prescriptive. As expounded by today's jurists, our concepts of law, a legal system, and legal obligation have less and less to do with the actual practices of courtrooms and states and ever more to do with the arcane inclinations of academics. The result is dogmatic definitions incompatible with the way we ordinarily think and talk. In a similar way, academics have not only fashioned impractical pre-scriptive theories of judicial decision-making that have little or no bearing upon how judges in fact decide cases; they have also taken it upon themselves to advise judges how they morally ought to decide future cases. For those who are dissatisfied with these characteristics of contemporary legal philosophy, Holmes's ideas (properly understood) provide a meaningful alternative.

II

UTILITY, MORALITY, AND LIABILITY

A few of the similarities between Holmes's legal philosophy and the utilitarians' might seem too general to substantiate any significant conclusions about the affinity of Holmes's ideas with utilitarian jurisprudence. For example, their agreement that the purpose of a legal order was utility and that law was best kept distinct from morality could be viewed either as coincidence or as commonplace. And in either case (the argument would continue), strong conclusions could not rest upon such vague premises. However, if it were found that both Holmes and the utilitarians used these general ideas concerning utility, morality, and law to establish specific and controversial conclusions, then we should see the entire matter in a different light. I shall argue that the external and general theory of legal liability shared by the utilitarians and Holmes gives their agreement about the purpose of the legal order and about the proper relationship between law and morality added significance; they are the premises from which Holmes and the utilitarians derived their specific and controversial theories of legal liability. Hence one should not ignore these general affinities between Holmes and the utilitarians concerning the purpose of the legal order and the proper relationship between law and morality, since they function as the foundation for their respective theories of legal liability.

For the utilitarians, a legal order or an individual law was justifiable only if it increased the amount of pleasure over pain that the members of a society experienced.[1] Though Holmes's views are somewhat less explicit than this principle, a common point of view is still discernible. His well-known distaste for those who conceived the development of law as "a theological working out of dogma" or as "a logical development as in mathematics" rested upon convictions about the utilitarian purpose of law. He condemned blind imitation of the legal past. A "body of law is more rational and more civilized when every rule that it contains is referred articulately and definitely to an end which it subserves."[2] Consequently, he preferred to traditional practice "a time when the part played by history in the explanation of [legal] dogma shall be very small, and instead of ingenious research we shall spend our energy on a study of the ends sought to be attained." For this reason, Holmes encouraged lawyers to study economics; in the future lawyers will be "called on to consider and weigh the ends of legislation, the means of attaining them, and the cost. We learn that for everything we have we give up something else, and we are taught to set the advantage we gain against the other advantage we lose, and to know what we are doing when we elect."[3]

Holmes's commitment to general utility as the purpose of law is obvious also in the way he evaluated different legal policies. The familiar questions concerning interpersonal comparisons of value were at issue: how does one compare the satisfactions of individuals having different sensibilities, different types of desire, or desires in varying degrees of intensity? Both the utilitarians and Holmes responded that science, the substitution of quantitative amounts for qualitative distinctions, was the answer. Bentham's criteria for this scientific reduction of normative propositions to factual quantitative ones are well known. Each person was to count as one, and each of the individual's pleasures was measured by its intensity, duration, certainty, propinquity, fecundity, purity, and extent.[4] Armed with this scientific set of criteria, a legislator evaluated policies quantitatively. A policy was preferable to the degree to which it exceeded another in the "lots" of pleasure over pain it created.

Many doubted the practicality of this utilitarian legislative ideal; Holmes was among them.

In the law we only occasionally can reach an absolutely final and quantitative determination, because the worth of the competing social ends which respectively solicit a judgment for the plaintiff or the defendant cannot be reduced to number and accurately fixed. The worth, that is, the intensity of the competing desires, varies with the varying ideals of the time, and, if the desires were constant, we could not get beyond a relative decision that one was greater and one was less. But it is the essence of improvement that we should be as accurate as we can.[5]

This healthy skepticism about the feasibility of exact scientific measurement of human desires does not detract from Holmes's endorsement of it as an ideal. However, though we should use science to be "as accurate as we can," Holmes thought the sciences of logic and mathematics were inappropriate; they were not suited to measure the utilitarian end of law. The "true science of law" consisted "in the establishment of its postulates from within upon accurately measured social desires instead of tradition."[6] Holmes's science of law dealt primarily with the quantification of desire; his conception of the purpose of law was correspondingly utilitarian.

Of course the utilitarians used the same standard and method in moral issues.[7] They believed in an objective, scientifically measured system of utilitarian morality. This Holmes could not accept. In his opinion, all moral theories from pacifism to the warrior's code of honor were ultimately reducible to the same status, to the same level of human preferences formed by the early association of ideas. There were no objective permanent moral rules. As the mere de facto products of association, these moral preferences were ultimately arbitrary, even if fervently held.

Deep-seated preferences can not be argued about—you can not argue a man into liking a glass of beer—and therefore, when differences are sufficiently far reaching, we try to kill the other man rather than let him have his way. But that is perfectly consistent with admitting that, so far as appears, his grounds are just as good as ours.[8]

But even if Holmes reduced morality to contingent human preferences, he never denied the existence either of common preferences or of common moral rules. He agreed with the utilitarians that certain moral rules were beneficial and others necessary for the very existence of society.[9]

Yet there is a basic difference between Holmes's view of morality and the utilitarians'. Holmes described the validity of moral rules as contingent upon the desire of men to live in society; the utilitarians thought them obligatory no matter the desires of the individuals involved. The utilitarians never questioned the moral validity of the principle of utility itself. The obligation to establish the "greatest happiness of the greatest number" was to them not conditional; it was to Holmes. Perhaps social integration and interdependence, as some of the utilitarians thought,[10] would eventually lead to the growth of an extensive human sympathy. People would then love others more than themselves; they would sacrifice their self-interest for the greatest happiness of the greatest number. Holmes doubted this scenario because a dog will "fight for his bone."[11] But whatever the future might bring, Holmes thought the moral obligation to obey the dictates of utility would not arise until after this natural sympathy had developed. The obligatory character of utility was contingent upon our natural inclinations, and morality's function was not to shape fundamentally or to suppress these inclinations, but to satisfy them in an acceptable or appealing manner.

The significance of this difference between Holmes and the utilitarians concerning the nature of morality is not overly great. In drawing parallels between the respective *legal* theories of Holmes and the utilitarians, we should assess the importance of any disagreement about moral theory by its bearing upon legal philosophy. In this context, their respective views of morality did influence how Holmes and the utilitarians separated law from morality. Since the utilitarians used the same standard for both law and morality, the content of their ideal system of law was included within their ideal system of morality, much as a smaller circle can be placed within a larger one. All legal infractions were necessarily immoral acts or omissions. But since it was not beneficial for the state to punish all violations of moral rules, the converse was not true. There were a great many moral rules, those within the larger but not the smaller circle, whose violation would not imply illegal acts.[12] Hence, the distinction drawn by the utilitarians between law and morals as they ought to be was not as sharp as the one made by Holmes.

Since he had no objective standard of morality, Holmes did not believe in a necessary relationship between ideal systems of law and morality. Of course Holmes never doubted that in every society, whether past, present, or future, moral considerations had or would have a great impact upon law. Indeed, he conceived the law as "the witness and external deposit of our moral life. Its history [was] . . . the history of the moral development of the race."[13] Therefore, in his denial of any necessary relationship between law and morality, Holmes's point was a small one. It was not that morality never affected law, for it often did so. But its status never rose above opinion, and how it coincided with an ideal system of law was never more than a matter of contingent fact.

Furthermore, Holmes was intellectually not much interested in ideal systems of law, in morality, or in their possible interrelationships. His interests centered upon positive law, which lessens further the significance of his dispute with the utilitarians' opinion about morality.[14] Here Holmes followed his utilitarian predecessors' footsteps closely, especially in regard to legal education. Both Bentham and Austin insisted that legal education required the strict separation of law from related sciences of legislation, positive morality, and deontology.[15] Holmes agreed wholeheartedly.

When I emphasize the difference between law and morals I do so with a single end, that of learning and understanding the law . . . But I do say that that distinction is of the first importance for the object which we are here to consider—a right study and mastery of the law as a business with well understood limits, a body of dogma enclosed within definite lines.[16]

Holmes's peculiar method of separating law from morality was to look upon law as a "bad man." "If you want to know the law and nothing else, you must look at it as a bad man, who cares only for the material consequences which such knowledge enables him to predict."[17] Holmes conceived the law as equivalent to these material consequences that one's actions brought down upon one's self or others. Since "a bad man has as much reason as a good one for wishing to avoid an encounter with the public force,"[18] the educational purpose of Holmes's bad-man theory of law becomes clear. A theoretical refinement of a utilitarian method for a utilitarian end, the bad-man theory of law was meant to improve legal education by the strict separation of positive law from morality. Here again of course no moral cynicism was implied. Both Holmes and the utilitarians had a deep appreciation for the influence that normative theories have had upon the law, even if they believed that a student's interests were best served by separating positive law from what it might become.

Law and morality were also sharply distinguished for another reason. As Holmes understood it, morality dealt "with the actual internal state of the individual's mind";[19] the law dealt with the individual's external acts. The utilitarians also restricted law to external activity. Since the law's purpose was utility, they limited

15

its field of operation to those acts that were dangerous, acts that reduced pleasure or produced pain. These were external acts.[20] Punishment for an internal act was thought an unjustifiable infliction of pain. Holmes agreed:

All law is directed to conditions of things manifest to the senses. And whether it brings those conditions to pass immediately by the use of force, as when it protects a house from a mob by soldiers, or appropriates private property to public use, or hangs a man in pursuance of a judicial sentence, or whether it brings them about mediately though men's fears, its object is equally an external result.[21]

By adding a generally efficacious motive, the threat of corporal punishment, the law aimed only at an external result.

But there was more than one sufficient reason why the law refused either to shape or to examine man's internal life. In the opinions of Holmes and the utilitarians, it was simply beyond man's abilities; it was not only inappropriate, but also impossible.

The law takes no account of the infinite varieties of temperament, intellect, and education which make the internal character of a given act so different in different men. It does not attempt to see men as God sees them, for more than one sufficient reason. It might be said that the investigation and just appreciation of the actual facts is beyond the power of a human tribunal, with far more truth than in accounting, as many have done, for the presumption that every man knows the law.[22]

Therefore, both for reasons of utility and man's incapacity, the law dealt only with external action. If it were to attempt more by punishing internal acts or omissions, the law would wander into an impossible and inappropriate field, and area beyond man's abilities and the purpose of a legal order.

Despite its innocuous appearance, this conclusion had radical theoretical consequences. The external utilitarian purpose of law and the strict separation of law from morality were thought to necessitate a distinctive theory of legal liability. Holmes and the utilitarians logically related principles of punishment to standards of legal liability.[23] For example, if the motive of punishment was vengeance (as it was in primitive societies according to Holmes), then punishment was "limited to the scope of vengeance. Vengeance imports a feeling of blame, and an opinion, however distorted by passion, that a wrong has been done. It can hardly go very far beyond the case of a harm intentionally inflicted: [for] even a dog distinguishes between being stumbled over and being kicked."[24] Holmes accepted this controversial opinion that primitive man's legal liability was limited to harmful acts committed with evil intentions, because he accepted the utilitarian connection between punishment and responsibility.[25]

Parallel reasoning is found in Holmes's analysis of modern legal liability, except that the external utilitarian purpose of punishment required drawing the line of legal liability elsewhere than at intentional acts. Even if certain primitive rules of law survived anomalously into the contemporary period, the general tendency of modern law favored a theory of legal liability suitable to its utilitarian purpose.[26] In Holmes's opinion, the theory that fulfilled this requirement was the external general knowledge-based theory of legal liability whose essentials were first formulated by the utilitarian jurists. An examination of these issues will show that Holmes not only adopted the utilitarian conceptual link drawn between punishment and responsibility, but also endorsed a variant of the utilitarian theory of legal liability because he accepted their view of the purpose of law as distinguished from morality.

But to consider these issues, to appreciate what the utilitarians and Holmes contributed, we must first look at the intellectual context. Of course the common-law lawyers of the eighteenth and nineteenth centuries had little interest in or patience for any comprehensive theory of legal liability. Since lawyers found these general theories of little practical value, they then (as now) ignored them. Even the jurists of the age were never so bold as to endorse a theory of legal liability applicable to all areas of the law. There were too many obstacles that frustrated generalization: first, the wide chasm separating civil from criminal liability overawed the most determined theorist; second, the division of law into common law and equity, the assignment of each to different courts, and the different remedies, exceptions, justifications, and rules applied in the different courts made a comprehensive theory of legal liability almost impossible to imagine; and third, the procedural structure of the common law prevented any common-law theory of legal liability from arising. No generalization could be stretched across the different forms of action. In an action on the case, the plaintiff had to prove the defendant's negligence before the latter incurred liability for any indirect damage he caused; but in an action of trespass involving directly inflicted damage, the plaintiff only had to prove causation—negligence was irrelevant. Therefore, since requirements of liability varied with the different forms of action, the possibility of fashioning a general theory of legal liability for the common law was nil. Here again the intellectual context discouraged generalization.

The only possible exception was criminal law. In the eighteenth century, Sir William Blackstone restated the essentials of the orthodox theory of criminal liability.

All the several pleas and excuses which protect the committer of a forbidden act from the punishment which is otherwise annexed thereto may be reduced to this single consideration, the want or defect of will . . . So that, to constitute a crime against human laws, there must be first, a vicious will; and, secondly, an unlawful act consequent upon such vicious will.[27]

The stress here placed upon a vicious will reflects the influence that canon and Roman law had upon the jurists who formulated this approach to criminal liability during the late fifteenth and early sixteenth centuries. The explicit purpose of the criminal law was to punish sin; the existence and degree of moral culpability indicated the propriety and the amount of punishment. *Mens rea* considerations were therefore especially important, since they defined the excuses accepted by the orthodox theory of criminal liability:

Now there are three cases in which the will does not join with the act. 1. Where there is a defect of understanding . . . 2. Where there is understanding and will sufficient residing in the party, but not called forth or exerted at the time of the action done . . . 3. Where the action is constrained by some outward force and violence . . . It will be the business of the present chapter briefly to consider all the several species of defect in will, as they fall under some one or other of these general heads: as infancy, idiocy, lunacy, and intoxication, which fall under the first class; misfortune and ignorance, which may be referred to the second; and compulsion and necessity, which may properly rank in the third.[28]

At the theoretical level, a prohibited act accompanied by a vicious will was not only sufficient, but also necessary for criminal liability.

Before this vicious-will theory of criminal liability arose in English law, it is difficult to speak of any theory of criminal liability. However, to understand this orthodox theory and the way that the utilitarians and Holmes radically modified it, we must briefly describe the history of criminal liability. Now Holmes believed that Angle-Saxon criminal liability was restricted to intentional acts (since the law's purpose was primarily vengeance and since even "a dog can distinguish between being stumbled over and being kicked"). Other historians have disagreed, arguing that even if the purpose of early primitive law was vengeance, the practice of compensation that bought off the vengeance placed almost exclusive attention upon the victim.[29] The question was who was hurt and how badly, not who did what and how and why did he do it. Consequently, even if the harm or death was accidental, done in self-defense, or caused by an insane person or child, compensation (the *bot*) was still payable to the victim or his kin according to the status of the victim (his *wergild*). Of course, there is no theory of criminal liability present in these compensatory procedures because there was no concept of crime. To the Anglo-Saxon, all harms were torts.[30] According to our conception of the term, we must wait until the state prosecutes harmful acts before we can speak of crime or criminal liability.

However, it is true that even in the Angle-Saxon period, those who had to pay *bot* according to the *wergild* of his victim often had to pay *wite* to the king for violating his peace. But it is difficult to find the origin of criminal liability here.[31] *Wite* was not always required, and apparently the sum was for troubling the king, with no punitive purpose or effect. Even if the act in some way offended the king's person (for example, if the act was done in his presence or in his house), *wite* still appears more as a revenue measure than anything else. Moreover, the agent paid similar fees to local lords and even to the owner of the house in which the deed was done. Clearly, if fees were payable to several persons besides the compensation paid to the victim, then there is no notion of a set of conditions according to which the state punishes its subjects. Hence there was no theory of criminal liability.

The more promising area to look for notions of criminal liability earlier than the sixteenth century is in the growing category of unemendable offenses. These were uncompensable crimes that were thought to deserve corporal punishment. At first these heinous crimes were limited to religious offenses, treason, and outlawry.[32] But by the end of the Anglo-Saxon period, unemendable crimes included murder (secret killing), robbery, coining, theft, rape, arson, aggravated assault, and forcible entry.[33] Such perpetrators were executed unless pardoned by the king. Here we have clear criminal liability. Morover, the exercise of the pardoning power reveals early ideas of criminal liability since we find that all crimes—whether accidental, done in self-defense, or committed by an insane person or child—needed a pardon. Even as the list of unemendable crimes grew longer in the Norman and Angevin periods, liability to capital punishment was theoretically as strict as the liability to compensation was in the Anglo-Saxon period. The pardoning power was the escape valve. It functioned as a useful bridge between the old popular notion that persons were strictly liable to their victims (or kin) for tort damages and the more modern idea that the state should punish morally culpable persons who have harmed others or their property.[34]

The pardoning power was also the channel through which the more civilized ideas of responsibility found in the canon and Roman law flowed into the common law.[35] Reasons why the state should pardon over time became reasons why the state should excuse. However, no theory of criminal liability existed yet. The king pardoned for reasons other than moral exculpability; he pardoned to satisfy political patrons, to recruit an army, to save his friends, and to finance his administration. Therefore, no theory of criminal liability lie hidden within the Angevin practice of pardoning. Pardons depended too much upon the king's grace.

Not until the early Tudor period does the king begin to excuse (rather than pardon) nonculpable agents, and only in the sixteenth century is there some recognition of degrees of culpability. Though infants (under seven years of age) were granted excuses as early as 1300,[36] those who killed by misadventure or in self-defense were not excused until the reign of Henry VII.[37] By 1500, the common law had therefore accepted the principle (inherited from the canonists and civilians) that guilt required moral culpability and *mens rea* became the central, if not the only, issue of criminal liability. Clearly, then, one effect of the vicious-will theory of responsibility inherited from the civil and canon law was to narrow liability to morally culpable acts.

However, the requirement of moral culpability also had a tendency to widen liability. While nonculpable agents were excused, agents who recklessly or negligently caused harm or death were now found culpable and therefore punishable. In previous centuries, the king prosecuted reckless or negligent acts, but then often pardoned (as a matter of course) the agents on grounds of misadventure. For felonies, the only real punishment was death and therefore, if a negligent felon's act was closer to misadventure than to an intentional willful act, he got off scot-free.[38] The vicious-will theory consequently widened criminal liability in the sense that crimes previously pardoned were now punished.

Since the new theory taught that punishment should coincide with the degree of moral culpability, noncapital crimes were established—for example the crime of manslaughter or "chancemedley." By the time of Henry VII, the term "murder" (which was before a specific kind of culpable homicide) became equivalent to all forms of intentional killings punished capitally.[39] Though at this time judges did not recognize degrees of culpability,[40] in the following century they began to punish accidental deaths that happened in the course of an unlawful violent act not directed at the party slain.[41] The judges then withdrew the benefit of clergy from murder, but retained it for the less culpable offense of manslaughter.[42] But there is no question that manslaughter was still a crime; culpable but unintentional killings were no longer excused as misadventure. Later in the sixteenth century, the judges began to read literally the requirement of "malice aforethought" in cases of murder. Therefore, while liability for murder required actual premeditation, judges reduced liability for deliberate and intentional killings that happened at a sudden encounter to manslaughter.[43] But despite the alteration of the respective criterions of murder and manslaughter, degrees of culpability remained. Heated blood could mitigate punishment but was no excuse, while willful premeditated murder was considered the height of wickedness punished properly with death.

A similar sensitivity to the degrees of culpability is evident in the new sixteenth-century practice of prosecuting as misdemeanors harmful acts to persons and property that were earlier left (usually) to a private civil action of trespass.[44] Parliament created some of these new minor offenses that were punished by imprisonment, the pillory and other corporal punishments, and by fines, but the prerogative courts of the King's Council also made significant contributions to English criminal law. Of course this growing area of criminal liability reflected the stabilization of the modern English state in the Tudor period. But one can nonetheless see, especially in the activities of the King's Council, how the interests of the modern state coincided with the demands of the increasingly popular vicious-will theory of criminal liability. The ecclesiastical chancellors of the late fifteenth and sixteenth centuries and other members of the King's Council were enamored with the idea of equity, the idea "that the court ought to compel each individual litigant to fulfil all the duties which reason and conscience would dictate to a person in his situation,"[45] even if this meant dispensing with the relevant provisions of positive law. Most of the councilors who were learned in the law were trained in canon and Roman law and therefore they subordinated human law to natural and divine law.[46] They perceived themselves as "executive agents in the work of applying . . . [relevant] dictates of the law of God and nature"[47] to the case at hand. Even if the substantive rules of equity that the councilors produced with this perspective in the court of Chancery were primarily components of civil law, we should not understand those portions of the criminal law that the court of Star Chamber developed apart from these same ideas. The same general group of canonists and civilists that developed the law of equity also created (even if in a different courtroom) the criminal law of libel, perjury, forgery, conspiracy, and attempts.[48] In these crimes, *mens rea* considerations were crucial since no physical harm to person or property need take place.[49] The conclusion is that the criminal law's purpose of punishing according to moral culpability encouraged the prerogative courts to extend liability to those evildoers who had neither harmed persons nor destroyed property. Those with minor culpability had also to receive their just deserts, and the criminal law stepped forward to fulfill this need.

The interests of the modern state at times conflicted with the requirements of the vicious-will theory of criminal liability. For example, in the sixteenth century the *mens rea* of murder was malice aforethought, but the state punished as murder unpremeditated killings in three different types of cases: (1) killings that involved deliberate cruelty, especially if there were inequalities of strength (killing a child) or lack of warning (striking from behind); (2) killings of an officer of justice performing his official duties (usually making an arrest); (3) and accidental killings that resulted from an unlawful act of violence. Some of these rules preserved the liability of earlier times when an intentional act sufficed for capital homicide.[50] But whether these rules extended or preserved traditional liability for murder, judges reconciled these practices with their vicious-will theory of liability by the use of legal fictions. When the facts provided no evidence of malicious premeditation, the law would intend, assume, or imply the malice. As Chief Justice Holt was to say in the seventeenth century, "He that doth a cruel act voluntarily does it of malice prepensed."[51] No doubt this is pure sophistry, but it shows the contemporary vitality of the vicious-will theory of criminal liability. Judges and theorists would distort the facts rather than give up the basic notion that the criminal law's purpose was to punish evildoers to the degree of their moral culpability.

The rationalization of the felony murder rule is perhaps the most striking evidence of this commitment to the vicious-will theory. The state no doubt extended criminal liability in the sixteenth century when it made an accidental death murder if it was the result of an unlawful act. At first the unlawful act had to be violent, but soon even poaching qualified as murder if an accidental death occurred.[52] The fact that judges would imply malicious premeditation in such a case shows how the state tried to provide more adequately for the public safety (and for the convenience of ruling social groups) without sacrificing the now popular belief that the criminal law's purpose was to punish sin. Despite its incompatibility with many facts of criminal prosecution and punishment, the vicious-will theory of criminal responsibility survived well into the nineteenth century. Blackstone was one of the last jurists to endorse the theory in its pure form, but many who followed him favored a similar moral-fault theory of criminal liability.

The utilitarian jurists were the first to criticize the vicious-will theory. They thought it impossible to base criminal liability upon a vicious will and ignoble to hide the true facts of punishment behind such a fiction-ridden theory. The utilitarians therefore replaced this archaic theory of criminal liability with one more in accord with current legal practice and the science of psychology. At the same time, they fashioned an unprecedented theory of legal liability that included both criminal and civil law. In this manner Bentham and Austin destroyed the obstacles to generalization mentioned earlier. The distinction between criminal and civil law, the division of English law into common law and equity, the procedural structure of the common law were all castigated as meaningless obfuscations.

For example, Bentham claimed that every law has a civil part, which defines the acts to be punished, and a criminal part, which specifies the punishment.

We come now to speak of what is called a civil law or jurisprudence on the one hand and penal law or jurisprudence on the other: or more properly to the art of legislation in civil matters on the one hand, and the art of legislation in penal matters on the other. Between these two branches which are so often set in opposition to one another where then lies the distinction? Nowhere. They are inextricably interwoven.[53]

Consequently, this distinction between civil and criminal law had no bearing upon a theory of legal liability that set forth the necessary and sufficient conditions for punishment. Austin also used the distinction between civil and criminal law in a way independent of principles of liability. It was a procedural distinction depending upon whether the state or the individual initiated the action: "An offense which is pursued at the discretion of the injured party or his representative is a Civil Injury. An offense which is pursued by the Sovereign or by the subordinates of the sovereign, is a Crime."[54] But whether the offenses were prosecuted by the state or by the individual, the same principles of liability were applicable.

Bentham and Austin condemned the arbitrary division of English law into common law and equity. Even Blackstone supported the fusion of law and equity, and the common-law judge Lord Mansfield tried to unify the law by providing equitable remedies in a common-law court. But their efforts were futile; Parliament did not completely unite law and equity until 1873.[55] Nevertheless, Bentham and Austin continued to call for a system of one law administered by courts of general jurisdiction. Austin was very emphatic:

It is obvious that equity arose from the sulkiness and obstinacy of the Common Law Courts, which refused to suit themselves to the changes which took place in opinion and in the circumstances of society ... I only adverted to these facts because they strikingly illustrate the absurdity of the distinction between equity and law.[56]

24

Here again the arbitrary distinctions that had blocked previous attempts at generalization were rejected in favor of a comprehensive theory of legal liability.

The last obstacle to a substantive comprehensive theory of liability was the procedural structure of the common law. It met a fate similar to the distinctions described above. Bentham's codes were always substantive in nature, moving from general principles to specific legal rules.[57] "Adjective" procedural law was kept strictly subordinate to substantive law: "It may be said that the course of procedure ought to have in every instance, for its main and primary end at least, the accomplishment of the will manifested in the body of substantive laws. For this is not only a use of it, but the only use for it"[58] In the same way, Austin insisted that the law of procedure was properly "distributed under" the substantive law of persons and things: "The law of civil and criminal procedure, really consist[s] of a variety of species belonging to those two genera [law of persons and things], and should therefore not be co-ordinated with *jus personarum et rerum*, but distributed under both."[59] Austin and Bentham would not tolerate any arbitrary division of the law that prevented the formation of a comprehensive theory of legal liability. According to them, the external utilitarian purpose of punishment necessitated a distinctive theory of legal liability; no archaic distinction inherited from the past was to obstruct this fundamental utilitarian goal.

Of course not everyone agreed with the utilitarians. The actual legal practice of their day and the weight of tradition insured the unpopularity of the utilitarian approach. It was just too radical. To be sure, law and equity were unified in 1873, and the dying forms-of-action were gradually replaced by a substantive division of the law into crime, contracts, torts, wills, and so on. But the great division between civil and criminal law still intimidated most nineteenth-century jurists. Either they retained some version of a moral-fault theory of criminal liability, or they criticized all theories as fallacious generalizations of a criminal law court's practice. For example, E. C. Clark argued that it was "evidently" only "in the case of criminal wrongs where the consciousness of the party is the chief point to be considered."[60] Civil legal liability did not require any examination of the moral qualities of the offender. At first James Stephen also required moral culpability as a condition for criminal liability, but he later softened this requirement because he could not find one particular moral quality in all criminal cases. Each statute or line of judicial decisions described the specific evil *mens rea* required for the offense; nothing was gained by searching for a common immoral quality.[61] William Markby agreed with Stephen. One may try to fashion a set of necessary and sufficient conditions for legal liability, but in the end one is thrown "back upon the original and inevitable inquiry— what is that which the law bids or forbids us to do—and leaves that inquiry unsolved."[62]

The utilitarian theory of legal liability was not popular in the nineteenth century primarily because it was so radically comprehensive. Hence, in showing that Holmes and the utilitarians adhered to a similar comprehensive theory of legal liability, we have shown a great deal. Holmes had many alternatives open to him; he could have followed Clark, Stephen, or Markby. If he chose instead to endorse the radical utilitarian theory of legal liability, then the general similarities noted earlier between Holmes and the utilitarians have a great deal of significance. From a shared understanding of the external utilitarian purpose of law, Holmes and the utilitarians derived a distinctive and radically comprehensive theory of legal liability.

There is to begin with no doubt that Holmes favored a comprehensive theory of legal liability. As he announced, "The first subject to be discussed is the general theory of liability civil and criminal."[63] By the time Holmes wrote *The Common Law*, history had made the old distinctions between law and equity and between the forms of action obsolete. Holmes welcomed these developments. However, the substantive divisions of civil law that had replaced the older forms of action were still difficult obstacles to Holmes's goal of a comprehensive theory. The difference between contract and tort was a case in point. Holmes's solution was the following: "The duty to keep a contract at common law means a prediction that you must pay damages if you do not keep it—and nothing else. If you commit a tort, you are liable to pay a compensatory sum. If you commit a contract, you are liable to pay a compensatory sum unless the promised event comes to pass, and that is all the difference."[64] Holmes reduced contract to a peculiar tort to preserve a comprehensive theory of legal liability.

But my argument is not only that Holmes found the utilitarian goal of a comprehensive theory of legal liability workable and attractive. Far from it. The real issue is one of substance. Was the comprehensive theory of legal liability endorsed by Holmes similar to the one fashioned by the utilitarians? The fact that their theories were comprehensive has little significance unless they were also substantively alike. However, if they are close in substance, then the radically comprehensive nature of the theories does have implications. Holmes went out on a very thin limb by supporting a comprehensive theory of legal liability. But if he went out upon the same thin limb as the utilitarians did, then the question is why did he do it? If we can show that Holmes endorsed a radically comprehensive theory of legal liability, which was similar to the one fashioned by the utilitarians, upon utilitarian grounds, then we have taken a large step in showing that Holmes was indebted to utilitarian jurisprudence.

The best method to ascertain a resemblance is to examine Holmes's theory of legal liability full-grown, so that the contrasts between it and the orthodox vicious-will theory of criminal liability (which we have described above) are explicit, and then to compare it to the views of the utilitarians. What Holmes proposed was an "external," "general," "knowledge-based" theory of legal liability. The question is, did the utilitarians endorse principles of legal liability (markedly different from those which preceded them) that later flowered into Holmes's more explicit external, general, and knowledge-based theory? The external and general features of Holmes's theory of legal liability were primarily negative; they denied the traditional vicious-will or moral-fault requirement of legal liability. The knowledge-based nature of the theory was positive; it clarified what facts were necessary to impute legal liability. I will first discuss the negative features, hoping to show that Holmes and the utilitarians had a similar critical perspective on the orthodox vicious-will theory of criminal liability, and then go on to address the positive issue of which facts were necessary for legal liability.

By "external" and "general" standards of liability, Holmes meant that, in an age where the prevention of harm seemed "to be the chief and only universal purpose of punishment,"[65] liability no longer required either an evil motive or a personal moral fault. A morally blameless man was culpable despite the fact that his motives were pure or that compliance was personally impossible for him. In Holmes's terminology, the standards of legal liability were external because liability was incurred regardless of the degree of evil in the agent's motives; they were general because liability was incurred despite the impossibility of compliance. An individual was legally liable for his acts even if he lacked the capacities of intelligence and prudence that were necessary to act in accordance with the law. The standards of legal liability "do not merely require that every man should get as near as he can to the best conduct possible for him. They require him at his own peril to come up to a certain height."[66] In Holmes's opinion, the height usually demanded was the due care that a man of ordinary intelligence and reasonable prudence would have. If an individual failed to meet this objective general standard of care, then he incurred liability even if he lacked the capacities necessary to conform to the standard. Hence, the question was not whether an individual harmed another because he did not use his native abilities; rather, the issue was whether the harmful consequence resulted from a particular individual's failure to use the capacities of reason and prudence found in an ordinary man. Whether the individual had these capacities was irrelevant. Just as any investigation of motive was unnecessary for legal liability (because the standards of liability were external), so also any examination of the actual intellectual capacities of the agent was superfluous (because these standards were also general).

Holmes's rationale for the externality and generality of the standards of legal liability was quite utilitarian. Indeed, from the fact that the legal order willingly sacrificed individuals for the public good, Holmes concluded that the agent's evil motives or personal shortcomings were relevant "only so far as the public welfare permits or demands."[67] The principle was to punish people in accordance with rules that served the public welfare. Since utility was better served by ignoring the motives and shortcomings of offenders, external and general standards of legal liability were more compatible with the currently accepted justification of punishment. When Holmes added the law's external purpose to this utilitarian argument, he thought that his rationale for an external and general theory of legal liability was indisputable.

Considering this external purpose of the law together with the fact that it is ready to sacrifice the individual so far as necessary in order to accomplish that purpose, we can see more readily than before that the actual degree of personal guilt involved in any particular transgression cannot be the only element, if it is an element at all, in the liability incurred.[68]

If the law were to concern itself with the internal acts of its subjects, public policy might require an internal theory of legal liability. The external role of the law prevented that possibility. According to Holmes, in a utilitarian legal order the standards of legal liability were external and general.

Because the utilitarians endorsed the principle of utility as the standard for both law and morals, they assigned an even greater role to external and general standards of responsibility. Bentham and Austin considered moral responsibility to have the same general and external characteristics as its legal counterpart. However, this general and external theory of responsibility was not always so explicitly stated as in Holmes's writings. For example, Bentham failed to distinguish between his theory of legal liability (that set forth the necessary and sufficient conditions for punishment) and his more general discussion of all the factors that contribute to the gravity of an offense and thus to the demand for punishment. In fact, in his *Introduction to the Principles of Morals and Legislation,* he discussed acts and circumstances, intentions, consciousness, motives, dispositions, and consequences in preparation for a chapter entitled "Of the Proportion Between Punishments and Offenses."[69] Austin's views also have their own peculiar difficulties of interpretation. Even so, we can still glean from their writings the external and general nature of their standards of legal liability.

First, to indicate the externality of the utilitarian theory of legal liability, we need only discuss their views on motive. Their psychology reduced all motives to the same level; all were ultimately desires of pleasure and avoidance of pain. The utilitarians had no basis to distinguish motives into absolute categories of good or bad. The most reprehensible motive (hate) could cause a beneficial act (informer betrays his underworld boss); the most meritorious one (love) could result in a pernicious act (a kidnapper who acts out of love for his family). As Bentham summed it up,"A motive is substantially nothing more than pleasure or pain, operating in a certain manner . . . It follows, therefore, immediately and incontestably, that *there is no such thing as any sort of motive that is in itself a bad one.*"[70] Therefore, Bentham reasoned, "as it is with everything else that is not itself either pain or pleasure, so it is with motives. If they are good or bad, it is only on account of their effects."[71] But the effects of motives were intentions. They filled the vacuum in the theory of liability created by the utilitarian exclusion of motive.

The only way, it should seem, in which a motive can with safety and propriety be styled good or bad, is with reference to its effects in each individual instance; and principally from the intention it gives birth to: from which arise, as will be shown hereafter, the most material part of its effects. A motive is good, when the intention it gives birth to is a good one; bad, when the intention is a bad one: and an intention is good or bad, according to the material consequences that are the objects of it.[72]

Motives therefore have no place in the utilitarian theory of legal liability. Society should punish harmful acts regardless of motive.[73]

However, the feature of generality was the more controversial issue. Few doubted, even if orthodox theorists hid the fact behind legal fictions, that a man who murdered another without malice or any other disreputable motive still deserved punishment. But the notion that an individual incurred liability for an act whose harmful consequences he could not have foreseen was far more controversial. Did the utilitarians believe it proper to punish an individual who, because of personal intellectual shortcomings, failed to attain the general standard required by law? Though the evidence is somewhat ambiguous, with Bentham's opinion more explicitly affirmative than Austin's, the utilitarian theory can be interpreted as favoring general standards of legal liability. But what utilitarian doctrines are relevant to this question? The utilitarians' views on intentional acts are, of course, irrelevant because such acts imply facts of knowledge and foresight that the question explicitly denies. However, the utilitarian jurists also endorsed liability for negligent, heedless, and rash acts. In these cases, the offender failed to foresee the consequences either of his omission (negligence), or action (heedlessness); or foresaw the harmful consequences but falsely believed that they would not ensue (rashness). The question is—did the utilitarians believe that punishment for such acts was proper, even if the agent was not morally culpable? Even if the knowledge required to foresee the consequences or to perceive the risk was beyond the capacities of the particular agent?

Bentham's response was definite. Since he preferred not to make the subtle Austinian distinction between negligent omissions and heedless acts, his views concerning the general nature of the standards of legal liability are found in his analysis of heedlessness and rashness. In both cases, the standard used to measure if an act was heedless or rash was not only general, but also identical to the one popularized by Holmes. The general Benthamite standard of legal liability was the due care of the rational man of ordinary prudence.

An act which is unadvised, is either heedless, or not heedless. It is termed heedless when the case is thought to be such, that a person of ordinary prudence, if prompted by an ordinary share of benevolence, would have been likely to have bestowed such and so much attention and reflection upon the material circumstances, as would have effectually disposed him to prevent the mischievous incident from taking place . . .

A misadvised act then may be either rash or not rash. It may be termed rash, when the case is thought to be such, that a person of ordinary prudence, if prompted by an ordinary share of benevolence, would have employed such and so much attention and reflection to the imagined circumstance, as, by discovering to him the non-existence, improbability, or immateriality of it, would have effectually disposed him to prevent the mischievous incident from taking place.[74]

These quotes indicate that Holmes was not the first to formulate a theory of legal liability that used general rather than personal standards. According to Bentham, we should punish a heedless or rash act even if the offender lacked the rational and prudential capacities of the ordinary person. Personal shortcomings were of no relevance; the standard of legal liability was general and objective. Also, it is clear that Bentham's views directly contradicted the orthodox vicious-will theory of criminal liability; men were properly punished for harms they could not have personally avoided.

Austin's opinions on the same subject are not as easily ascertained. Since it failed to appear in his writings, there is no doubt that Austin never endorsed the standard of the rational and prudent man. Yet he could have supported general standards of legal liability even though he never endorsed Bentham's and Holmes's

31

particular test of the rational prudent man. However, orthodox opinion is to the contrary. Even Holmes has argued that Austin adopted personal standards of liability:

Austin is compelled to regard the liability to an action as a sanction, or, in other words, as a penalty for disobedience. It follows from this, according to the prevailing views of penal law, that such liability ought only to be based upon personal fault; and Austin accepts that conclusion, with its corollaries, one of which is that negligence means a state of the party's mind.[75]

But this interpretation of Austin's theory of legal liability is either wrong or unsubstantiated.[76] No doubt Holmes was correct in saying that Austin considered negligence, heedlessness, and rashness as distinctive states of mind. But this hardly distinguishes Austin's theory of legal liability from Holmes's; nor is it relevant to whether Austin thought it justifiable upon utilitarian grounds to punish a person of meager abilities for acts the harmful consequences of which he could not have foreseen. Even with Holmes's theoretical device of the rational and prudent man, a judge who finds an individual negligent implicitly makes negative claims about the state of mind of the offender; the offender lacked the knowledge of the circumstances that a rational and prudent man would have known. Hence both a general and a personal theory of legal liability have implications concerning the mental states of offenders. A finding of negligence upon a personal standard implies that the offender was in an avoidable state of ignorance; a finding upon a general standard implies the same state of mind, but not the fact that the ignorance was avoidable. Consequently, Austin's language describing negligence as a state of mind does not substantiate the claim that Austin's standards of liability were personal.[77] Austin could still have adhered to a theory of legal liability that ignored the personal capacities of the agent.

The issue is not states of mind, but the nature of the standard of liability. Did Austin believe that the limits of legal liability were defined by the personal capacities of the agent or by some general objective standard? When the proper issue is in focus, the evidence begins to support the view that Austin favored a general standard of liability. As with Bentham, Austin's requirements of legal liability in cases of negligence, heedlessness, and rashness are the crux of the matter.

Unlawful intention or unlawful inadvertence, is, therefore, of the essence of injury . . . [for] the sanction could not have operated . . . to the fulfillment of duty, unless . . . [the agent] had been conscious that he was violating his duty, or unless he would have been conscious that he was violating his duty, if he had adverted or attended as he ought.[78]

Here the individual was required to advert as he ought, not as he could; the test was objective not personal. However, one might argue that Austin thought the personal intellectual capacities of the agent formed the basis for defining what he ought to advert to, and therefore held that personal abilities established the limits to an individual's legal liability. But this argument is unconvincing for a number of reasons: first, it runs counter to Austin's insistence that ignorance of fact was excusable only if inevitable or invincible; second, a personal standard of liability is incompatible with the nature of eighteenth-century civil liability; and, third, Austin's related remarks about the ignorance of the law indicate that his standard was general. A discussion of each of these matters will contribute greatly to our understanding of Austin's theory of legal liability.

Austin thought ignorance of circumstances that made an act dangerous was excusable only if it was inevitable or invincible. This implied that an ignorant offender was legally culpable unless he was inevitably ignorant. In the Thomist tradition of ethics, invicible ignorance meant that the individual did not have the personal capacities to overcome it.[79] But Austin's sense of the term was otherwise.

For unless the ignorance of error was inevitable or invincible (or, in other words, unless it could not have been removed by due attention or advertence), the act, forbearance, or omission, which was the consequence of the ignorance of error, is imputable to negligence, heedlessness or temerity . . . That is to say, to error which could not have been prevented by any attention or advertence, practicable under the circumstances.[80]

Austin's penchant for precise expression justifies close attention to the wording. Ignorance was invincible "unless it could not have been removed by *due* attention." The person was negligent if he did not pay the attention *due*, not the attention of which he was capable. Legal liability was *imputable* to negligence, heedlessness, or temerity if the harm "could not have been prevented by *any* attention *practicable* under the circumstances." But what is practicable is a matter of averages, a question of general standards. "Practicable under the circumstances" does not mean that an idiot could do it. Hence, the judgment is not dependent on the personal capacities of an agent. Moreover, the agent must give *any* attention practicable, not just the attention of which he is capable. By invincible ignorance Austin therefore meant ignorance that most or all men could not overcome. The standard was general; men must attain it at their peril.

Eighteenth-century civil liability supports our interpretation of Austin as favoring general standards of legal liability. According to Holdsworth, "The central idea of the medieval common law was that civil liability was based upon an act causing damage, if that act fell within one of the causes of action provided by the law."[81] Of course by the eighteenth century, certain of the forms of action also required the defendant's negligence. For example, in actions on the case negligence was a necessary condition of liability even if the burden of proof rested with the defendant. But despite its important role in eighteenth-century civil liability, negligence did not easily lose the strict-liability features of the medieval civil law. As Holdsworth describes it:

In the first place, they naturally, from the first, adopted the objective standard of the ordinarily prudent man, for they were not trying to determine whether this or that defendant had been negligent, but whether having regard to what any ordinarily prudent man would have foreseen, a particular damage, flowing from a given defendant's acts, was a sufficiently proximate consequence of those acts to entail liability. This principle was not indeed formally laid down till 1837 [Vaughan v. Menlowe (1837) 3 Bing. N.C. 468]; but, as Sir F. Pollock says, the idea "pervades the mass of our authorities" [*Torts*, (12 ed.) p. 444]; and it pervades them, because this manner of regarding negligence was necessitated by the way in which the conception came into the common law.[82]

The concept of negligence thus entered the common law as a criterion to determine if an indirect consequence of an act was sufficiently proximate to the act to incur liability in an action on the case. It had nothing to do with the personal capacities of the agent.[83] It is too much to believe that Austin was unaware of this objective measurement of negligence. He was a theorist of the positive law. Unless the textual evidence gives us no choice but to reduce Austin to a positive theorist who knew nothing of the actual law, we should interpret his theory of legal liability as reflecting the general standards found in eighteenth-century civil liability.

Austin's description of the only case that was, in his opinion, in contradiction with his theory of liability helps to make the point. The example was one of contracts in which performance was automatically due from the instant the obligation was undertaken. In English law, the creditor could sue for breach of contract without a previous demand of performance. Austin considered this rule absurd and reprehensible.[84] But clearly he would not have described this example as the only case that violated his theory (which required for liability either unlawful intention or inadvertence) if his standard of liability was personal. He could not have been that ignorant of the law. Austin was not claiming that all or some men could have intuited their creditor's demand of payment; rather, he was claiming that no man, no matter how rational or prudent, could know the facts or foresee the injury without a previous demand. Consequently, the reason why Austin thought this example violated his theory was not because it required a person to know things that were beyond his particular capacities, but because it punished people for the consequences that no man could know or foresee. The test was general.

Indeed, even if Austin could be interpreted as supporting general standards of negligence, his opinion that only one case violated his theory would still be fallacious. We have already noted that some forms of action did not require negligence; in actions of trespass, liability was incurred if the defendant caused the harm. But if we adopt the view that Austin adhered to general standards of legal liability, we can at least explain why his theory departed from the view that causation sufficed for civil liability. It was his aim to provide a general theory of criminal and civil liability. To generalize over this field, Austin opposed the strict rule found in trespass because it conflicted with criminal law requirements.[85] He favored reforming the strict forms of action by making inadvertence a necessary condition for civil liability. Austin was therefore a critic of the English law of torts, but a reasonable critic with one foot in reality. On the other hand, if we adopt the view that Austin adhered to personal standards of legal liability, then his theory becomes so incompatible with the practice of his day that we have no choice but to describe him as a confused utopian and a fool—a positive theorist who knew little of what he was about. This is an unreasonable conclusion. A layman would have known more law. Therefore, the nature of eighteenth-century civil liability strongly suggests that Austin's standards of legal liability were general.

Austin's related discussion of ignorance of the law further supports our view that he measured the degree of advertence necessary to escape legal liability by an objective standard. Though he endorsed the traditional presumption that all men know the law, Austin rejected the customary rationale that the law was in fact knowable by all men, that ignorance of it was never inevitable. Indeed, in its present uncodified form the law was necessarily unknowable; even lawyers could not know all of it. Austin thought a better justification of this legal presumption was the utilitarian ground that a case-by-case analysis of the agent's legal knowledge and capacities was impractical.

Now either of these questions were next to insoluble. Whether the party was *really* ignorant of the law, and was *so* ignorant of the law that he had no *surmise* of its provisions, could scarcely be determined by any evidence accessible to others. And for the purpose of determining the *cause* of his ignorance (its *reality* being ascertained), it were incumbent upon the tribunal to unravel his previous history, and to search his whole life for the elements of a just solution.[86]

The court would have to decide if the agent knew the rule and, if not, if he ever had the opportunity and the capacity to know the rule. This was impossible, according to Austin; courts would squander their time on "questions of fact, insoluble and interminable."

Circumstantial facts were a different matter. Here the court's inquiry, in Austin's words, "is limited to a given incident, and to the circumstances attending that incident, and is, therefore, not interminable."[87] The question is, would the individual have known the relevant facts of his situation if he had attended as he ought? Notice that the question is still objective in nature, but specific and concrete. What should a person have known in those circumstances? But in cases of ignorance of law, the parallel question was open-ended. Did the agent know the rules or did he ever have the opportunity and capacity to know them? A person can know rules years before the culpable act; he knows facts only when he comes upon them. Consequently, Austin treated ignorance of law differently from ignorance of fact because of this vital difference between knowledge of rules and knowledge of facts. The court therefore reasonably inquires into what facts a person should know, but properly avoids the unanswerable question of what rules he should know.

Austin's position upon ignorance of the law is important because it involves the principle of punishing the morally innocent. It is indisputable that Austin was willing to punish individuals upon utilitarian grounds who were inevitably ignorant. Even if agents had no chance to know the rule, they were liable. But it seems doubtful that Austin adhered to personal standards of legal liability if he gave them up so readily when he went from ignorance of fact to igorance of law. The same principle was involved. The fact that Austin used general standards of legal liability in cases of ignorance of the law should therefore encourage us to interpret his views on ignorance of fact in a consistent manner. To formulate a comprehensive theory of liability, Austin ignored the distinctions between law and equity, criminal and civil law, and the various forms of action. Hence he would not have allowed the minor distinction between ignorance of law and ignorance of fact to bifurcate his theory by ascribing general standards to the former and personal ones to the latter. Austin's theory was meant to encompass the width and breadth of the law; therefore his discussion of liability for ignorance of the law can buttress our interpretation of Austin's principles of legal liability.

The role that legal presumptions played in Austin's discussion of ignorance of the law is crucial to understanding his general theory of legal liability. He claimed "that wherever ignorance of law exempts from liability, the ignorance is presumed to be inevitable, and the party, therefore, to be clear from unlawful intention and inadvertence."[88] Legal presumptions (or, if you will, legal fictions) were the key to defining what was invincible ignorance.[89] It was not one's personal capacities, but the law that determined who had to know what rules. Austin cited examples of special legal presumptions of Roman law that exempted women, soldiers, and persons under twenty-five years of age from the general requirement of knowing the law. They were exempt "not by reason of their general imbecility, but because it is presumed that their capacity is not adequate to a knowledge of the law."[90] Clearly, Austin adhered to a general standard for assessing the invincibility of ignorance of the law.

This suggests that legal presumptions were similarly used in cases involving ignorance of fact. For example, consider Austin's discussion of liability for acts done in a state of drunkenness. In English law drunkenness was not an exemption, but in Roman law it was, even in criminal matters. Austin identified the ground for this exemption as the same one found in the case of infancy or insanity. "The party is unable to remember the law if he knew it, or to appreciate distinctly the fact he is about, or to subsume it as falling under the law."[91] Roman law presumed that a drunken man was ignorant of the facts about him and therefore relieved him of legal liability. But Austin could only have understood this ignorance as a case of legal presumption because he knew English law held otherwise. In the common law, drunkenness was no excuse. Now if Austin was adverse to a general standard of legal liability, then he would have objected to one of these views. If liability for ignorance of fact was assessed by each individual's capacities, then why did he discuss these various legal presumptions as if nothing was amiss? The evidence indicates Austin's recognition of legal presumptions that assumed a particular offender either ignorant or cognizant of the facts that made his act dangerous.[92] Each legal system could define its general standard of legal liability by choosing the legal presumptions it preferred. Austin had no objection to an objective test, nor even to some diversity in the tests used by various legal systems. For this reason, Austin never endorsed the general standard of the rational and prudent man favored by Bentham and Holmes. It was not because he opposed objective standards of liability, but because he did not believe in a correct standard for all legal systems. The theorist of positive *universal* jurisprudence thought that it was improper of him to endorse any particular standard.

However, Austin did think that in those legal systems where drunkenness is "not a ground of exemption; the party, it is evident, is liable in respect of heedlessness . . . He has heedlessly placed himself in a position, of which the probable consequence will be the commission of a wrong."[93] Yet this position is hardly detrimental to my interpretation of Austin's theory of legal liability. Indeed, it confirms it by indicating how Austin used legal presumptions to assess heedlessness. Of course punishable acts were heedless: the important question was how to determine if the agent was heedless. Was it by ascertaining his intellectual capacities or by noting the legal presumptions of English law? Austin no doubt used legal presumptions to decide the matter because in Roman law drunken illegal acts were not considered heedless.

Other examples described by Austin require a similar interpretation. Wrongs done in furious anger incur liability because the offender "neglected that self-discipline, which would have prevented such furious fits of anger." In a malpractice case, heedlessness was not imputed to a doctor's inadvertence at the time of the act; but to the "neglect of the previous duty of qualifying myself by study for the profession I affect to exercise." And even injuries done by one's employees or by one's children were imputable to that person, "because it is generally in my power not to employ persons of such a character, or to form them by discipline and education so as to be incapable of the commission of wrong."[94] But in these cases, Austin was not such a dreamer as to claim that every drunken offender could have developed the self-discipline necessary to abstain from alcohol, that every doctor has the abilities to prepare himself for every unexpected disease, or that every employer or father has the powers of insight to hire only virtuous employees or to shape only spiritually well-developed children. However, if we interpret these statements as clarifying certain legal presumptions of the common law of negligence, then we can credit Austin with a substantive (though partial) analysis of the general standard of English legal liability. But in following this course the only alternative is to admit that Austin did have a general standard of legal liability. The above drunk, doctor, and employer are liable for damage despite their personal incapacities. As Austin clearly stated in the case of the employer, he was liable because he generally has the power to employ prudent employees. "Generally" does not mean invariably. Therefore Austin thought it proper to punish offenders for acts they could not have avoided given their personal capacities: his standard of legal liability was general.

To complete our discussion of the affinity between Holmes and the utilitarians concerning legal responsibility we need only clarify the positive feature common to their respective theories of liability. Until now what Holmes and the utilitarians had in common was their rejection of the traditional requirements of the vicious-will theory of criminal liability. No evaluation of the agent's will or capacities was necessary. Also, the subordination of civil law to the same general and external theory forced the utilitarians and Holmes to reject the medieval view of civil liability (which held that a man was liable for all the damage he caused, that he acted at his peril). Before civil liability was incurred, the agent had to have acted knowingly, recklessly, or negligently. But what test did Holmes, Bentham, and Austin use to decide these issues of knowledge, recklessness, and negligence? What kinds of facts were required before the law could properly punish an offender? The answer given in Holmes's and the utilitarians' theory of legal liability was knowledge, either of the probability of the harm that ensued or of the circumstances of the act that would have enabled a prudent man to foresee the harmful consequences.

But before discussing the nature of this condition more precisely, it is useful to note the similar justifications for the role assigned to knowledge. Holmes's rationale for his knowledge-based theory of legal liability was deceptively simple and subtly utilitarian.

An act cannot be wrong, even when done under circumstances in which it will be hurtful, unless those circumstances are or ought to be known. A fear of punishment for causing harm cannot work as a motive, unless the possibility of harm may be foreseen. So far, then, as criminal liability is founded upon wrong-doing in any sense, and so far as the threats and punishments of the law are intended to deter men from bringing about various harmful results, they must be confined to cases where circumstances making the conduct dangerous were known.[95]

Because the purpose of punishment was to deter crime through fear, it was senseless to punish individuals for harmful consequences which they could not have foreseen (based upon the knowledge that they either had or should have had). Bentham anticipated Holmes's reasoning in his analysis of "cases unmeet for punishment." He argued that punishment was inefficacious when it could not deter an individual "with regard to the individual act he is about to engage in: to wit, because he knows not that it [the act] is of the number of those to which the penal provision relates." Examples of such cases were: unintentionality, where the individual "knows not that he is about to engage in the act in which eventually he is about to engage"; unconsciousness, where the individual "may know that he is about to engage in the act itself, yet, from not knowing all the material circumstances attending it, he knows not of the tendency it has to produce that mischief"; and missupposal, where, even if the individual "may know of the tendency the act has to produce that degree of mischief, he supposes it, though mistakenly, to be attended with some circumstance, or set of circumstances, which, if it had been attended with, it would . . . not have been productive of that mischief."[96] For the same reason, Austin also narrowed the requirements of legal liability to either actual knowledge or culpable ignorance:

For unless the party knew that he was violating his duty, or unless he might have known that he was violating his duty, the sanction could not operate, at the moment of the wrong, to the end of impelling him to the act which the Law enjoins or of deterring him from the act which the Law forbids.[97]

Hence, for Holmes, Bentham, and Austin the utilitarian principles of punishment were thought to limit legal liability to certain cases of knowledge and ignorance. All three were committed to the same utilitarian principles that shaped their respective theories of legal liability accordingly.

But what of details? Did the utilitarians and Holmes agree about the exact nature of the knowlege or lack of knowledge requisite for legal liability? Their analyses of the relationship existing among malice, intent, and foresight of consequences provide us with a convenient starting point. Since the law punished illegal acts even if not done maliciously, the term "malice" had to have a legal sense. In the law, the term "malicious" meant only intentional. Austin fumed against the tendency of the orthodox theory of criminal liability to confuse malice with intention: "Of this confusion the law of England affords a flagrant instance when it lays down that murder must be committed of malice aforethought; by which is only meant that it must be committed intentionally."[98] Holmes agreed with Austin that the law would be better off without the word "malice," but that if it remained its meaning was the same as intention.[99]

But neither Holmes nor Austin was satisfied with this reduction of malice to intention. In common speech, intent implied a wish for the consequences working as a motive for the act. An act was intentional when its consequences were desired. This meaning was not acceptable in the law. A harmful act done with a wish that the foreseen harm not happen was still legally culpable. A poor sick mother who abandoned her baby on a doorstep in December hoping that a better provider than she would care for the infant was yet guilty of murder if her hopes went unfulfilled. Therefore, the utilitarians and Holmes separated the legal sense of "intent" from the ordinary sense of "acting with a wish." But what did this leave to the meaning of the legal sense of "intentional"? Austin and Holmes addressed this precise issue and reduced intent to foresight or expectation of consequences.

> To desire the *act* is to *will* it. To *expect* any of its *consequences* is to *intend* those consequences.

> The question then is, whether intent, in its turn, cannot be reduced to a lower term. Sir James Stephen's statement shows that it can be, and that knowledge that the act will probably cause death, that is, foresight of the consequences of the act, is enough in murder as in tort.[100]

Hence, both Holmes and Austin defined the criterion of legal liability as the expectation or foresight of harmful consequences, that is, as knowledge that the act will probably cause harm. Upon this basis, Austin distinguished intentional acts from rash acts. Rashness involved an awareness of the possible consequences, but not a belief in its probability. An intentional act was committed even if the offender thought the consequence only slightly probable.[101] In sum, the agent's knowledge of probable harm was determined from his knowledge of the circumstances of the act. Therefore, any question of the malicious or intentional character of an act was ultimately answered by ascertaining if the individual knew enough of the circumstances of the act to have foreseen the probability of harm.[102]

However, an act need not be malicious or intentional to incur legal liability. Negligence, heedlessness, and rashness were also punishable. Obviously, in these cases the actual knowledge of the probability of harm was denied. A negligent, heedless, or rash person should have foreseen the harm but did not. But here, the external and general standard of liability enabled knowledge to play a key role despite the ignorance of the agent. For Bentham and Holmes, the knowledge of the probability of harm that a rational and prudent man would have had was the test of legal liability. If a rational and prudent man would have known the probability of harm, then he is liable even if ignorant.

Holmes extended even further the role that knowledge played in his theory of legal liability. For him, the standard of the rational and prudent man did not operate in a vacuum. The issue was, what knowledge did the average man have? Does he know the gun is loaded? Does he know that people frequently walk behind the fence upon which his target hangs? Does he know the fence to have weak spots or holes? According to Holmes, these questions must be answered before we can ask what a rational and prudent man would have foreseen. Moreover, Holmes thought these questions were usually answered in accordance with the offender's actual knowledge of the circumstances.[103] From what the agent knew of the circumstances at the time of the act, would a reasonable man of ordinary prudence have known the probability of harmful consequences? Or, in a more complex case, from what the agent knew, would a prudent man have inferred the existence of other facts unknown to the agent that would (in turn) have revealed the harmful probability of the act? If either answer was in the affirmative, then Holmes found the offender guilty of negligence. Consequently, what the agent actually knew played an important role in Holmes's theory and was usually the ultimate test of legal liability.

But there were exceptions to this criterion. While the general limit of legal liability required men to use their knowledge reasonably and prudently, the law could set the limit higher, according to Holmes. People could be required to foresee harms the probabilities of which are very unlikely. For example, the felony-murder rule has made the act of poaching on a neighbor's chickens murder if a stray shot has killed the ungracious host. It was murder even if the harmful consequences of the act could not have been foreseen by a man of ordinary prudence and rationality acting with the actual knowledge of the agent.[104] Here the law requires us to act with more prudence and foresight than the ordinary person has. Also, Holmes thought it possible for the law to demand that we know particular facts surrounding us at our peril. In the case of the unlawful abduction of girls under sixteen years of age, the law would still punish the agent even if he had every reason to believe that the girl was over sixteen.[105] When the law wanted to, it could set the limit of legal liability higher than our average capacities of foresight or knowledge.

But these cases were exceptional. The general theory of legal liability, if for no other reason than that the higher standard would bear too hard upon the community,[106] was otherwise, according to Holmes. In the majority of cases, men were punished for the harmful consequences of their acts only if the agent knew the probability of harm; or, if he did not, only if the average man of the community either would have known the probability of the harm (upon the facts known by the agent) or would have (from facts known) inferred other facts that would have revealed the danger of the act.

However, the endorsement of this weaker theory of legal liability does not mean that Holmes opposed strict liability. He was against it only in its general form that held a man liable for all the consequences of his acts, that a man acted at his peril. Holmes in fact welcomed particular rules of strict liability as the culmination of legal development.

It is the coarseness, not the nature, of the standard which is objected to. If, when the question of the defendant's negligence is left to a jury, negligence does not mean the actual state of the defendant's mind, but a failure to act as a prudent man of average intelligence would have done, he is required to conform to an objective standard at his peril, even in that case. When a more exact and specific rule has been arrived at, he must obey that rule at his peril to the same extent.[107]

Hence the standard of the prudent man entailed strict liability to the same extent as specific rules of strict liability, which fleshed out the duties of the rational and prudent man. Holmes thus considered his external and general theory of legal liability perfectly compatible with strict liability. He opposed only those rules of strict liability, unless justified upon specific grounds, that were too far beyond the ordinary capacities of the average member of the community.

Holmes's endorsement of strict liability does not, moreover, separate him from the utilitarian theory of legal liability. Bentham's endorsement of the standard of the rational prudent man rendered his theory of legal liability just as compatible with strict liability as Holmes's. In both cases, individuals were required to conform to an objective standard at their peril. Austin accepted even more explicitly the practice of strict liability because his theory omitted the complexities of the standard of the rational prudent man. Austin's legal presumptions required individuals to come up to the objective standard at their peril. The negligent doctor was assumed to know the deficient areas of his medical knowledge, to know all the kinds of cases that might come his way, to know where and how the patient could attain the proper medicine or treatment. The drunken criminal was also presumed to know the effect that alcohol had upon him, to know that what he consumed was alcohol, to know how he could prevent such incidents. And even more so, the legally liable employer was assumed to know the abilities, true character, and motivations of his employees. In these cases, the legal presumptions demanded that agents achieve an objective standard. Holmes thought the last rule of strict liability unconscionably high.[108] Hence, it is possible that Austin accepted an even more severe standard of strict liability than Holmes did; in any case, there is no doubt that he accepted the practice of strict liability. Although he preferred to express it in the language of fiction, of presumed foresight that Holmes avoided religiously,[109] he too believed that individuals must come up to an objective standard at their peril.

These specific similarities between Holmes's, Bentham's, and Austin's theories of legal liability place into proper relief the more general areas of agreement discussed earlier. All agreed that the general purpose of law and punishment, conjoined with the external field of action proper to law, required a corresponding theory of legal liability. As Bentham was the first to phrase it, "In proportion as an act tends to disturb that happiness, in proportion as the tendency of it is pernicious, will be the demand it creates for punishment . . . The general tendency of an act is more or less pernicious, according to the sum total of its consequences."[110] Rather than the vicious will of the agent, the tendency of the act became the central condition of legal liability. Holmes, upon similar utilitarian premises, concluded that "the known tendency of the act under the known circumstances to do harm may be accepted as the general test of conduct."[111]

The factual nature of this test of legal liability and its significance as an indication of a deeper methodological debt that Holmes owed to the utilitarians will be discussed in a later chapter. We need here only point out how the resemblances hide an important difference between Holmes's theory of legal liability and the utilitarians'. Both theories emphasized the factual tendency of the act (as opposed to the nature of the will), but the utilitarians required more for legal liability. According to them, an agent was not punished no matter the tendency of his act, unless he violated another person's legal right. The utilitarian theory of legal liability required an illegal, overt act that caused injury before an intentional, rash, or negligent agent could incur legal liability. No doubt this requirement was accepted tradition. Bentham's and Austin's contribution in the development of legal liability was to shift attention from the vicious will of the agent to the general tendency of the act. But none of the earlier utilitarians imagined that this tendency alone sufficed for liability. The act must also be prohibited.

This was the requirement that Holmes abandoned. By placing exclusive attention upon the tendency of the act, Holmes thought it possible to arrive at the simplest comprehensive theory of legal liability possible. Holmes summarized his theory of legal liability in a sentence:

I think that the law regards the infliction of temporal damage by a responsible person as actionable, if under the circumstances known to him the danger [tendency] of his act is manifest according to common experience, or according to his own experience if it is more than common, except in cases where upon special grounds of policy the law refuses to protect the plaintiff or grants a privilege to the defendant.[112]

By following the utilitarian example of a comprehensive theory of legal liability, Holmes had gone out on an intellectual limb. Indeed, he took a few steps beyond the utilitarians into an area where no theorist had yet dared to tread. We must realize the radical nature of this theory if we are to appreciate Holmes's contribution to the philosophy of legal responsibility. In short, Holmes widened the boundaries of legal liability by decreasing to one the number of conditions required. If the tendency or the danger of the act was manifest, then (but for a few exceptions and privileges) the agent was liable. Maliciousness, intent, or negligence were not additional requirements because "commonly malice, intent, and negligence mean only that the danger was manifest to a greater or less degree, under the circumstances known to the actor."[113] Hence, while the utilitarians relied upon the factual tendencies of acts as one of the conditions for legal liability, Holmes based liability exclusively upon them.

This emphasis upon dangerous tendencies of acts is Holmes's contribution to the development of the utilitarian theory of legal liability. No doubt Holmes chose this radical approach consciously. He could have opted for the orthodox approach of requiring moral fault for criminal liability, while finding causation sufficient in civil law; or he could have accepted a moderate variant of the external, general, knowledge-based theory of the utilitarians. But for Holmes the appeal of the universal was irresistible. He wanted a theory that would explain legal liability by one set of facts. Holmes made this clear not only in his theoretical writings, but also in his personal reminiscences of a conversation with an English judge.

But when I stated my view to a very eminent English judge the other day, he said: "You are discussing what the law ought to be; as the law is, you must show a right. A man is not liable for negligence unless he is subject to a duty." . . . [In] his opinion, liability for an act cannot be referred to the manifest tendency of the act to cause temporal damage in general as a sufficient explanation, but must be referred to the special nature of the damage, or must be derived from some special circumstances outside of the tendency of the act, for which no generalized explanation exists. I think that such a view is wrong, but it is familiar, and I dare say generally is accepted in England.[114]

Holmes was a self-consciously radical theorist of legal responsibility. His premises were utilitarian, but (here as elsewhere) his ultimate conclusions were his own. He adopted the utilitarian rationale of law and punishment, the utilitarian separation of law from morality, and the external, general, knowledge-based theory of legal liability. Therefore Holmes's radical theory of legal liability is best understood through utilitarian eyes; sensitivity to the utilitarian origins of Holmes's doctrines is the best way to appreciate the content and purpose of his theory of legal liability. On the other hand, Holmes was an insightful and innovative theorist who expanded upon the assumptions he shared with the utilitarians in ways they never imagined.

III

LAW, SOVEREIGNTY, AND LEGAL OBLIGATION

While the utilitarians and Holmes derived very similar and controversial theories of liability from shared premises about the purpose of law as distinct from morality, the relation of Holmes's conceptions of law, sovereignty, and legal obligation to utilitarian jurisprudence is more ambiguous. Many commentators, from Mark DeWolfe Howe to Martin Golding, have detected disparities between Holmes's and the utilitarians' views of law, sovereignty, and legal obligation.[1] Though there is no doubt that differences do exist, what matters is their significance. If these disagreements are minor relative to broad areas of congruence, then they should have little weight in assessing Holmes's debt to the utilitarian tradition. Unfortunately, orthodox interpretations have not even broached the issue of whether any important similarities exist between Holmes's ideas of law, sovereignty, and obligation and those of the utilitarians. On the basis of a few incongruities, the reviewers have usually characterized the more historically minded Holmes as a virulent critic of analytical jurisprudence.[2] The assumption is that a historical jurist could have learned nothing from Bentham and Austin.

A more balanced approach is needed. For example, if it can be shown that Holmes endorsed more utilitarian conclusions than even the explicit followers of Austin did, a number of implications would follow. Clearly, if the historically minded Holmes was more utilitarian than the later utilitarians concerning the nature of law, sovereignty, and obligation, then the standard assumption about the incompatibility of the English historical school of juris-

48

prudence with the older analytical school of the utilitarians requires reexamination. Such a reappraisal may show that the assumption is anachronistic, and that it reveals more about present-day attitudes than about the perspectives of nineteenth-century jurists. The rationale for discussing a few of Holmes's contemporaries therefore becomes clear. The ideas of Sir Henry Maine, the founder and leading exponent of the English historical school, are relevant because they indicate to what degree historical jurists were still Austinians. Conversely, the theories of Thomas E. Holland and William Markby reveal to what degree the later nineteenth-century utilitarian jurists diverged from their mentor, John Austin. In short, the argument is a form of *reductio ad absurdum;* if the significance of the intellectual differences that exist between Holmes and the utilitarians outweighs the significance of the similarities, then *a fortiori* it will also be necessary to separate the later utilitarian jurists' theories of law, sovereignty, and obligation from the earlier utilitarian tradition. The more reasonable conclusion is to abandon the questionable assumption that the English historical and utilitarian schools of jurisprudence were mutually exclusive, that no individual could have adopted assumptions and methods from both schools of thought. It will then become clear that Holmes's debt to the early utilitarian views of law, sovereignty, and obligation was more a matter of degree, requiring close attention to the nuances of late nineteenth-century English jurisprudence, than a matter of all or nothing.

The utilitarian theories of law, sovereignty, and obligation formed a nexus of interlocking concepts. The first of these, the imperative theory of law, was introduced into England by Hobbes, seconded by Bentham, but received its classical shape only with John Austin. While all these theorists thought laws were a "species of commands," Austin described this definition as the key to jurisprudence.[3] On the one hand, the distinctive characteristics of the "legal commander" established a sharp distinction between law and the related sciences of morals, deontology, and legislation with which it was often confused, according to Austin. Compared to his counterparts in morals and deontology, the legal commander's definite criteria gave to the student of law a clear conception of the boundaries of his discipline. While the demands of a highwayman, the dictates of God, and the orders of parents were all commands, lawyers were only interested in the commands set "by a sovereign person, or a sovereign body of persons, to a member or members of the independent political society wherein that person or body is sovereign or supreme."[4] On the other hand, besides furnishing a clear delimitation of the boundaries of jurisprudence, the concept of command gave Austin his theory of legal obligation. The existence of a command implies that "the party to whom it is directed is liable to evil from the other, in case he comply not with the wish."[5] If we are liable to such an evil (a sanction) for noncompliance, we are "bound," "obliged," or "under a duty." Hence legal obligations were a subset of commands. All commands produced obligations, but only the commands of the sovereign enforced by coercive sanctions resulted in legal obligations. As this triad of concepts formed the core of Austin's jurisprudence,[6] their significance as a defining feature of utilitarian jurisprudence is assured. Any attempt to examine Holmes's debt to the utilitarian tradition of jurisprudence must therefore examine these issues.

Austin's definition of sovereignty (criticized often and severely) is relatively well known in its general form. The sovereign whose commands defined the lawyer's subject and the existing set of legal obligations was that person or group of persons fulfilling the following two conditions: first, the *"bulk* of the given society are in a *habit* of obedience or submission to a *determinate* and *common* superior"; and second, that "certain individual, or that certain body of individuals, is *not* in a habit of obedience to a determinate human superior."[7] Only when these two conditions were true of the same determinate human superior (assuming a sufficient number of subjects), did a legal system of valid obligatory law exist. For our purposes, the crucial features of this conception of sovereignty were its factual and determinate nature. The sovereign was determinate; "all the persons who compose[d] it . . . [were] determined and assignable"[8] because only such a body had a capacity for corporate activity; only such a body could issue sovereign commands. Commands were "significations of desire"; only natural or artificial persons could have desires or signify them.[9] Consequently, all the individuals who formed a sovereign, whether one or many, had to fall within either a specific or generic description.[10] Only then were the relevant individuals capable of corporate activity and sovereignty.

The factual nature of Austin's definition of sovereignty is also implicit in his criterion that assessed which of several determinate persons was sovereign. Objective facts, the subjects' habits of obedience, were all that were relevant to decide this question; they sufficed to indicate the existence and the identity of a legal system. The sovereign of a society was not discovered by analyzing the constitutional law, the customary morality, or any other norms of the society. Perhaps in stable political societies, the bulk of the population used norms—whether customary, moral, religious, or revolutionary—to identify who the sovereign was. But in Austin's view this was not necessary.[11] Provided the two factual conditions of habitual obedience were fulfilled, the society still constituted a legal system even if the bulk of the population obeyed their sovereign out of fear, greed, prejudice, or hatred. Motives for the subjects' obedience were simply irrelevant to the question of whether a legal system existed. Only objective facts were necessary for a system of valid law to exist. Hence, even if there was controversy about whether the facts of obedience were sufficient to constitute the habit necessary for the existence of a sovereign, Austin insisted that this was no excuse to ignore the nature of the relevant facts.[12] The norms identifying the sovereign and the subjects' motives for obedience were no doubt interesting topics. But legal theorists inferred the existence of a sovereign, a legal system, and a body of valid obligatory laws exclusively from the presence or absence of external facts.

From this definition of law and sovereignty Austin understood a number of seemingly radical implications to follow, which were roundly criticized and ultimately responsible for the demise of his theory of law in the latter half of the nineteenth century. The first implication was that legal absolutism was inevitable in every legal system.[13] It seemed indisputable that if laws were the commands of a sovereign (who obeyed no other person), then the sovereign was not legally limitable because he was not habitually subject to anyone. Hence, legal limitations of sovereignty were impossible by definition. The second implication concerned the legal indivisibility of the sovereign powers. If no law could limit the sovereign, then a fortiori no law could legally divide the powers of the sovereign. Since a legal division of powers implied a limitation of sovereign powers to either distinct territories or functions, it was logically impossible: "in every society political and independent, the sovereign is *one* individual, or *one* body of individuals: that unless the sovereign be *one* individual, or *one* body of individuals, the given independent society is either in a state of nature, or is split into two or more independent political societies."[14] Even in federal states, the several united governments were sovereign *"as forming one aggregate body."*[15] The sovereign powers were not legally divisible because the sovereign, subject to no one, suffered the pain of no law.

This brief characterization of Austin's views on law and sovereignty suffices to evaluate Holmes's debt to utilitarian jurisprudence. But before entering these waters, a few cautions are in order. One must guard against certain misunderstandings of the utilitarian theories of law and sovereignty that are all to prevalent. Despite clear textual evidence to the contrary, there is an apparently irresistible temptation to interpret the utilitarian doctrines of legal absolutism and indivisibility to mean that the sovereign could not suffer any limitations or divisions of its power. This is a serious error. First, while the sovereign was incapable of legal limitations, its "component parts" could be subject to a legal duty. Austin argued that, though "considered in its corporate character, a sovereign number is sovereign and independent . . ., considered severally, the individuals and smaller aggregates composing that sovereign number are subject to the supreme body of which they are component parts." Hence, "though the [sovereign] body is inevitably independent of legal or political duty, any of the individuals or aggregates whereof the body is composed may be legally bound by laws of which the body is the author."[16] Since a part of the sovereign was susceptible to a legal limit, the sovereign as a whole could assign it special political functions and grant it legally limited powers. Austin's key criterion for determining the existence of such legal limitations or divisions was whether they were enforceable in a court of law. Like the noted English constitutional lawyer A. V. Dicey, Austin used judicial enforcement as the basis for distinguishing constitutional law from positive morality (or constitutional maxims).[17]

However, the more important misconception of Austin's views involves the question of de facto limits and divisions of the sovereign power. Commentators have claimed that Austin's sovereign was an irresistible arbitrary power that monopolized the use of political power. The most important critic who so errs is H. L. A. Hart. Indeed, he compounds the dilemma by claiming that Bentham never thought that the sovereign power was legally indivisible or illimitable. If true, his argument would seriously compromise the value of my claim concerning Holmes's debt to utilitarian jurisprudence. A bifurcated utilitarian theory of law and sovereignty would be of no use as a backdrop upon which to sketch Holmes's relationship to utilitarian jurisprudence if Austin's and Bentham's opinions diverged so widely. But fortunately there are serious problems with Hart's interpretation. He claims that Bentham "in very emphatic terms" insisted that the sovereign could be legally limited and divided.[18] Further, though Bentham first required the existence of an "express convention" for a legal limitation of sovereignty, he later abandoned this condition. Whether embodied in such a convention or not, a limited disposition to obey the sovereign sufficed to limit a sovereign legally. Moreover (Hart's interpretation continues), Bentham also thought that if subjects were disposed to obey different persons in different spheres of activity, then the sovereign powers were legally divided, presumably whether the division was contained within an "express convention" or not. Hart concludes: "Bentham, unlike Austin, always insisted that the habit or disposition to obey might be present with regard to one sort of act and absent with regard to another, and limited sovereignty is simply the correlative of a limited habit and disposition to obedience."[19] Bentham believed in legal limitations and divisions of the sovereign power; Austin did not.

Hart, however, has distorted Bentham's opinions by confusing de facto limits and divisions of sovereignty with legal limits and divisions. The context of Bentham's remarks and other textual evidence make this quite evident. First, Bentham's views concerning the limitations and divisions of sovereignty are found within his discussion of the moral obligation to obey the law. Now there is no question that Bentham thought it futile to try to solve this moral issue, as Blackstone had done, through the language of rights and duties—the respective rights and duties of the sovereign and his subjects.[20] Since (for Bentham) long-term interest and duty coincided, the moral dilemma of when to disobey was resolved by patient and sober examination of the utility of disobedience. That is why Bentham did not make a sharp distinction between legal and de facto limits and divisions of sovereignty. Having explicitly stated that all talk of rights and duties of the sovereign (in cases of civil disobedience) was rather puerile and useless, he assumed that his readers would not misunderstand his position that a sovereign could suffer only de facto limitations and divisions of power.

Additional textual evidence buttresses this interpretation. Any claim that the subjects' "dispositions to obey" limited the sovereign power would seem on the face of it to concern only de facto limits and divisions. It is unreasonable to interpret Bentham to have said (as Hart's view requires) that the *legal* authority of the sovereign varied with the mood of the public, that it expanded in cool weather upon the complacency of the populace and contracted in hot upon the bellicosity of uncomfortable urban dwellers. And last, we must note Bentham's analysis of the relative powers of despotic versus free governments: "Is it that those persons in whose hands that power is lodged which is acknowledged to be supreme, have less power in the [despotic] one than in the other, when it is from custom that they derive it [free governments]? By no means."[21] Now clearly, if both free and despotic governments have the same power, face the same limits, then Bentham was referring to de facto limitations that exist in every society and lie embedded within the subjects' limited dispositions to obey. No one would say that a despot and a free government face the same *legal* limitations of their powers. Therefore, the conclusion is that Bentham believed that the subjects' dispositions to obey, whether embodied in an "express convention" or not, was the key to defining the de facto limitations or divisions of the sovereign powers. This position is identical in substance to Austin's. The early utilitarian theory of law and sovereignty can thus serve as the backdrop upon which to assess Holmes's debt to utilitarian jurisprudence.

My claim is that critics who have heaped so much abuse upon Austin for imagining that an irresistible arbitrary power must exist within every legal order have only buried a straw man. Austin never endorsed any such requirement, either of arbitrary power or of a factual monopoly of power. To the contrary, Austin believed that in political sovereignty "the relation of superior and inferior are reciprocal. Or (changing the expression) the party who is superior as viewed from one aspect, is the inferior as viewed from another." The implication is that "the governed, collectively or in mass, are also the superior of the [sovereign] monarch: who is checked in the abuse of his might by his fear of exciting their anger; and of rousing to active resistance the might which slumbers in the multitude."[22] Consequently, the legally absolute sovereign's power was always checked by the customs, prejudices, and opinions of the public. Austin's favorite examples of checks upon the sovereign power were duelling and fervent religious obligations.[23] Duelling, which survived for centuries despite a legal sanction, was an example of public opinion checking the power of the sovereign, and Austin thought religious obligations especially efficacious because of their awful sanction. But in either case, there is no doubt that Austin believed that de facto limitations of the sovereign's power existing in the beliefs, opinions, and prejudices of the public were perfectly compatible with legal absolutism.

To show how completely wrongheaded the orthodox interpretation of Austin's theory actually is, we need only point out that Austin accepted Hume's insight into the controlling role of public opinion in politics.[24] Indeed, it was Austin's position that every political sovereign was in a state of habitual obedience to public opinion: "habitual deference to opinions of the community, or habitual and especial deference to opinions of a portion of the community, is rendered by every aristocracy, or by every government of a number, as well as by every monarch."[25] Legal absolutism of the sovereign was not only compatible with overpowering moral and religious obligations, but also with paying habitual obedience to public opinion. Only obedience to a determinate superior was incompatible with the sovereign's legally absolute nature. Indeed, Austin thought the only kind of independence which the sovereign could attain was a slavish submission to the indeterminate person of the general public. The conclusion was that when legal theory was set aside, when the legal supremacy of the sovereign was not at issue, the sovereign's power was checked, limited, and even controlled by public opinion. There was no arbitrary irresistible sovereign in Austin's theory of law.

Austin's views about the legal divisibility of the sovereign powers also require reinterpretation. Here again the commentators have mistaken Austin's claims about legal indivisibility for claims about the sovereign's de facto indivisibility. Fortunately, the textual evidence is again overwhelming. Austin admitted that "various constituent members of the heterogeneous and sovereign body may share the sovereign powers in any of infinite modes."[26] Indeed, except for legal divisions of the sovereign, Austin accepted the most extensive divisions of the sovereign power imaginable; it was divisible along lines of persons, territory, or function. For example, Austin's aplomb and ingenuity were clearly in evidence when he described how composite and federal states (including the United States and possibly the German Empire) were perfectly compatible with his requirement of legal indivisibility. The only de facto divisions that were incompatible with the sovereign's existence were those that undermined or destroyed the habit of obedience that constituted the sovereign. But this was a very weak condition. Even in states where the sovereign's power was divided among persons who rarely if ever met—for example, the sovereign of the United States, that is, the state governments (that is, the body of citizens of the respective states)[27]—the habit of obedience that constituted the sovereign still existed. It continued tacitly in the day-to-day obedience of individuals to the sovereign's political subordinates—the federal and state governments. Hence, even if the sovereign never met in formal session, even if it was divided extensively along geographical and functional lines, it was yet according to Austin the legally indivisible sum of sovereign powers. It was destroyed only if anarchy or rebellion eroded the general habit of obedience paid to the sovereign's agents. Of course while certain de facto divisions of power were preferable as more conducive to stability, in the end any de facto divisions were compatible with Austin's legally indivisible sovereign. In sum, Austin thought violence, disobedience to political superiors, and conflicts among political subordinates extinguished sovereignty, not de facto divisions of the sovereign power as such.

In Austin's doctrine of legal absolutism and indivisibility, a sovereign was legally absolute and indivisible because it was not subject to a law. But why not? Because all laws were commands of a sovereign. The logical requirements of legal indivisibility and legal absolutism arose from Austin's narrow definition of law. Once it was abandoned—for example, once custom was accepted as law—then the same factual and determinate sovereign was legally limitable and divisible. The appropriate custom had only to evolve. The main fact was that Austin's definition of law was distinct from his conception of sovereignty. It is important to keep this in mind in following the course of Austin's ideas of law and sovereignty into the latter half of the nineteenth century.

Sir Henry Maine, the founder of the English historical school, no doubt criticized many doctrines held dear by the utilitarians. He doubted the value of their pleasure-pain morality and the validity of the psychology underlying it; he deplored their insensitivity to history's role in human affairs, especially since it encouraged them to support impractical radical reforms.[28]

However, for our purposes Maine's most significant objection was against the Austinian definition of law. It was a disagreement over a central issue of jurisprudence; the others were not. Indeed, Maine began a line of criticism that quickly became standard. By pointing out examples of laws that existed apart from a sovereign, he destroyed Austin's reduction of all laws to commands of a sovereign. Village communities that preserved the ways of their forefathers, and tax-gathering empires that respected the customs of their individual communities were Maine's primary counterexamples. In the first case a sovereign did not exist, and in the second the sovereign failed to promulgate general commands. The essential point was that customary law was a reality, a fact ignored only by dogmatists.[29]

It was not that Austin's theory of law was inconsistent or unworkable; Maine in fact believed that once the assumptions of the theory were admitted, the majority of Austin's conclusions would "follow as of course and by ordinary logical process."[30] But to judge properly the value of a theory so overladen with strong assumptions, one had to assess the significance of the facts that the assumptions excluded from consideration. In the end, Maine rejected Austin's definition of law because it placed the historical facts of how a sovereign arose, moral limitations of a sovereign's power, and customary societies past and present outside the boundaries of jurisprudence. The objection was academic. Where should we draw the boundaries of jurisprudence? Should they include or exclude customs?

The fact that Maine objected more to Austin's narrow conception of jurisprudence than to his analysis of contemporary law is also indicated by Maine's characterization of Austin's theory of law as an accurate depiction of progressive societies. Austin's definition of law as a command of the sovereign was in regard to customary societies "only verbally true, and therefore without the value which it possesses in societies of the type to which our own [England] belongs."[31] Indeed, Maine thought that as the "capital fact in the mechanism of modern States is the energy of legislatures,"[32] the laws "with which the student of Jurisprudence is concerned in our own day are undoubtedly either the actual commands of Sovereigns . . . or else they are practices of mankind brought under the formula 'a law is a command,' by help of the formula, 'whatever the sovereign permits, is his command.' "[33] Therefore Austin's theory of law approximated the truth more and more as the course of history proceeded; as societies moved from status to contract, their laws gradually came to consist only of commands of a sovereign.[34] As early as 1855, in a paper read before the Juridical Society of London, Maine made his position clear. He stated that the "ultimate analysis of every positive law inevitably resolves it into a command of a particular nature, addressed by political superiors, or *sovereigns,* to political inferiors, or *subjects.*"[35] Despite the orthodox interpretation to the contrary, Maine never wrote anything to contradict this early opinion. The Austinian imperative theory of law, though of little value in regards to customary societies, was to Maine an accurate representation of the positive legal systems of modern progressive societies.

Holmes, like others of his generation, accepted the validity of Maine's objection to Austin's definition of law. No philosophical basis existed for denying customs the status of law. The issue of who enforced the law, whether by an identifiable political superior or not, was of less importance than the definiteness of the law's expression and the certainty of its enforcement. If in opposition to this view, "it be said that an indefinite body cannot directly signify a command," Holmes would have us remember "that the rules of judge-made law are never authentically promulgated as rules, but are left to be inferred from cases."[36] But since these are no doubt laws, it is also possible to have laws that are the commands of other indefinite bodies, for example, the commands of the general public. "The further difficulty which might be suggested, of fixing the line when the desires of indefinite bodies become so certain in form and sanction as to come within the category of laws (philosophically speaking), is no greater than that which a court encounters in deciding whether a custom has been established."[37]

However, this criticism of Austin had become quite commonplace. By 1880, the publication date of *The Common Law,* even self-described followers of Austin had doubts about Austin's reduction of custom to positive morality. By this time, German theories of law (but especially Savigny's) that gave custom a prominent place had swept through English jurisprudence. No legal theorist could stand up against this tide. Sir William Markby in 1871, with proper citations to Maine and Savigny, admitted that customs were in fact laws prior to judicial enforcement. In later editions of his work entitled *Elements of Law,* after he became aware of the inconsistency between an Austinian definition of law and recognition of a non-Austinian source of law, he conceded that there were serious flaws in Austin's theory of law.[38]

Thomas Erskine Holland confronted the same dilemma—how could one square Austin's definition of law with the prominence given to custom by German jurists? Though Holland thought it "convenient to recognize as laws only such rules as are enforced by a sovereign political authority," he also acknowledged that courts give effect to customs, "not merely prospectively from the date of such recognition, but also retrospectively; so far implying that the custom was law before it received the stamp of judicial authentication."[39] These attempts to reconcile the Austinian definition of law with German ideas show the overall influence of the German historical school upon English jurisprudence. While Maine accepted the status of custom and adjusted his philosophical definition of law accordingly, the later Austinians tried to square a circle, to incorporate new doctrines into the old analytical framework, with limited success. Nevertheless, Markby and Holland accepted the validity of these German doctrines no less than did Holmes or Maine. Consequently, one should not magnify unduly the significance of Holmes's abandonment of Austin's definition of law. Very few could still stomach such dogmatism.

Moreover, as Holmes generally ignored such philosophical definitions of law, the commentators who have visualized a gap existing between Holmes and the early utilitarians may have overestimated its breadth. Indeed, though Maine favored a new philosophical definition of law that included custom, Holmes doubted the value of such speculations; like Austin before him, Holmes was more practically oriented. With his definition of law, he wanted to establish the boundaries of jurisprudence by clarifying what modern lawyers meant by the term "law." Holmes was a "jobbist." What must a lawyer know to do his job? From this practical point of view, Holmes believed Austin's "definition of what lawyers call law is doubtless accurate enough."[40] But, Holmes should have added, "not as accurate as it could have been." He thought that Austin's practical definition of law as "the command of the sovereign" was reducible even further because most sovereigns enforced their commands through courts. In the present day, Holmes thought it no surprise that the lawyer's "only concern is with such rules as the courts enforce. Rules not enforced by them, although equally imperative, are the study of no profession."[41] Consequently, Holmes "doubted whether law, in the more limited meaning which lawyers give to the word, possessed any other common attribute than of being enforced by the procedure of the courts."[42] This reasoning indicates that Holmes came to his famous definition of law as the "prophecies of what the courts will do in fact,"[43] not by applying new scientific or pragmatic principles to the law, but by further refining the Austinian tradition of delimiting the boundaries of jurisprudence. The ultimate aim was practical: to know what to teach a lawyer. Austin limited the lawyer's subject matter to the general commands of the sovereign; Holmes narrowed further this practical definition of law. Law was "what a body of subjects, namely, the judges, by whom it is enforced, *say* is his [the sovereign's] will."[44] Judicial enforcement was the key criterion to the boundaries of positive law.

But even more to the point, Holmes's practical definition of law did not constitute a major departure from the utilitarian tradition. Though Austin defined laws as the commands of the sovereign, he often used judicial enforcement as the criterion of what rules were sovereign commands. Judicial enforcement had already fulfilled the important function of identifying laws within previous utilitarian theories. For example, Austin used the courts to distinguish constitutional law from maxims and customary laws from mere customs. Only when a court enforced a custom did its status shift from one of positive morality to one of positive law; only when a court applied constitutional maxims did they achieve the legal status of constitutional laws.[45] A. V. Dicey, an admirer of Austin, also used judicial enforcement as the criterion to distinguish between law and constitutional maxims.[46] So Holmes's practical definition of law as "the prophecies of what the courts will do" did not diverge much from Austin's views. Both the utilitarians and Holmes saw judicial enforcement as the key to defining the lawyer's subject matter. Austin, it is true, did not let this criterion shape his definition of law. He retained his definition of law as "the command of the sovereign" with the fiction that "whatever the court enforced was the command of the sovereign." Holmes detested fiction in the law[47] and saw no value in tracing all laws to a sovereign. Rather than accept this definition, Holmes took the opposite course; he shifted the definition of law to Austin's criterion of judicial enforcement, a criterion that had made Austin's more abstract definition of law workable. The conclusion is not only that Holmes's practical definition of law was inspired by the utilitarian interest in a sharply demarcated body of positive law, but also that its substance was not far removed from the early utilitarian view.

* * *

The second of the triad of Austinian concepts under discussion is the concept of sovereignty. Maine's opinions are again relevant here because they challenge the validity of a sharp distinction between the utilitarian and historical schools of jurisprudence, so the assumption that Holmes learned much from the utilitarians becomes all the more credible. In fact, as early as 1855, Maine explicitly endorsed Austin's definition of the sovereign.[48] It was that *Determinate* human superior *Immune* from punishment to whom the *Bulk* of a society were in a *Habit* of obedience. In 1875 Maine added a fifth requirement: the sovereign had to control "irresistible force." But since by this condition Maine only meant that the sovereign's power was irresistible by individuals, not by the society in general, it was already implicit in Austin's definition.[49] Maine's was only a stylistic refinement. More important, all of Austin's substantive criteria were preserved, and it is Maine's attitude toward the determinate and factual characteristics of Austin's sovereign that requires examination.

Though a group-sovereign was possible, Maine insisted with Austin that the sovereign had to be a determinate person. The reasoning was identical: "For otherwise such [a] superior could not address a command to, or in other words impose a law upon, his subjects. A command can only emanate from an individual or from a number of individuals conjoined in a corporate capacity."[50] Moreover, Maine used this Austinian reasoning for a purpose dear to Austin's heart, to undermine the intellectual foundations of the democratic movement in England. Maine attacked the popular conception of democracy—the rule of the people by the people—as nonsensical. Democracy was just another form of government, in essence no different from monarchy according to Maine, in which the "Many not the Totality ruled over the Few."[51] But Maine thought democracy faced an even more serious theoretical objection. Even if cleansed of obscurity, the popular notion of democracy was still at odds with the needs of a modern progressive state. It lacked that determinate sovereign who was the center, the *sine qua non*, of the contemporary state.

In all governments acts of State are determined by an exertion of will. But in what sense can a multitude exercise volition? . . . No doubt the vulgar opinion is, that the multitude makes up its mind as the individual makes up his mind; the Demos determines like the Monarch. A host of popular phrases testify to this belief . . . But what do such expressions mean? . . . On the complex questions of politics . . . the common determination of a multitude is a chimerical assumption; and indeed, if it were really possible . . . it is probable that . . . all social progress would be arrested. The truth is, that the modern enthusiasts for Democracy make one fundamental confusion. They mix up the theory, that the Demos is capable of volition, with the fact, that it is capable of adopting the opinions of one man or of a limited number of men, and of founding directions to its instruments upon them.[52]

The theoretical objection was that the multitude could not attain sovereign status because, unlike a determinate person, it was not able to "exercise volition." Maine used the Austinian definition of sovereignty for an Austinian end—to thwart democracy in England.

But though Austin was as severe a critic of democracy as Maine, he never used his theory of sovereignty to claim that pure democracy was impossible. Indeed, Austin admits that a society "governed by a sovereign body consisting of the whole community, is not impossible"; but he immediately adds that "the existence of such societies is so extremely improbable, that, with this passing notice, I throw them out of my account."[53] In every actual society, Austin continued, the "sovereignty can hardly reside in *all* the members of a society: for it can hardly happen that some of those members shall not be naturally incompetent to exercise sovereign powers." Austin concludes that in "most actual societies, the sovereign powers are engrossed by a single member of the whole, or are shared exclusively by a very few of its members: and even in the actual societies whose governments are esteemed popular, the sovereign number is a slender portion of the entire political community."[54] In short, Austin made practical rather than theoretical objections to the claim that "government for the people by the people" was possible.[55]

Even so, it is still possible to speculate that Maine's theoretical objection to democracy grew out of an Austinian conception of sovereignty. Though Austin may have been imaginative enough to see that a government of all by all was not logically incompatible with his definition of a determinate sovereign, those who followed him may well have begun to doubt whether a multitude was ever a determinate person. The issue was only one of fact. To find the Austinian sovereign one asked which determinate person the bulk of the population habitually obeyed. For those who thought the multitude was not a determinate person, the Austinian definition of sovereignty became a handy shovel to heap scorn upon the democrats. Had not Austin himself said that a political society "is divisible into two portions: namely, the portion of its members which is sovereign or supreme, and the portion of its members which is merely subject"?[56] This dualist view of political society (inherent in Austin's conception of sovereignty) yielded a convenient means of undermining the intellectual foundations of democracy once certain facts about the incapacities of multitudes were added.

The factual characteristic of Maine's conception of sovereignty also requires consideration. When the bulk of a society were in a habit of obedience to a determinate person, only then would that person having "irresistible power" over the individual members of the society achieve sovereignty. As with Austin, only objective facts of obedience were relevant to ascertaining if a sovereign existed. In Maine's words:

The question of determining his [the sovereign's] character is, you will understand, always a question of fact. It is never a question of law or morals. He who, when a particular person or group is asserted to constitute the Sovereign in a given community, denies the proposition on the ground that such Sovereignty is an usurpation or a violation of constitutional principle, has completely missed Austin's point of view.[57]

Of course this did not mean that moral considerations or constitutional principles accepted by public opinion never had any bearing. For both Maine and Austin, the bulk of the population often identified the sovereign in accordance with certain rules, whether called constitutional laws or positive morality. But a legal theorist need not examine the motives of the subjects in order to identify the sovereign. Objective facts sufficed. Maine no doubt thought that the motivation of obedience was a proper subject for jurisprudence; Austin, committed to a utilitarian psychology that treated the issue of motive brusquely and dogmatically, did not think it deserved a place within the study of positive law. Nevertheless, despite these discrepancies about where to draw the boundaries of jurisprudence (should they include custom, constitutional law, international law?), Austin and Maine agreed that habits of obedience were the criterion for identifying the sovereign; both were committed to a factual theory of sovereignty.

With a new sensitivity to the utilitarian origin of Sir Henry Maine's theory of sovereignty, it is now easier to see the resemblance between Holmes's ideas and the concepts of the utilitarians. First, it is clear that Holmes, like Maine and Austin before him, believed firmly in legal absolutism. From the legal point of view, from the view of courts and lawyers, law in the contemporary world was "not a brooding onmipresence in the sky but the articulate voice of some sovereign or quasi-sovereign."[58] Law implied an identifiable source, which (to avoid an infinite regress) was neither legally limitable nor legally divisible. "I simply say that the ultimate source of law when you find it, is subject to such laws or resolutions only as it chooses to impose upon itself, from a legal point of view, and that therefore the state is not subject to legal claims except so far as it seems fit to submit itself to them— and I should think that that was obvious."[59] This conclusion was required by both the "logical and practical ground that there can be no legal right as against the authority that makes the law on which the right depends."[60] However, this does not mean that Holmes considered the sovereign an arbitrary absolute power without any de facto limits; he agreed with Austin that when legal theory "is left to one side sovereignty is a question of strength and may vary in degree."[61] In Holmes's view, no human power is unlimited. Therefore any sovereign is necessarily susceptible to de facto limits and divisions of its power.[62]

I agree that although the lawmaker cannot admit that anything it enacts is not law, there is a large margin of *de facto* limit in the common consciousness that various imaginable enactments would provoke a general uprising. But that is an extra-legal fact of uncertain boundaries. The only limit that I can see to the power of the law-maker is the limit of power as a question of fact.[63]

Holmes's favorite example of this kind of limit to a sovereign power was the price of beer in Germany. Now obviously the price of beer was not a legal limitation of the German sovereign. It was a de facto one; if it was crossed, if the price of beer was raised, the German people would rise as one.[64] These were the only kinds of limits that the sovereign could experience. The sovereign was legally subject to no one for he was the source of all law; but as an organization of power, he was confronted by a wide variety of de facto limitations.

Holmes accepted the above reasoning because of his commitment to the utilitarian conception of a determinate and factual sovereign. As offsprings of courts established by a sovereign, judges conceived law to have an identifiable determinate source. Holmes believed that this practical orientation of judges should predominate in jurisprudence. But he denied Maine's claim that the "identifiability" of the sovereign precluded the sovereignty of the people. If a smaller number formed into a corporate aristocracy could will a command, then so could a majority or totality of a country. "It is true," Holmes insisted, "that if the will of the majority is unmistakable, and the majority is strong enough to have a clear power to enforce its will, and intends to do so, the courts must yield."[65] Courts and lawyers could therefore identify the will of the majority as a source of law. However, the more important feature of Holmes's theory was that all laws in contemporary societies were understood by lawyers and judges to have had an origin in a definite, assignable will. Factual disagreements over the capacities of multitudes should not hide theoretical affinities. Holmes's sovereign was as determinate[66] as Maine's or Austin's.

But which determinate person or group was the sovereign? How was he identified? Holmes's factual criteria indicate the utilitarian source of his ideas. Though the language changed slightly over the fifty years separating Austin from Holmes, both believed that objective habits of obedience were the key to the sovereign's identity, and coercive power was the substance of his authority.

Now it is admitted by every one that who is the sovereign is a question of fact equivalent to the question who has the sum of the political powers of a state in his hands. That is to say, sovereignty is a form of power, and the will of the sovereign is law, because he has power to compel obedience or punish disobedience, and for no other reason.[67]

The shift from Austin's facts of habitual obedience to Holmes's facts of political power was only terminological. Austin of course believed that habits of obedience were crucial because they established the power of the sovereign; and Holmes never doubted that a sovereign's power was based ultimately upon habits of obedience. Both contended that the factual nature of the sovereign prevented all restrictions of sovereignty except de facto limitations of power. As the sovereign was a form of power, its limits were of a similar nature—de facto dispositions to obey. Both theorists agreed that the subjects' dispositions to obey—their habits of obedience—were the key to identifying the sovereign and its limitations because sovereignty was a matter of power and coercion.

Holmes's relative debt to the utilitarian conception of a determinate and factual sovereign is further revealed against the background of the relevant ideas of his contemporaries. Once the German conception of custom as law became commonplace, attention shifted to how this definition related to the English theory of sovereignty inherited from the utilitarians. A paradox developed when the implications of the Germanic conception of the state were noted.[68] If the state was as much a product of law as a source of law, if the existence of a state implied the evolution of customary laws that defined and constituted the respective institutions of the state, then why could not these customary laws legally limit or divide the sovereign powers? If customs were valid laws, then a sovereign could face legal limits and divisions. Indeed, to the degree to which the Germans were right that such customs were necessary to constitute the state, to that degree Austin's theory of the legally absolute, determinate, and factual sovereign was necessarily wrong.

Later nineteenth-century English jurists, responding to this predicament, tried to reconcile Austin's theory of sovereignty with the increasingly popular German conception of law. For our purposes, two general approaches were the most important. The first resolved the contradiction by making the sovereign and the origin of custom coincide; the people became the sovereign. All customs were then the direct commands of the people, while statutes, executive orders, and judicial decisions were the indirect commands of the people's agents. Often popular for political reasons, this kind of reconciliation of the paradox seeped into more than one scholar's theory. Both Sir Frederick Pollock, the noted historical jurist, and William E. Hearn, a little know Austinian, were jurists who took this option.[69] Their method of reconciling Austin with the German theories significantly altered the English theory of sovereignty and corresponding conception of the state. As noted above, the Austinian theory of sovereignty that was followed by Maine and Holmes required the existence of a determinate person (even if corporate) that was superior in power to all other persons. This theory was wedded to a dualist notion of the state as a hierarchy of power subjecting all to the power of one "person." However, in Pollock's and Hearn's reconciliation, the sovereign was not a determinate person; it was "the indeterminate People." Consequently, the English no longer conceived the state as essentially a matter of political inequalities of power. The dualist view of the state was replaced with the more organic German conception.

The second option for resolving the contradiction between the Germanic definition of law and Austin's theory of sovereignty was more popular and (for our purposes) more important because it formed the basis for the twentieth-century understanding of a legal system. The Germans not only separated law from the existence of a sovereign, but also claimed that customary law established the political institutions and practices of a state. In contrast to Austin's position, the sovereign was necessarily defined and limited by law. The customary constitutional laws would define who has what sovereign powers. Facts of obedience or power were not relevant. The Austinian factual political sovereign was either replaced or (the more usual case) supplemented by a new legal sovereign. Though this distinction is now closely associated with James Bryce, the difference between a political and a legal sovereign was widely accepted in legal circles.[70] For example, the noted Austinian A. V. Dicey made the same distinction. He insisted that sovereignty was a legal fact independent of the reality of who exercised the de facto political power of the society, and independent also from the external facts of habitual obedience and coercive power.[71] Who was the legal sovereign and what powers it held were legal questions decided by laws, not by habitual facts of obedience. In Dicey's opinion, the English sovereign was legally undivided and unlimited except for the definition of who it was. But this was only a contingent legal fact subject to change. If and when customary laws that limited or divided the sovereign evolved, they would legally limit or divide the English sovereign.

This distinction between Austin's political sovereign and the Germanic legal sovereign was quite popular. It gave the term "sovereignty" a role in an intellectual world where the legal status of customary constitutional law was assured. But the victory of Germanic ideas was not instantaneous or unanimous. Besides Holmes, the English judge James F. Stephen also preserved intact the Austinian theory of sovereignty.[72] He too was convinced that contemporary lawyers should understand law as having a determinate and factual source itself not legally defined or constituted. Sovereignty was an extralegal fact.

However, there is no doubt that since the late nineteenth century the legal conception of sovereignty has won the day. The pre-eminence of John Salmond's *Jurisprudence* has done much to this end, by popularizing Germanic conceptions in jurisprudential circles of common-law countries. Salmond distinguished a state from other associations not only by its function, the fact that it alone waged war and administered justice, but also by its permanent structure and method of operation. The existence of the state "implied a permanent and definite organization—a determinate and systematic form, structure and operation."[73] Of this structure, the more fundamental elements were enshrined in constitutional law, which consisted of "the body of those legal rules which determine the constitution of the state."[74] Consequently, as the validity of a law depends upon its derivation from constitutional laws, "there can be no law without a state and a constitution."[75]

Moreover, the rules of constitutional law that defined and constituted the authority of the legal sovereign marked the boundary of jurisprudence. The jurist as jurist had no interest in the de facto political realities that exist beneath the de jure sovereign. He was only concerned with "the theory of the constitution, as received by courts of justice." His interest was in "the constitution not as it is in itself, but as it appears when looked at through the eye of the law."[76] The law identified the sovereign, not the facts of power and coercion: "all questions as to civil and supreme power are questions as to what is possible within, not without, the limits of the constitution. If there is no constitution which meets with due observance, there is no body politic, and the theory of political government is deprived of subject matter to which it can apply."[77] The conclusion was that if there was no constitutional law, then there was no sovereign, no state, and no system of valid law. Without a constitution, jurisprudence lost its subject matter.

By the turn of the century, the Germanic theory of law and the state had completely replaced the once orthodox utilitarian theory. Rather than recognizing the need of an extralegal political fact (sovereignty) for the existence of a system of law (as the nineteenth-century utilitarians had done), twentieth-century theorists have agreed that constitutional law—a "legal fact"—is necessary for the existence either of a state or of a legal system. Almost imperceptibly, a radical change has taken place in how people came to conceive the nature of law and the state.

It is within this context that one must assess Holmes's debt to the utilitarian theory of sovereignty. Holmes's endorsement of a legally absolute, determinate, and factual sovereign made him one of the last defenders of the utilitarian theory against the overwhelming influence of German ideas upon Anglo-American jurisprudence in the latter half of the nineteenth century. Since he despised German philosophy, German jurisprudence, and much of the German system of thinly veneered Roman law, Holmes deeply regretted this importation of continental ideas and fought against it throughout his life. And when the utilitarian origins and purposes of Holmes's practical definition of law are recalled, one is in an even better position to appreciate the degree to which Holmes was indebted to utilitarian jurists. His definition of the law as "the prophecies of what the courts will do in fact" and his conception of the sovereign as legally absolute, determinate, and factual were antithetical to German ideas, and together form convincing evidence that Holmes worked from utilitarian premises. However, it still remains to examine the third concept of the interrelated triad that formed the core of utilitarian jurisprudence: legal obligation. How did the early utilitarians along with Holmes and his contemporaries think of legal obligation?

The general contours of the early utilitarian theory of legal obligation rested upon the conviction that one should understand and explain human behavior scientifically. Moral activity was not excluded from this perspective. David Hume had set the precedent for applying the experimental method of reasoning to moral subjects, and the utilitarians followed his example. Consequently, the utilitarian theory of obligation had a psychological orientation. The sanction that motivated a person to fulfill his obligation became an essential requirement for the existence of an obligation. The utilitarian classification of duties into religious, moral, and political (legal) obligations reflected its importance. Depending upon whether the sanction was enforced by the hand of a superior invisible being, by the whim of public opinion, or by a judge acting in accordance with the will of the sovereign, the obligation was respectively religious, moral, or legal. With these general assumptions, the utilitarians understood legal obligation to mean "being obliged by the sovereign's threat of punishment."[78] However, this reduction of "having an obligation" to "being obliged" did not imply that an obliged person was bound to abide by his obligation. A legal obligation existed even though neither the force nor the probability of the sanction was either strong or likely enough to deter the commission of the prohibited act. Therefore, the utilitarians did not equate "being obliged" with "being obliged to act." The smallest chance of the offender incurring the smallest evil from the sovereign sufficed to establish a legal obligation, even if other motives induced the agent to act contrary to it.[79]

Holmes began with the same psychological approach. However, in following out the theory's implications, he went beyond the specific conclusions of the utilitarians. He thought it an error to suppose that the smallest likelihood of incurring the smallest sanction still constituted a legal obligation; the criterion was set too low relative to what the term meant in ordinary discourse. For Holmes, the term obligation included "something more than a tax on a certain course of conduct."[80] Something extra was therefore needed; but what was it?

The word [duty] imports the existence of an absolute wish on the part of the power imposing it to bring about a certain course of conduct, and to prevent the contrary. A legal duty cannot be said to exist if the law intends to allow the person supposed to be subject to it an option at a certain price. The test of a legal duty is the absolute nature of the command.[81]

Consequently, even a substantial sanction was not necessarily sufficient to establish a legal obligation. (Taxes, for instance, are often quite severe.) Besides a sanction, the command had to be absolute. The nature of this requirement, which Holmes added to the utilitarian theory of legal obligation, is defined as follows: an absolute command existed if "a breach of it is deprived of the protection of the law . . . such as the invalidity of contracts to do the forbidden act."[82] Therefore, in the criminal law, we have a legal obligation to refrain from murder, rape, robbery, and so on, because the state does not enforce contracts to perform such acts. The sovereign gives no legal option; he insists upon compliance.

But the liability found in civil law is not of this sort. "Liability to pay the fair price or value of an enjoyment, or to be compelled to restore or give up property belonging to another, is not a penalty; and this," Holmes added, "is the extent of the ordinary liability to a civil action at common law."[83] The agent has a legal choice: return the property (or enjoyment) or pay the price. The law, indifferent to the outcome, has no absolute wish that the agent take either course. So also in contracts. "The duty to keep a contract at common law means a prediction that you must pay damages if you do not keep it—and nothing else."[84] Since the law cares not whether a person fulfills his contract or pays for his omission, Holmes finds it pure sophistry to say that the agent has promised to do something, or that he has an obligation to keep his contract, or that the state punishes with damages anyone who breaks his agreement, or that a person is morally culpable for not keeping his contract. To the contrary, Holmes did not "think a man promises to pay damages in contract any more than in tort. He commits an act [the contract] that makes him liable for them if a certain event does not come to pass, just as his act in tort makes him liable *simpliciter.*"[85] Only in the remedies provided by a court of equity was Holmes willing to describe civil liabilities as imposing duties or obligations. With the injunction, the court would enforce its will "by putting the defendant in prison or otherwise punishing him unless he complies with the order of the court."[86] Here the agent has no legal choice: he must comply or go outside the law and face punitive legal reaction. But Holmes thought it foolish "to shape general theory from the exception" of equitable remedies. Accordingly, based upon what the term "obligation" ordinarily meant, Holmes concluded that there were no civil obligations at common law.

Holmes's modification of the utilitarian concept of legal obligation was therefore no small refinement. The utilitarians were right that legal obligation needed a sanction, but something more was required. The sovereign had also to deprive the act of any protection of the law. The agent must be obliged, but his legal alternatives must also be reduced to one, that is, to obey the sovereign's absolute wish. This alteration of the utilitarian theory of legal obligation may seem so fundamental that little is gained by associating Holmes's theory with the utilitarian tradition. However, the fact that Holmes made these refinements to further a utilitarian end helps to justify our conclusion. No theorist (for professional reasons) was more deeply committed to the utilitarian doctrine of the separation of law from morality than Holmes.

All moral terms were either thrown out of the law or given a distinctive meaning relevant to the needs and beliefs of the legal profession. But Holmes thought the lawyer ought to be concerned only with the actual operations of the law: what liabilities were imposed, in what manner, upon the commission of what acts. To guarantee that the lawyer did not wander from his true subject matter (perhaps into morality), Holmes's advice was to look upon the law as a "bad man" would, as a man who was only interested in the material consequences of his acts.

It was from this perspective that Holmes analyzed the concept of (obligation) duty—a word that still had "all the content which we draw from morals."[87] But what would the bad man mean by the term legal obligation? Holmes thought it would have no meaning to him (beyond a tax on a course of conduct) unless further material disadvantages followed upon the commission of the act. Holmes found those added disadvantages only in the criminal law, when the sovereign made it impossible for a person to act legally otherwise than as enjoined. Hence, Holmes's bad-man approach to law reduced radically the number of existing legal obligations. Many lines of conduct were taxed, many civil actions imposed liability, but few had no legal alternative. As Holmes described it, "the vague circumference of the notion of duty shrinks and at the same time grows more precise when we wash it with cynical acid and expel everything except the object of our study, the operations of the law."[88] This passage reveals clearly the utilitarian premises of Holmes's conception of legal obligation. A psychological orientation and the insistence upon the separation of law from morality were the utilitarian assumptions that shaped Holmes's distinctive theory of legal obligation.

A comparison of Holmes's views of legal obligation with those of his contemporaries further supports the conclusion that Holmes's refinements were not radically divergent from the utilitarian tradition. Other jurists departed even further from the earlier utilitarian antecedents. In fact, explicit utilitarian theorists like Holland and Markby[89] could not fully accept Austin's psychological analysis of legal obligation. Here again the troubling issue was the status of custom. Both of these utilitarian jurists accepted customs as valid laws. Hence a law was obligatory even when not enforced with an organized sanction; its validity was not derived either directly or indirectly from the will of the sovereign. This conclusion fitted poorly with Austin's theory, which held that a legal obligation required a command of the sovereign enforced with a sanction. In a later edition of his work, Markby expressed doubt about the value of deriving the validity of all laws from the sovereign's personality, and admitted that Austin's theory failed as a scientific conception.[90] These signs of wavering faith indicate that Austin's theory of legal obligation was in a serious dilemma. If customs were deemed obligatory laws, then Austin's factual source of legal validity and his psychological requirement of an obliging sanction were superfluous.

New theories arose to replace the old utilitarian ideas. If neither a sovereign nor a sanction was necessary for a valid law, then what were the requirements? The responses of Holmes's contemporaries point out the relative proximity of his views to those of the early utilitarians. For example, John Salmond gave answers that were radically different from the traditional utilitarian responses. He replaced the psychological theory of legal obligation with a normative theory. Salmond had concluded that all states were based upon constitutional laws that defined and constituted the legal authority. Consequently, the source of the law's validity was not a factual and determinate personality that existed at the top of the legal system. Indeed, Salmond thought there could be no such person unless fundamental laws superior to it existed. The validity of law was not derivable from persons, whatever power they might have, but only from legal persons. The norms underlying the legal sovereign's personality therefore became the foundation of legal validity. Salmond concluded that "there must be found in every legal system certain ultimate principles, from which all others are derived, but which themselves are self-evident. Before there can be any talk of legal sources," Salmond continued, "there must be already in existence some law which establishes them and gives them their authority."[91] This new theory of legal obligation that arose at the end of the nineteenth century thus had a normative explanation of legal validity. The source of all legal validity was not a factual and determinate person, but a basic norm.

As for sanctions, the psychological theory of the utilitarians had stated that we had an obligation because we were obliged. Did this new theory, in which legal validity was deduced from a law's relationship to deeper norms, require a sanction? The answer is no. "A duty is legal because it is legally recognized, not necessarily because it is legally enforced or sanctioned."[92] A law therefore need not "oblige us" for us to incur a legal obligation. According to the new perspective, the psychological inducements that cause us to act according or contrary to our legal obligations are an empirical scientific issue irrelevant to the subject matter of jurisprudence. Jurisprudence is the study of law, which is the study of ought-statements; ought-statements are derived only from other ought-statements. Because the question of their existence cannot rest upon empirical facts, neither can legal obligations (a subset of these legal ought-statements) rest upon the presence or absence of a contingent sanction. The only possible conditions for the existence of legal obligations are other normative considerations. If a law has the proper relationship to deeper, more fundamental laws, then the law is obligatory despite the lack of a sanction. With this conclusion, obligation became a rule-dependent concept.

The twentieth century has warmly received this normative theory of legal obligation, and contemporary legal philosophy has accepted it as its own. Hans Kelsen and more recently H. L. A. Hart and Joseph Raz have followed the example of Salmond.[93] Kelsen, Hart, and Raz agree that the obligatory character of a valid law is explained by that law's relationship to a more fundamental principle, whether called a basic norm, a secondary rule, or a power-conferring norm. The assumptions of this theory of legal obligation have become so widespread that it has influenced our conception of a legal system. In Hart's terminology, if a valid primary law requires the existence of a secondary rule, then a legal system can be best characterized and defined as a "union of primary and secondary rules."

There are therefore two minimum conditions necessary and sufficient for the existence of a legal system. On the one hand, those rules of behaviour which are valid according to the system's ultimate criteria of validity must be generally obeyed, and, on the other hand, its rules of recognition specifying the criteria of legal validity and its rules of change and adjudication must be effectively accepted as common public standards of official behavior by its officials.[94]

While the utilitarians and Holmes understood a legal system as a factual and determinate sovereign imposing legal duties upon its subjects through threats, twentieth-century thinkers describe a legal order as a system of primary and secondary rules in which the valid obligatory character of substantive laws is derived from the acceptance of more fundamental norms. More radically different views are hard to imagine: a hierarchy of persons is now considered a hierarchy of norms; a factual origin of legal validity and obligation is replaced with a normative one.

It is within this context that one should consider the relationship of Holmes's theory of legal obligation to utilitarian jurisprudence. The new normative theory of obligation and new definition of a legal system arose in the late nineteenth century as a result of Germanic ideas of law and the state influencing English jurisprudence. Given Holmes's distaste for German legal philosophy, his theory of legal obligation (like his concepts of law and sovereignty) is properly understood as a refinement of the utilitarian tradition. Indeed, Holmes is best described as a defender of English utilitarian assumptions against the invading army of continental jurisprudential ideas. He preserved the utilitarians' legally absolute, factual, and determinate sovereign; he adapted the practical utilitarian definition of law without violating its integrity; and he refined their theory of legal obligation for reasons that the utilitarians also endorsed. Of course Holmes was not a slavish follower of his utilitarian predecessors. He was an original and inventive jurist who made distinctive contributions to jurisprudence by working from utilitarian premises. Only in this sense is Holmes's work a part of the nineteenth-century utilitarian tradition of jurisprudence. But it is important nonetheless to give credit where credit is due. Many of the insights of Holmes's jurisprudence are historically explicable as direct inferences from explicit utilitarian doctrines or as indirect inferences from implicit utilitarian ideas of law, sovereignty, and legal obligation.

IV

JUDICIAL IDENTIFICATION, INTERPRETATION, AND LEGISLATION

It was not difficult to find the relatively well-known utilitarian ideas of law, sovereignty, and obligation reappearing in slightly modified forms in Holmes's legal philosophy. Now the task will be to examine familiar Holmesian insights into judicial decision-making and try to uncover similar ideas in the rather unexplored areas of utilitarian jurisprudence. But to appreciate the significance of any resemblance between Holmes's and the utilitarians' theories of judicial decision-making, it is necessary to consider the intellectual context. The orthodox theory was deductive; judges never made law, but only applied the right rule to the case and deduced the appropriate legal consequence. Legal interpretation was therefore crucial. If judges only applied law, then their activity required an extended theory of legal interpretation to explain the power which judges indisputably had.

The utilitarians and Holmes did not reject this theory entirely. When certain definite statutes or precedents were involved, they agreed that judges only applied the law to the case and deduced the consequence. But, in their opinion, legal identification and interpretation constituted only one facet of judicial activity, and the orthodox theory thus mischaracterized many important relevant facts. To capture these salient features of judicial activity, the utilitarians and Holmes proposed an inductive theory of judicial decision-making. This theory gave a new description of how judges ascertained controversial precedents, endorsed the view that judges did in fact make law, and thereby relieved the traditional theory of interpretation of its intellectual burden. And underlying the inductive approach of Holmes and the utilitarians, there were common attitudes toward syllogistic reasoning, the role of general principles, the significance of the particular case, and the course of legal development.

However, the center of the disagreement between the deductive versus the inductive characterizations of judicial activity was whether judges only applied existing laws to cases or whether they made laws upon calculations of utility. The utilitarian jurists were the first to adopt the perspective that judges made law; Holmes later broadened, deepened, and refined this inductive approach. His well-known insights into judicial decision-making were gained through a utilitarian understanding of judicial activity.

In Austin's and Bentham's day, the most popular adherent of the orthodox deductive theory of judicial decision-making was William Blackstone. He assumed a strict separation of legislation from execution; the former function belonged to the sovereign Parliament, the latter to the king and his courts.

Municipal law is "a rule of civil conduct prescribed *by the supreme power in a state.*" For legislature, as was before observed, is the greatest act of superiority that can be exercised by one being over another. Wherefore it is requisite to the very essence of a law, that it be made by the supreme power. Sovereignty and legislature are indeed convertible terms; one cannot subsist without the other.[1]

This strict separation of powers reduced the judicial function to one of identifying and interpreting statutes and precedents, applying them to cases, and deducing legal consequences. If judges ever altered or circumvented statutory provisions, then that "set the judicial power above that of the legislature, which would be subversive of all government." Blackstone concluded that there was "no court that has power to defeat the intent of the legislature."[2] Judges applied law; they did not make it.

Blackstone conceived of the unwritten common law in the same way. Judges were only the "living oracles" of this law, not its makers.

[How] . . . are these customs or maxims to be known, and by whom is their validity to be determined? The answer is, by the judges in the several courts of justice. They are the depositaries of the laws; the living oracles, who must decide in all cases of doubt, and who are bound by an oath to deciding according to the law of the land . . . For it is an established rule to abide by former precedents . . . as well as to keep the scale of justice even and steady, and not liable to waver with every new judge's opinion; as also because the law in that case being solemnly declared and determined, what before was uncertain, and perhaps indifferent, is now become a permanent rule, which it is not in the breast of any subsequent judge to alter or vary from according to his private sentiments . . . but according to the known laws and customs of the land; not delegated to pronounce a new law, but to maintain and expound the old one.[3]

There was only one apparent exception to the rule that judges merely applied the law of the land to cases. If a common-law rule contradicted the natural or divine law, the judge should not apply it: "But even in such cases the subsequent judges do not pretend to make a new law, but to vindicate the old one from misrepresentation. For if it be found that the former decision is manifestly absurd or unjust, it is declared, not that such a sentence was bad law, but that it was not law."[4] Judges never legislated according to Blackstone; they only applied the proper interpretation of the rule to the case and deduced the appropriate legal consequence.

Throughout the nineteenth century, different variants of this deductive theory of judicial decision-making retained their popularity. For example, conservative justices of the late nineteenth century defended the United States Supreme Court against charges that it was obstructing the people's will by affirming a "mouthpiece" theory of constitutional adjudication. The justices argued that they only compared statutory provisions against constitutional guarantees and deduced the appropriate legal consequence. The constitution, not the justices, invalidated legislation.[5] Holmes's opinion of this reasoning is familiar and needs no special emphasis here. However, Holmes's critique of another variant of this deductive approach is less well-known and a description of it will reveal the breadth of the orthodox deductive theory. For example, C. C. Langdell, the distinguished dean of the Harvard Law School during the late nineteenth century, assumed that every branch of the law consisted of a set of consistent interlocking principles. He preferred the case-book method of teaching law because it showed the student how the principles "hung together."[6] For this reason, Holmes described Langdell as the "greatest living legal theologian." He placed too much emphasis on the importance of logic and consistency in the law.

But in this word "consistency" we touch what some of us at least must deem the weak point in Mr. Langdell's habit of mind. Mr. Langdell's ideal in the law, the end of all his striving, is the *elegantia juris*, or *logical* integrity of the system as a system. He is, perhaps, the greatest living legal theologian. But as a theologian he is less concerned with his postulates than to show that the conclusions from them hang together . . .

If Mr. Langdell could be suspected of ever having troubled himself about Hegel, we might call him a Hegelian in disguise, so entirely is he interested in the formal connection of things, or logic, as distinguished from the feelings which make the content of logic, and which have actually shaped the substance of the law.[7]

According to Langdell, the judges only applied legal principles to cases and deduced the appropriate legal consequences. The legislative role of judges was ignored.

But if judges did not legislate, how were their power and influence explained? Blackstone and Langdell responded that legal interpretation sufficiently described the judicial function. In their view, judges could range far and wide to identify the intention or purpose of a statute. They could even narrow or widen statutory provisions under the guise of interpreting the law's reason or spirit.[8] Holmes's description of Langdell's work assesses accurately the discretionary power that Langdell granted to judges and theorists. If judges only applied legal principles to cases, they must have liberty to put the material into order.

Every line is compact of ingenious and original thought. Decisions are reconciled which those who gave them meant to be opposed, and drawn together by subtle lines which never were dreamed of before Mr. Langdell wrote. It may be said without exaggeration that there cannot be found in the legal literature of this country, such a *tour de force* of patient and profound intellect working out original theory through a mass of detail, and evolving consistency out of what seemed a chaos of conflicting atoms.[9]

In Holmes's estimation, Langdell admired judges who subtly and imaginatively manipulated principles. He certainly practiced this in his own work; he could hardly have understood the judge's task differently.

The deductive theory of judicial decision-making was therefore conjoined to a discretionary theory of legal interpretation. The utilitarians and Holmes disagreed with both elements of this traditional view. First, they thought Blackstone's and Langdell's understanding of judicial activity defective because it misleadingly gave syllogistic deductive reasoning a greater role than the facts substantiated. Holmes believed that history clearly showed "the failure of all theories which consider the law only from its formal side, whether they attempt to deduce the *corpus* from *a priori* postulates [Blackstone and other natural-law jurists], or fall into the humbler error of supposing the science of law to reside in the *elegantia juris,* or logical cohesion of part with part [Langdell]."[10] In either case, these theories distorted the facts by overemphasizing deductive reasoning. Second, the utilitarians and Holmes claimed that the characterization of all forms of judicial activity as deductive interpretations and applications of law was delusional. To their minds, it was clear that judges not only interpreted but also made law. Therefore, they believed that a theory of judicial legislation had to supplement a restricted theory of legal interpretation. The utilitarians, but especially Austin, were the first to perceive these problems in the traditional outlook, and to solve them they fashioned a new inductive approach to judicial decision-making and a literal theory of interpretation. Holmes accepted these utilitarian premises, strengthened their conclusions, and clarified the implications of the inductive theory.

However, the utilitarians and Holmes accepted that some facets of judicial activity were ably described by the deductive theory. When a simple case arose under a clear precedent or statute, the judge deferred usually to the wisdom of his predecessors and always to the sovereign's will. Austin's distinction between supreme and subordinate legislators reveals the deductive element in judicial activity. Though he thought the Lockian-Blackstonian distinction between legislative and executive (that is, judicial) power "too palpably false to endure a moment's examination,"[11] Austin favored a distinction between the supreme sovereign's power and legislative or executive powers subordinate to the sovereign. Subordinate officials, whether called legislative or executive, had to defer to the wishes of the sovereign. According to Austin, English judges were subordinate executive officials subject to the control of the sovereign. Perhaps in some societies the sovereign would consist of judges; then they would only be

subject to public opinion. English judges, however, were subordinate; whenever the sovereign spoke, they were only to listen, to
interpret his intention, to apply the rule, and to deduce the appropriate legal consequence: "but there it is, the solemn and unchanged will of the legislator, which the judge should not take
upon himself to set aside, though he may think it desirable that it
should be altered."[12] Austin therefore limited the judicial discretion of judges. Judges did make law, but not all the time; often
they deferred to the sovereign's will.

Holmes followed this Austinian tradition of judicial deference
to the sovereign's will and encouraged his fellow justices not to
overstep their authority when invalidating legislation upon constitutional grounds. Though he too conceded that judges made
law, he immediately cautioned that they "do so only interstitially;
they are confined from molar to molecular motions."[13] They legislate within the intervals left by the sovereign's commands, not
against the commands themselves. In many of his dissents from
Supreme Court decisions that invalidated economic and social
legislation, Holmes acted because he believed his job was to "help
the country go to hell if it wanted to."[14]

There is nothing that I more deprecate than the use of the Fourteenth
Amendment beyond the absolute compulsion of its words to prevent the
making of social experiments that an important part of the community
desires . . . even though the experiments may seem futile or even noxious
to me and to those whose judgment I most respect.[15]

According to Holmes, the Supreme Court should not declare a
law unconstitutional "unless it can be said that a rational and fair
man necessarily would admit that the statute proposed would in-
fringe fundamental principles as they have been understood by
the traditions of our people and our law."[16] Holmes's attitude towards the constitutional role of the Supreme Court arose from the
Austinian tradition of judicial deference to the sovereign, a tradition that insisted upon a monopoly of power for the existence of a
legal order. Moreover, Holmes assumed that law "being a practical thing, must found itself on actual forces,"[17] on the actual sovereign power that exists in every legal order. These dominant
forces of society were reflected in the legislature; judges should
generally defer to their wishes.

But how to ensure that judges in simple cases only applied the relevant rule and deduced the proper legal consequence? What was to keep them from extending or narrowing the law? Blackstone and Langdell granted large amounts of discretion to judges through a theory of legal interpretation. Since Austin and Holmes opposed judicial discretion, they hoped to obtain judicial subservience by a strict theory of legal interpretation. To ascertain the legislature's intention, the judge need only consult the written word, the actual statutory provisions.

The discovery of the law which the lawgiver intended to establish, is the object of genuine interpretation . . . For the reasons which I have given in the text, the literal meaning of the words wherein the statute is expressed, is the primary index or clue to the intention or sense of its author.

Now the literal meaning of words (or the grammatical meaning of words) is the meaning which custom has annexed to them. It is the meaning attached to them commonly by all or most of the persons who use habitually the given language.[18]

Even if the literal meaning of the words departed from the sense (found through other means) of the legislator's intention, Austin advised judges to limit themselves to the explicit statutory provisions. It was better to ignore the scope, purpose, and history of a statute, and to avoid extrapolating from clear statutes the meaning of an ambiguous but similar one. Austin's reasoning was simple: "The terms through which the legislature tried to convey its intention, were probably measured as carefully as the intention which it tried to convey."[19] If the provisions were vague, the intention was likely vague also; nothing was gained by searching for the sovereign's intention by other methods.

However, Austin had another reason for a strict theory of legal interpretation. In his own words,

If the literal meaning of the words were not the primary index, (or were not scrupulously regarded by the interpreter,) all the advantages (real or supposed) of statute legislation would be lost. For the purpose is, to give an index more compendious, compact, (or lying together,) and therefore less fallible, than is that to a judiciary rule. But if the interpeter might, *ad libitum*, desert the literal meaning, no such index could be given.[20]

Codification was advantageous only if the code was strictly interpreted. However, if the judge had reason to believe that behind the vague language of a statute hid a relatively clear intention, then Austin advised judges to abide by the sovereign's wishes. This does not amount to an inconsistency; Austin's doctrine of judicial deference required judges to act in accordance with the sovereign's intention if known. In case of a vague statute, judges would justify their decision by pointing to the obscure but clear intention of the sovereign. But this was the exceptional case. Normally the customary sense of the terms used would indicate either the sovereign's clear intention or as much as possible of a sovereign's vague intention.

At first, Holmes seems to have favored a theory of legal interpretation even stricter than Austin's. While in exceptional cases Austin had permitted the judge to ascertain the sovereign's intention through methods other than the statute's provisions, Holmes apparently denied to judges this option. They were to stick to the written word. "We do not inquire," Holmes insisted, "what the legislature meant; we ask only what the statute means." Consequently, "if the same legislature that passed it should declare at a later date a statute to have a meaning which in the opinion of the court the words did not bear," Holmes supposed "that the declaratory act would have no effect upon intervening transactions."[21] Holmes thought too much discretion was granted to judges if they could interpret the sovereign's will according to speculative historical matters, or according to statutes addressing the same topic, or according to the statute's scope or purpose. Judges were to attend only to the written statutory provisions.

But this seems a very difficult theory to live with. What if the legislature made a small misstatement that had significant consequences? Would the legislature have to enact an amendment or a corrected statute? Why not simply allow the judge to correct this kind of slip of the pen? Holmes was far too commonsensical to disagree.

The Legislature has the power to decide what the policy of the law shall be, and if it has intimated its will, however indirectly, that will should be recognized and obeyed. The major premise of a conclusion expressed in a statute, the change in policy that induces the enactment, may not be set out in terms, but it is not an adequate discharge of duty for the courts to say: We see what you are driving at, but you have not said it, and therefore we shall go on as before.[22]

Holmes's theory of legal interpretation came very close to Austin's. The judge should depart from the statutory record only if he knew the provisions did not express the true and clear intention of the legislator. Given his commitment to the Austinian doctrine of judicial deference to the sovereign, Holmes had little choice; given his assumptions concerning the requirements of a legal order and the necessity of sovereignty, Holmes could not allow the judge to ignore, even if poorly expressed, the specific will of the sovereign. Of course in the normal case the sovereign's intention was known from what he said; only if there was clear evidence that intention and text diverged did the judge have the right to depart from the customary meanings of statutory provisions.

Moreover, statutes were not the only factor limiting judicial discretion, according to Holmes and Austin. Precedents also deserved respect. When not legislating, judges were in Austin's view applying "either some statute law, or else the general ground of some anterior decision by which a new rule had been already introduced and created."[23] Holmes even described himself as "slow to consent to overruling precedent."[24] His favorite example was the common-law requirement of consideration in contracts. The rule was settled; judges should tamper with it only if historical developments rendered the law obsolete.

But respect for precedent seems too commonplace to prove much. Blackstone and Langdell certainly adhered to this principle, so the fact that both Austin and Holmes accepted the validity of precedents hardly seems noteworthy. However, just as their strict theory of statutory interpretation differentiates their views from the orthodox approach, so also Austin's and Holmes's peculiar method of identifying precedents distinguishes their opinions from Blackstone's and Langdell's. The older deductive theory assumed that judges identified precedents or legal principles much as they ascertained statutes. When a relevant case came up, the judge took down the judiciary rule, interpreted it, applied it to the case, and deduced the proper legal consequence. Conversely, Austin and Holmes thought precedents so different from statutes that they required an inductive method of identification and interpretation.

Legislatures deliberately framed statutes in abstract and general terms that "are *parcel* of the law itself. And, consequently," Austin argues, "the proper end of interpretation is the discovery of the meaning which was actually annexed by the legislator to those very expressions."[25] For this reason, Austin favored the strict theory of statutory interpretation described above. But judicial precedents do not have these abstract and general characteristics. When legislating the judge does not fashion a clear abstract rule, but decides a particular case; he "legislates *as properly judging*, and not *as properly legislating*."[26] The purpose of judicial legislation is concrete. Moreover, the general propositions found within a judge's opinion are usually unauthoritative or so crudely expressed that they have little significance. In Austin's opinion, these characteristics of judicial legislation and judicial opinions limit the way judges should identify and interpret precedents:

> For as the proper purpose of the judge is the decision of the specific case, any general proposition which does not properly concern it is extrajudicial and unauthoritative. And (moreover) as the judge is not (like the legislator) occupied in constructing a rule, his general propositions are often crudely expressed, and must be carefully construed by a constant reference to his direct and proper purpose.[27]

These effects necessitated a method to identify and interpret precedents that was very different from the strict theory of interpretation suitable to statutes. This new method gave judges wide discretion to interpret precedents by the particular facts of the cases.

> As taken apart (or by themselves), and as taken with their literal meaning, the terms of his entire decision (and, *a fortiori*, the terms of his general propositions) are scarcely a clue to the rule which his decision implies. In order to an induction of the rule [*sic*], which his decision implies, their literal meaning should be modified by the other indices to the rule, from the very commencement of the process. From the very beginning of our endeavor to extricate the implicated rule, we should construe or interpret the terms of his entire decision and discourse, by the nature of the case which he decided; and we should construe or interpret the terms of his general or abstract propositions, by the various specific peculiarities which the decision and case must comprise.[28]

Austin criticized the Roman jurists for having failed to interpret inductively the general principles of their judiciary law. By separating the principles from the particular facts to which they were applied, the Roman jurists lost the requisite guides to their import.[29] The proper way to identify and interpret a precedent required an examination of the different situations of fact to which the principle was applied.[30] Only by this inductive method would the judge know the meaning of the principle.

However, Austin did not think an inductive comparison of cases sufficed to know the meaning of a principle. If legal principles were linked without qualification to each particular situation of fact, then precedents were impossible. Therefore, after considering a number of cases, the judge had to abstract the rule from the irrelevant facts of the specific cases.

In short, although a rule or principle is established by the decision or decisions ... that rule or principle lies *in concreto,* and must be gotten from the decisions by which it was established, through a process of abstraction and induction. Before we can find the import of the general principle or rule, we must exclude the peculiarities of the cases to which it was applied, and must consider the decision to which the tribunal would have come, if its decision had not been modified by those specific differences.[31]

It was a dual process. First, to identify and interpret a precedent, the judge inductively observed and considered the relevant particular cases; second, to fashion a rule of conduct, the judge abstracted the rule from the immaterial facts.

The similarity of Holmes's method of identifying and interpreting precedents to Austin's procedure of induction and abstraction is most easily discerned in one particular implication of the above approach. If, according to Austin, legal principles were meaningless apart from particular cases, if they were identified, interpreted, and even established by a method of induction and abstraction, then they arose after the fact. I do not mean merely that Austin believed judiciary law to be *ex post facto* in the sense that judges often meted out punishment for acts that became illegal only with the delivery of the judge's opinion. Though both Austin and Holmes recognized this aspect of judiciary law as inevitable, I mean something more: legal principles themselves were established after the fact of the judicial decision. Because legal principles (the *rationes decidendi*) were identifed, interpreted, and established by a method of induction and abstraction, they did not attain existence—they had no body or meaning—until a number of similar cases were decided.

Successive judges therefore established the *rationes decidendi* of previous cases. Legal principles were extrapolated through a method of interpretation; they arose only after several analogous cases were reconciled. Holmes saw this implication of Austin's method of induction and abstraction clearly.

It is the merit of the common law that it decides the case first and determines the principle afterwards. Looking at the forms of logic it might be inferred that when you have a minor premise and a conclusion, there must be a major, which you are also prepared then and there to assert. But in fact lawyers, like other men, frequently see well enough how they ought to decide on a given state of facts without being very clear as to the *ratio decidendi*.[32]

Holmes therefore thought Lord Mansfield's advice to a businessman suddenly appointed judge, that he should state his conclusions but not his reasons, good advice for more educated courts. The underlying insight is that a "well settled legal doctrine embodies the work of many minds,"[33] and consequently, that "just in proportion as a case is new and therefore valuable, no one, not even judges, can be trusted to state the *ratio decidendi*."[34] Holmes therefore thought legal principles were established as precedents not by the presiding judge, but by those who followed him. Given their underlying similar method, Austin and Holmes admired the common law because it preferred having contemporary judges identify, interpret, and thereby establish the legal precedents of an earlier era.

Holmes's specific attitudes toward general principles further clarify how his view that "the common law decides the case first and determines the principle afterward" flowed from Austin's method of induction and abstraction. First, Holmes also considered that legal principles divorced from the circumstances to which they were applied were meaningless. In his view, to make "a general principle worth anything you must give it a body; you must show in what way and how far it would be applied actually in an actual system."[35] Judges should not therefore be restricted to the specific language of any previous case; they interpreted a legal principle inductively from all the cases, from all the similar but different circumstances to which it was applied. Accordingly, Holmes concluded that "only after a series of determinations on the same subject matter," does it become "necessary to 'reconcile the cases', as it is called, that is, by a true induction to state the principle which has until then been obscurely felt."[36] Because precedents were identified and interpreted inductively, they did not exist until later judges provided the rationale for earlier cases. Because judges established precedents by an inductive method of reconciling cases, legal principles arose ex post facto, after the judicial decision. Judicial successors determined the precedents of their predecessors.

The discretion granted to judges by this inductive method of identifying and interpreting judiciary law far exceeded what Austin and Holmes thought proper to grant to judges interpreting statutes. The judge more or less ignored the specific language of previous cases, familiarized himself with any number of "similar" cases, and excluded any "irrelevant" facts when he reconciled the cases. Though judges were subordinate to the sovereign's statutes, sovereigns in common-law jurisdictions had granted to their judges authority to interpret and develop judiciary law independently. These assumptions therefore enabled the utilitarians and Holmes to provide a realistic theory of judicial decision-making, one that insisted upon judicial subservience to the sovereign without ignoring the discretionary power of judges. In turn, their sensitivity to judicial power made them suspicious of the distinction between interpretation (execution) and legislation. Was the judge's power of interpretation so extensive that he at times made rather than applied laws? The utilitarians' and Holmes's affirmative answer to this question provides us with another area of comparison: their conception of judicial legislation. How did it relate to legal interpretation, to the distinction between substance and the form of law, to the standard of utility, to legal principles and distinctions? Answers to these questions will show that Holmes's ties to the utilitarian theory of judicial decision-making were not limited to a strict notion of statutory interpretation and an inductive method of interpreting precedents. They included a theory of judicial legislation.

Many commentators think the insight that judges do in fact make law is a twentieth-century discovery of the legal realists. Holmes, an early adherent to this new scientific and pragmatic approach to law, was only slightly ahead of his time. However, this myth survives only because the facts go unexamined. Legal philosophy did not have to wait for the twentieth century for either a scientific approach to law or an awareness that judges made law. The utilitarian jurists consciously adapted jurisprudence to the scientific methods of their time and examined the then unexplored topic of judicial legislation. Bentham himself caricaturized the unwritten common law as "an assemblage of fictitious regulations" made by judges: "I hope it is by this time apparent, that what is called the Unwritten Law is made not by the people but by Judges: the substance of it by judges solely: the expression of it, either by Judges or by Lawyers who hope to be so."[37]

Austin's sense of judiciary law was somewhat different than Bentham's, but he too saw that English judges made law. The "mode of origination" was the key criterion to Austin's concept of judiciary law, whether it was the sovereign or his subordinate judges who legislated. Austin thought it clear that as "a subordinate body clothed by the sovereign with legislative power may make laws by direct enactment, so the sovereign, acting in the capacity of a judge may make them in the indirect mode of judicial decision."[38] But Austin distinguished between "direct" and "oblique" legislation (rather than between judge-made law and sovereign-made law) mainly to account for the Roman assembly's practice of delegating legislative powers to subordinate *praetors* and the Roman emperor's practice of making law judicially.[39] It had no bearing upon his understanding of the English judge. He lamented the "childish fiction employed by our [English] judges, that judiciary or common law is not made by them, but is a miraculous something made by nobody, existing, I suppose, from eternity, and merely *declared* from time to time by the judges."[40] Hence, both Bentham and Austin clearly understood that English judges made laws.

But this common insight into the fact of judicial legislation hides an important difference between Bentham and Austin. Bentham condemned judiciary law as unknowable and uncertain.

They are made known thus. The Judge in a narrow, ill-contrived room, where a hundred perhaps can see, where fifty perhaps can hear, where twenty perhaps can bestow themselves at such ease as to profit from their hearing, announces these judicial acts *viva voce:* Of these twenty, if anyone publish what is announced, he is to be punished: so saith the Law. Thus it is that the acts of Judges are made known by them to 8 millions of people.[41]

According to Bentham, the ex post facto qualities of the law burdened the people even more than its unknowable and therefore uncertain character. In a comparison of judiciary laws to rules made for pets, Bentham expressed his contempt for the retroactive quality of the common law. The master waits for his dog to do something he does not like and then punishes him for it.[42] In sum, Bentham condemned judge-made laws as an inefficacious use of punishment in direct contradiction with the principle of utility.[43]

Austin agreed that judiciary laws were ex post facto and generally unknowable, even by lawyers.[44] However, notwithstanding these objections, Austin valued judicial legislation as "highly beneficial and even absolutely necessary."

I cannot understand how any person who has considered the subject can suppose that society could possibly have gone on if judges had not legislated, or that there is any danger whatever in allowing them that power which they have in fact exercised.[45]

Consequently, although both Austin and Bentham favored codification, they had different ideas about the role judges should play afterward. Bentham wanted to restrict judges to deductive applications of the code. Though (as Austin reports it) Bentham "again and again declared in his works that the reports of the decisions of the English Courts are an invaluable mine of experience for the legislator,"[46] he no doubt wished to shut this mine down. Hence Bentham has little to say about the practice of judicial legislation; the censorial jurist generally ignored what he condemned. In his visionary society, judges were to report defective laws to the Ministries of Justice and Legislation; but they were to apply them nonetheless until formally changed.[47] Austin, on the other hand, thought that "the growth of judiciary law explanatory of, and supplementary to, the code, cannot indeed be prevented altogether, but it may be kept within a moderate bulk, by being wrought into the code itself from time to time."[48] Moreover, Austin's more descriptive orientation encouraged him to study the existing practice of judicial legislation. By what method did judges in fact make law was the question Austin tried to answer. For these reasons, an examination of the relationship of Holmes's theory of judicial legislation to that of the utilitarians must revolve around Austin's writings.

Austin distinguished two types of judicial legislation: one he associated with the interpretation of statutes, the other with the interpretation of precedents. He had little use for the first type of legislation. He described it as a "bastard" or "spurious" type of interpretation "which lays all statute law at the arbitrary disposition of the tribunals."[49] By this means the judge extended or restricted a statute's unequivocal provisions *ex ratione legis*. For example, the sovereign "expresses exactly the intention with which he is making it, but conceives imperfectly and confusedly the end which determines him to make it." Therefore, "the judge who finds that a statute is thus defective or excessive, usually fills the chasm, or cuts away the excrescence"; he thereby "completes or corrects the faulty or exorbitant intention with which it actually was made."[50] But Austin refused to describe this practice as Blackstone had done—as the *"interpretation* of a statute by its reason or spirit"—because in his own opinion it was "a palpable act of judicial legislation."

Instead of interpreting a statute obscurely and dubiously worded, the judge modifies a statute clearly and precisely expressed: putting in the place of the law which the lawgiver indisputably made, the law which the reason of the statute should have determined the lawgiver to make.[51]

Austin thought that certain forms of statutory interpretation merged into judicial legislation; the judge made rather than interpreted law.

Whether Austin entirely condemned this spurious kind of judicial activity is doubtful. He admitted that sovereigns often delegated powers of legislation to judges and admired the harmony and consistency of the law which this practice had produced.[52] But Austin's doctrine of judicial deference to the sovereign's will permitted a judge to extend or restrict a statute's provisions only if he knew the sovereign's purpose in enacting the law, in what way the sovereign's intention was faulty, and that the sovereign would agree with his alterations. If the judge had the delegated authority to correct statutes, if he identified faulty statutes correctly, if he understood the sovereign's purpose properly, and if he provided a remedy agreeable to the sovereign, no problem existed. But Austin was suspicious. "It may indeed be doubted," he cautioned, "whether the so-called interpretation, which *restricts* the operation of statutes . . . ought to be permitted by any"[53] system of law. It may have been suitable for earlier legal periods, but the time for codification had arrived. Experts like himself were now able to draft unequivocal statutes that would both express exactly the sovereign's intention and attain successfully its purpose. Therefore, judicial legislation through the extension or restriction of statutory provisions *ex ratione legis* not only involved a dangerous grant of discretionary power to judges, but was also unnecessary. Austin believed the practice would die out.

The other type of judicial legislation associated with the interpretation of precedents faced a far happier future. Austin considered judiciary legislation inevitable because no code could foresee all possible cases. The presiding judge had to legislate if none of the code's provisions applied and no clear precedents existed:

When the law or rule is introduced obliquely, the proper purpose of its immediate author or authors is the decision of a specific case or of a specific point or question. Although this specific case is decided by a new rule, the proper purpose of the judge is not the introduction of that rule, but the decision of the specific case to which the rule is applied, and so, speaking generally, the shew of legislation is avoided. Generally the new rule is not introduced professedly, but the existing law is professedly ascertained by interpretation or construction . . . and is then professedly applied to the case or question which awaits decision. If the new rule obtains as law thereafter, it does not obtain directly, but because the decision passes into a precedent: that is to say, is considered as evidence of the previous state of the law; and the new rule, thus disguised under the garb of an old one, is applied as law to new cases.[54]

In many instances of judicial legislation new rules were introduced, though they were "professedly" only interpretations of existing precedents. The logical form of the law remained the same, while its substance changed. Consequently, the logical consistency of judiciary law, which the traditional deductive theory had admired so profusely, was actually a fiction; the substance of the law was continually adapting itself to the changing needs of society under the guise of logical necessity.

No one popularized this distinction between the form and the substance of law more than Holmes. He also believed that the logical form of legal continuity was no more than appearance, even using the same metaphor as Austin had done:

The form of continuity has been kept up by reasonings purporting to reduce every thing to a logical sequence; but that form is nothing but the evening dress which the new comer puts on to make itself presentable according to conventional requirements. The important phenomenon is the man underneath it, not the coat; the justice and reasonableness of a decision, not its consistency with previously held views.[55]

But Holmes drew this distinction between form and substance of the law not merely to instill in his readers an appreciation for the subtleties of legal development. He aimed to provide a new theory of judicial law-making so that judges would have a realistic guide to follow in making their decisions.[56] The deductive theory with its emphasis upon the syllogism could not account for judicial legislation. There was no major premise. Consequently, how did judges decide certain cases and how should they decide them? Austin and Holmes again resorted to the inductive method they had endorsed for ascertaining precedents, in developing their theory of judicial legislation.

According to Holmes, the answer depended upon the fact that law had become "a conscious reaction upon itself of organized society knowingly seeking to determine its own destinies."[57] Holmes saw that the logical (deductive) method of judicial decision-making flattered our longing for certainty and repose, but insisted that "certainty generally . . . [was an] illusion, and repose . . . not the destiny of man."[58] Judges needed to look under the logical form of the law to see if its substance helped to attain organized society's goals. Unfortunately, too often judges "have failed adequately to recognize their duty of weighing considerations of social advantage. The duty is inevitable, and the result of the often proclaimed judicial aversion to deal with such considerations is simply to leave the very ground and foundation of judgments inarticulate, and often unconscious."[59] As the purpose of law and a legal order was utility, Holmes therefore applied the same standard to judicial legislation: "The very considerations which judges most rarely mention, and always with an apology, are the secret root from which the law draws all the juices of life. I mean, of course, considerations of what is expedient for the community concerned."[60] No matter what the logical form, the substance of judiciary law developed in accordance with utility. Judges made law by inductive calculations of utility, not be deductive syllogistic reasoning. Hence, Holmes advised lawyers to study economics, for then they could "consider and weigh the ends of legislation, the means of attaining them, and the cost."[61] But clearly, if utility was the standard of law, then judges legislated according to an inductive method. And, just as Holmes considered induction the key to identifying and interpreting precedents, so also he believed that it was the essence of judicial legislation.

Austin was the first to see this connection between the standard of judicial legislation and its method. For this reason, he denied the justificatory value of history; judges should not decide cases according to what the law was, but according to what it should be. Whenever the utilitarian rationale of a precedent disappeared, the precedent itself ceased to exist. In "the case of judiciary law, if the ground of the decision has fallen away or ceased, the *ratio decidendi* being gone, there is no law left."[62] Holmes had identical opinions. Precedents that survived "long after the use they once served was at an end" deserved no respect: they were to be overruled.

But just as the clavicle in the cat only tells of the existence of some earlier creature to which a collarbone was useful, precedents survive in the law long after the use they once served is at an end and the reason for them has been forgotten. The result of following them must often be failure and confusion from the merely logical point of view.[63]

According to Holmes, the strict rule of agency—an employer held liable for his employees' acts—was an example of such an outworn precedent and should be overturned.[64]

Austin's favorite example recalled sixteenth and seventeenth-century judges preserving outdated rules rather than properly introducing beneficial ones; by doing so, they caused the growth of equity and an unhappy division of the English court system. In his words, the distinction between law and equity "arose because the Judges of the Common Law Courts would not do what they ought to have done, namely to remodel their rules of law and of procedure to the growing exigencies of society, instead of stupidly and sulkily adhering to the old and barbarous usages."[65] In sum, since the standard of legislation was utility, history could not justify the substance of judiciary law.

However, Holmes and Austin did ascribe an important role to history. Holmes's appreciation of the historical dimension is well known, and Austin's admiration for German historical jurisprudence should dispel the common assumption that Austin's analytical approach precluded any appreciation of history.[66] Indeed, from the following long but interesting quote, it is evident that

Austin tended to identify the inductive utilitarian school with the German historical school.

> And here I would remark that a great mistake is often made with respect to Bentham's notions of law. Bentham belongs strictly to the historical school of jurisprudence. The proper sense of that term as used by the Germans is, that the jurists thus designated think that a body of law cannot be spun out from a few general principles assumed *a priori*, but must be founded on experience of the subjects and objects with which law is conversant. Bentham therefore manifestly belongs to this school. He has again and again declared in his works that the reports of the decisions of the English Courts are an invaluable mine of experience for the legislator. The character of the historical school of jurisprudence in Germany is commonly misconceived ... The meaning of their being called the historical school is simply this, that they agree with Bentham in thinking that law should be founded on an experimental view of the subjects and objects of law, and should be determined by general utility, not drawn out from a few arbitrary assumptions *a priori* called the law of nature. A fitter name for them would be the *inductive* and *utilitarian* school.[67]

Though Austin may have been wrong about Bentham's historical sensitivity and about the nature of the German historical school, the passage indicates clearly that the utilitarians were not in principle hostile to history. They only opposed its inappropriate use as the standard of legislation. Its proper uses were: "To explain the origin of laws, which are venerated for their antiquity. To explain much of the law, which now exists; and to enable us to separate the reason of modern times from the dross of antiquity."[68] History teaches what the law now is, and how it arose. It cannot say what it ought to be.

Holmes agreed entirely. He dedicated much of his life to exploring the origins of the common law because he thought it "perfectly proper to regard and study the law simply as a great anthropological document."[69] But Holmes assigned a more important practical task to history; he agreed with Austin that history could separate useful laws from the "dross of antiquity." "History is the means by which we measure the power which the past has had to govern the present in spite of ourselves, so to speak, by imposing traditions which no longer meet their original end."[70] Therefore, though "it may help us to know the true limit of a doctrine," history's "chief good is to burst inflated explanations";[71] it is to discover and explode those "survivals" in the law that (like the clavicle in the cat) have outlived their usefulness. "History sets us free and enables us to make up our minds dispassionately whether the survival which we are enforcing answers any new purpose when it has ceased to answer the old."[72] But it could not do more; it was not a standard for legislation. Holmes too accepted the limited role granted to history by the utilitarians, of separating "the reason of modern times from the dross of antiquity" and discovering the useless "survivals" in the law. But as he repeatedly advises us, "historic continuity with the past is not a duty, it is only a necessity."[73]

An earlier discussion showed that Austin and Holmes endorsed a doctrine of judicial deference to the sovereign. But judicial deference could come into conflict with the judge's calculation of utility. Should he apply the rule that he believes is most beneficial or defer to general opinion reflected in the sovereign's will? Both Austin and Holmes preached submission. Anyone's calculations of utility were far from indisputable. "Views of policy," in Holmes's words, "are taught by experience of the interests of life. Those interests are fields of battle."[74] There are no Archimedean points of view. But since law is

a practical thing, [it] must found itself on actual forces. It is quite enough, therefore, for the law, that man, by an instinct which he shares with the domestic dog, and of which the seal gives a most striking example, will not allow himself to be dispossessed, either by force or fraud, of what he holds, without trying to get it back again.[75]

The judge should then grant legal remedies to possessors even if he believes that an owner's monopoly of legal rights would better serve the general interest. Judicial deference to the community's beliefs was justified upon similar grounds. Holmes would not invalidate legislation he thought unwise; he would "help the country go to hell if it wanted to" because law was a practical thing.[76] A judge's private opinion should not obstruct the community's wishes or instincts.

Judicial deference also predominated in Austin's theory of judicial legislation. He agreed that law was practical; it had to agree with human nature and public opinion: "Legislation must be bottomed in general principles drawn from an accurate observation of human nature, and not in the imperfect records called history."[77] Holmes may not have approved of the utilitarian pleasure-pain psychology, but he took as his own this principle that law must rest squarely upon human nature. Judicial respect for a community's general opinions received a similar utilitarian endorsement. Even the sovereign had to follow the wishes of the community; Austin's belief that judges were (and should be) obedient to public opinion is therefore not surprising.

For the *arbitrium* of subordinate judges (like that of the sovereign legislature) is controlled by public opinion. It is controlled, moreover, by the sovereign legislature: under whose inspection their decisions are made: by whose authority their decisions may be reversed: and by whom their misconduct may be punished.[78]

Holmes and Austin therefore agreed that generally accepted beliefs and desires of the community should dictate legal development. The judge should introduce rules generally desired or thought beneficial by society.

But desires or beliefs uniform throughout a society are exceptional; the community is usually divided into conflicting groups. Here the court cannot defer to a general consensus, but must evaluate what is in the public interest. "Whatever decisions are made must be against the wishes and opinion of one party."[79] There are always two sides to every case, and usually more than one assessment of the costs and benefits of a policy. According to Holmes, to measure these costs and benefits "needs not only the highest powers of a judge and a training which the practice of the law does not insure [scientific measurement of social desires and their possible satisfaction], but also a freedom from prepossessions which is very hard to attain."[80] Hence judges should strive to attain impartiality and humility. They do not deduce indisputable conclusions from known premises—"general propositions do not decide concrete cases." Rather, judges make more or less controversial judgments of social policy upon an inductive factual basis—"the decision will depend on a judgment or intuition more subtle than any articulate major premise."[81] Therefore, to carry out his task in Holmes's inductive utilitarian fashion, a judge should be a humble and impartial "spectator."

Holmes also thought legal distinctions were a matter of degree. Because a decision rested upon an inductive judgment of fact, there was no dispute about general principles. The only question "is whether this case lies on one side or the other of a line which has to be worked out between cases differing only in degree."[82] The judge decides if a particular case is a slightly darker shade of gray than another, if it is slightly more analogous to one cluster of cases than to another set. This is another reason for judicial modesty. Not only do these decisions rest upon contingent controversial judgments of fact, but they distinguish and treat very differently cases that closely resemble one another. Indeed, Holmes thinks they are so close that the line of illegality might "well have been drawn a little farther to the one side or the other."[83] Humility is in order because judges draw arbitrary lines; lines that are necessary and (one hopes) philosophical, but nonetheless arbitrary.

But if the judge's job is to draw arbitrary but philosophical lines, he ought to have some guidelines to follow. Should the judge attend primarily to the language or general form of several proposed rules? Should he make cost-benefit analyses for each of these rules, choose the seemingly most beneficial one, and apply it to the case? Holmes's answer was that the judge had a far more humble task. Legal distinctions already exist; lines of authoritative precedents are always relevant if not directly applicable to the case. The judge legislates under the guise of interpretation and must decide whether this case is grayer than that one. His attention is not on rules or generalities, but on the facts of the particular case at hand. "When the question of policy is faced it will be seen to be one which cannot be answered by generalities, but must be determined by the particular character of the case."[84] The judge must ask himself whether his particular case with all its relevant circumstances is more analogous to the cluster of cases in which the agents were held liable or to a different set in which the agents escaped liability. This is how judges should and do legislate according to Holmes; they should legislate through the comparison of different factual settings.

Holmes's emphasis upon the factual orientation of judicial legislation influenced his theory of legal development. A judge decides a particular case by comparing it to others. But having done so, the judge has (more or less unintentionally) extended the line of illegality a little further. He has narrowed the field of legal uncertainty by infinitesimally clarifying a distinction of degree that separates two clusters of cases. So, according to Holmes, the growth of law usually takes place in the following way:

Two widely different cases suggest a general distinction, which is a clear one when stated broadly. But as new cases cluster around the opposite poles, and begin to approach each other, the distinction becomes more difficult to trace; the determinations are made one way or the other on a very slight preponderance of feeling, rather than articulate reason; and at last a mathematical line is arrived at by the contact of contrary decisions, which is so far arbitrary that it might equally well have been drawn a little further to the one side or to the other. The distinction between the groups, however, is philosophical, and it is better to have a line drawn somewhere in the penumbra between darkness and light, than to remain in uncertainty.[85]

In other words, legal development resembles "an approach of decisions towards each other from the opposite poles."[86] As legal distinctions grow old, doubtful cases (the only ones likely to go far in court) arise which explore the gray penumbra of the concepts involved. The result is more legal certainty achieved by an arbitrary legal line; not complete legal certainty however, for that is impossible to attain. The "complexity of life makes it impossible to draw a line in advance without an artificial simplification that would be unjust."[87] But the important point concerns judicial legislation. Judges legislate (and thereby extend the line of illegality) by comparing the relevant facts of different cases. They legislate "only interstitially; they are confined from molar to molecular motions."[88] The particular facts of the case—whether they are more similar in important ways to cases in which the agent is held liable or to cases in which the agent is set free—are the judge's primary concern. He does not legislate general rules; he legislates by deciding particular cases.

Austin suggested similar guidelines. In his opinion, the distinctive element of judicial legislation was its emphasis on the individual case. Though he decided the case by a new rule, the judge's purpose was not the introduction of the rule, but the decision of the specific case. For this reason, the judge avoided the "shew" of legislation. He legislated "obliquely"; he did not "professedly" introduce any new rule, for "professedly" he only ascertained existing law by interpretation or construction. Hence Austin's advice to judges was similar to Holmes's. Judges should not legislate general abstract rules; that was the legislature's job. Rather, they decided specific controversial cases justly in accordance with utility. Moreover, since new rules were not "professedly" introduced, the judge legislated under the guise of interpretation. He adapted the substance of the law to the changing needs of society by deciding specific controversial cases.

Austin's method of judicial legislation also led him to believe that legal distinctions were only a matter of degree. If judges decided cases requiring legislation under the guise of interpretation and with their attention directed to the individual case, then their job consisted of comparing individual cases. The judge would ask himself if the facts of the case before him were more similar to those cases controlled by precedent X or to those controlled by precedent Y. By his decision, the judge would legislate "obliquely" under the guise of interpretation by extending a precedent to a new case. However, he extends the line by way of inductive reasoning. Utility demands that the resemblances of the controversial case to the set of precedents governed by rule X override any similarities that the case may have to those governed by rule Y. But no matter how clear the distinction is at first, in time cases arise that are analogous to previous sets of cases treated differently. The judge decides the case inductively according to these differences and similarities; he extends the line of legality a little further; he legislates by deciding how particular cases resemble or differ from one another. Austin was equally aware that in the end the line could have been drawn a little further to either side; that the resemblances of particular cases requiring rule X could well have been subordinated to those requiring rule Y; that legal distinctions, no matter how forcefully stated, ultimately had a gray penumbra in which the judge must draw the arbitrary but philosophical line of legality. Legal distinctions were arbitrary because of the inductive method of judicial legislation; they were still philosophical because of the need to separate night from day.

Citations that not only substantiate this interpretation of Austin, but also reveal similarities between his and Holmes's understanding of legal development can be found in Austin's discussion of analogical reasoning, especially in his analysis of the competition of analogies.

But with regard to the application of the law to the case awaiting solution, "the competition of opposite analogies" may certainly arise. For the case awaiting solution may resemble in some of its points the case or cases to which the rule of law has actually been applied. But it may also resemble in some other points a case or cases from which the application of the law has been withheld. Now, with reference to the rule of law . . .

the resemblances of the case to the cases to which the law has been applied, and the resemblances of the case to the cases from which the law has been withheld, are "opposite and competing analogies."[89]

According to Austin, analogical reasoning was at the center of controversial judicial decision-making, both at the level of applying and legislating law. Because laws were often inconsistent or indefinite, the judge had to decide the case according to which set of competing analogies was stronger.[90] Here the judge did not make a law; he used the analogies to interpret and apply an indefinite or inconsistent statute or precedent. But Austin understood that interpretation merged with legislation. Therefore, the competition of analogies also operated at the level of legislation.

In truth, when it is said that a litigated case is *analogous* to another case, one of the following meanings is commonly imported by the phrase. It is meant that the litigated case bears to the other case, a specific and proximate resemblance; and that the former ought to be decided, on account of the alleged resemblance, by a given statute or rule in which the latter is included. Or else it is meant that the litigated bears to the other case a generic and remoter resemblance; and that the former should be brought or forced, on account of the alleged resemblance, within a statute or rule by which the latter is comprised: that is to say, that a new rule of judiciary law, resembling a statute or rule by which the latter is compromised, ought to be made by the Court, and applied to the case in controversy.[91]

If the case was closely analogous to previous cases, then the judge only applied the law; if it was remotely analogous, then the judge made a new rule, even if he avoided the "shew" of legislation.[92] But in either case, the judicial decision depended upon a comparison of particular cases, making legal distinctions matters of degree.

Austin's discussion of the competition of analogies also clarifies how similar his conception of legal develpment was to Holmes's. Just as Holmes thought that judiciary law grew by "an approach of decisions towards each other from opposite poles," Austin described it as developing through a "competition of competing and opposite analogies." Though the language is different, the similarity of ideas is striking. An explicit distinction exists between rule A and rule B. But as the law grows, doubtful cases lying between the rules arise; these new cases resemble both the cases to which rule A was applied and those to which rule B was applied; analogies therefore come into competition with one another to control the case at hand; the law grows by decisions approaching from opposite poles. Holmes and Austin believed the law developed in this way because new cases resemble old ones decided in conflicting ways, and because the judge should and does decide the new case according to these resemblances. In their minds, comparisons of cases formed the essence of judicial legislation. Eventually the cases growing from opposite competing analogies or poles would meet; the judge would draw an arbitrary line, an arbitrary legal distinction of degree. A few more resemblances of the present case to those to which rule A was applied, or a different judicial estimation of the significance of the resemblances that do exist, would lead to a different decision. The line of illegality could be drawn a little further to either side. But the arbitrariness of the line drawn does not affect its value. It is necessary to draw the line, but important not to mischaracterize the arbitrary basis of the distinction.

The problem is how to get this analogical reasoning in judicial legislation to coincide with the standard of utility. If judiciary law is made under the guise of interpretation and justified accordingly through analogical reasoning, then what becomes of utility as the standard of judicial legislation? The solution to this paradox lies in how the resemblances are evalutated. To a utilitarian judge, the consequential implications of the resemblances were of central importance.

The life of the law has not been logic: it has been experience. The seed of every new growth within its sphere has been a felt necessity The form of continuity has been kept up by reasonings purporting to reduce everything to a logical sequence; but that form is nothing but the evening dress which the new-comer puts on to make itself presentable according to conventional requirements. The important phenomenon is the man underneath it, not the coat; the justice and reasonableness of a decision, not its consistency with previously held views.[93]

Here Holmes was not encouraging judges to decide cases according to utility and then to justify them by some fictitious and hypocritical line of legal reasoning. Holmes did not want legal newcomers to arrive naked. Even if the important phenomenon was the man underneath the coat, he should still appear properly attired. Since legal form and substance were not necessarily antagonistic, it was far better to have a just and reasonable decision suitably adorned than to have either a correct decision without any justification or a bad decision dressed up with glittering legal generalities.

But even though Holmes and Austin preferred to have legal decisions suitably adorned, utility was still the real ground of the decision. According to Holmes, "decisions follow earlier decisions that are not identical on the ground that the policy implied covers the present case."[94] Holmes is here advising us not to forget that earlier cases and distinctions were (presumably) also decided and formulated according to utility. Consequently, in deciding whether a case is a light enough shade of gray to require a white decision, the judge does not divorce his decision from utility. Indeed, by deciding that the case has more important consequential resemblances to the set of cases controlled by rule A, the judge is in fact pursuing the social policy implied in rule A. According to Holmes and Austin, legal principles implied policies and therefore the logical justification of a case was not something apart from a utilitarian assessment of policy. Pulling down a legal principle to decide a case was equivalent to pursuing a policy. Therefore, according to Holmes and Austin, judicial legislation did not contain two procedures—one of utilitarian decision and the other of logical justification. A judge decides the case upon utilitarian grounds through the resemblances it has to previous cases; the line he draws "must be justified by the fact that it is a little nearer than the nearest opposing case to one pole of an admitted antithesis."[95] But the grounds for the judge's assessment of proximity were ultimately utilitarian judgments. While Holmes distinguished between the logical form and substance of the law, they were not to oppose one another. The form and substance of law were to walk hand-in-hand.

Hence Holmes's platitude that "the life of the law has not been logic, but experience" did not imply anything about man's irrationality. In the next chapter, I shall examine Holmes's conception of human rationality and explain why he described a judge's inductive beliefs of policy as "felt necessities." Here I wish only to emphasize the rational nature of judicial law making. When they legislated, judges reasoned inductively and experimentally upon the costs and benefits of various policies that were reflected in the resemblances of the case at hand to those that preceded it. The utilitarians were the first to endorse this new inductive and experimental theory of judicial legislation and legal development. In Austin's words: "Law (as it ought to be) is not deducible from principles knowable *a priori,* but from principles which must be obtained (through induction) from experience."[96] Austin also emphasized the experimental basis of analogical reasoning. Whether the resemblances (that ultimately decide the case) be specific or generic, the reasoning was "built on experience."[97] Austin therefore castigated natural-law jurists, praised Bentham's method of censorial jurisprudence, admired the German historical school, and considered the reports of English judges a "mine of experience for the legislator."

Holmes followed this tradition. He too thought that judiciary law developed (and should develop) according to inductive truths of utility, learned from experience, that were reflected in the resemblances of particular cases. Therefore he dismissed purely formalistic theories for their misplaced emphasis upon generalities and for their silly rejection of experience.

What has been said will explain the failure of all theories which consider the law only from its formal side, whether they attempt to deduce the *corpus* from *a priori* postulates, or fall into the humbler error of supposing the science of law to reside in the *elegantia juris,* or logical cohesion of part with part.[98]

Formal theorists erred fundamentally by ignoring the facts of judicial legislation and by overlooking the connection between the utilitarian end of law and an inductive experimental method of judicial decision-making. It was for this reason that Holmes described Langdell as the world's greatest living legal theologian, and that Austin scorned Blackstone's deductive theory of judicial decision-making.

As long as the law was conceived as a mysterious logically related "omnipresence in the sky," the deductive theory was attractive if misleading. But once the utilitarian reformers came upon the scene, once the facts were examined and the discrepancies between the law as it was and how it ought to have been were noted, once law had to justify itself before the standard of utility, the deductive syllogistic theory of judicial decision-making was dismissed as a fictitious piece of nonsense that ignored the utilitarian end of law. The early nineteenth-century utilitarians had a fondness for facts and a bold vision for the future. In this tradition, Austin fashioned a new theory of judicial decision-making resting upon induction and experience. Holmes undoubtedly contributed to this theory, by clarifying its assumptions and conclusions, by exploring the theory's implications, and even by supplementing it with compatible methods and conclusions drawn from other schools of thought. But the essentials of the inductive and experimental theory of judicial decision-making that Holmes popularized were ultimately derived from utilitarian jurisprudence. Exploration of the relatively uncharted areas of Austin's legal philosophy helps us to understand Holmes's well-known theory of judicial decision-making in this light.

V

REALITY, IDEAS, AND LANGUAGE

Holmes and the utilitarians shared a common philosophical method. By this I mean that the utilitarians and Holmes used comparable procedures to discern, clarify, and ultimately define important but ambiguous concepts. The method itself was Lockian in origin: first, it assumed that all ideas and knowledge arose from the experience of real objects; and second, it held that the meanings of words consisted in the ideas for which they stood. This empirical epistemology and ideational theory of meaning implied that controversial terms were clarified and defined by identifying the ideas to which they were obscurely linked. But since all ideas were of real objects, the theorist most easily accomplished this task by reducing the controversial term to a name of a real object, to a name that was obviously linked to the relevant idea.

The man who first clearly saw these implications of Locke's epistemology and theory of meaning was John Horne Tooke, an eighteenth-century English philologist. Both Bentham and Austin accepted Tooke's theory of language, especially his program of linguistic reductionism. Clarity demanded the reduction of all vague and ambiguous words to the names of real objects. The issue of what constituted reality was therefore central to the utilitarian philosophical method; ontological commitments determined which ideas were possible and which words needed reduction. Therefore changes in ontology marked the primary line of development of this utilitarian philosophical method. Bentham and Austin were ontologically moderate, with a relatively generous class of names of real objects from which to derive the meanings of controversial terms; however, James Mill's contributions to associationist psychology soon necessitated a narrower ontology, and John Stuart Mill explored the implications of this psychology for language, reason, and ideas. The development of this utilitarian philosophical method must be described before we can assess Holmes's adherence to it. But the general assumption is that the substantive similarities described in previous chapters were not accidents. The utilitarians and Holmes came to their conclusions because they had the same outlook upon the interrelationships of reality, ideas, and language.

Bentham called his manner of clarifying and defining controversial concepts the "paraphrastic method." It was an especially useful procedure when the common method of definition *per genus et differentiam* failed. "Among abstract terms we soon come to such as have no *superior genus*. A definition, *per genus et differentiam*, when applied to these, it is manifest, can make no advance: it must either stop short, or turn back, as it were, upon itself, in a *circulate* or a *repented*."[1] Faced with such a predicament (or even for other reasons), Bentham used paraphrasis:

A word may be said to be expounded by *paraphrasis*, when not that *word* alone is translated into other *words*, but some whole *sentence* of which it forms a part is translated into another *sentence;* the words of which latter are expressive of such ideas as are *simple*, or are more immediately resolvable into simple ones than those of the former . . . This, in short, is the only method in which any abstract terms can, at the long run, be expounded to any instructive purpose: that is in terms calculated to raise *images* either of *substances* perceived, or of *emotions;*—sources, one or other of which every idea must be drawn from, to be a clear one.[2]

Elsewhere Bentham labeled these two subsidiary operations "phraseoplerosis" and "archetypation."[3] Phraseoplerosis or "filling up the phrase" involved the placement of a controversial term into a suitable proposition. For example, the legal theorist would place the term obligation into a phrase like "An obligation is incumbent upon a man." Archetypation consisted of the discovery of the image of some real action or state of things that the proposition called to mind. In the case of obligation Bentham thought the image called to mind was of a heavy bar pressing down upon a man, restricting his activity either totally or partially.[4] Once the theorist ascertained this image, he would formulate a defining proposition more able to bring the archetype to mind. When the archetypal image was associated with the controversial term contained within the controversial proposition, the paraphrastic method was completed and the word (presumably) clarified.

C. K. Ogden and more recently H. L. A. Hart have tried to rescue this Benthamite philosophical method from obscurity by emphasizing its compatibility with twentieth-century linguistic theories.[5] But a quick look at the assumptions underlying Bentham's paraphrastic method will more than prove that it was embedded in an eighteenth-century linguistic perspective. First, Bentham's theory of meaning was ideational; words were only arbitrary signs for ideas. "When considered apart from the ideas, no very considerable instruction . . . is accordingly derived from the consideration of them."[6] Of these names or signs of ideas, some were names of subjects of propositions—the noun-substantives. But not all of these referred to real objects. Despite their grammatical position, certain noun-substantives did not imply the existence of corresponding objects. For example, "cat" in the proposition "the cat is black" was the name of a real entity, while space in the proposition "space is empty" was the name of a fictitious entity.

Real entities were therefore those ideas or impressions of real objects that functioned as the subjects of propositions: "entities are either *real* or *fictitious:* real, either *perceptible* or *inferential:* perceptible, either *impressions* or *ideas:* inferential, either *material,* i.e. *corporeal* or *immaterial,* i.e. *spiritual."*[7] Hence Bentham divided the class of real entities into perceptible and inferential entities. The former category encompassed objects experienced by the senses; rocks, emotions, and pain were such entities to which perceptible real objects were correlated.[8] Inferential real entities, however, were not experienced by the senses; rather their existence was inferred by reflection on the real entities that could in fact be experienced. Bentham thought God, souls, and matter were examples of such inferential entities.[9] But he realized that the existential status of inferential objects depended upon whether the theorist experienced the perception or idea upon which the inference was based or accepted the reasoning involved in the inference. For example, George Berkeley had denied that he perceived abstract ideas, while David Hume had cast doubt upon the proofs of the existence of the human soul and of God.[10] Therefore, Bentham's distinction between names of real versus fictitious entities rested upon ontology, upon our perception of reality and valid inferences made therefrom. One part of language required its elucidation by another part because all our ideas were derived from sense experience. Far from anticipating twentieth-century linguistic theories, Bentham came upon his paraphrastic method through a Lockian epistemology and theory of meaning.

Fictitious entities were impossible ideas having no real object from which they could have arisen. The parallel levels of name linked to an idea and to a real object did not reappear with fictitious entities. Since there was no real object, no corresponding idea could exist. Therefore, to the question of their origin, Bentham responded that it was "to language alone . . . that fictitious entities owe their existence—their impossible, yet indispensable, existence."[11] But this introduced the paradox: if words meant ideas, then how could fictitious terms mean anything, how were they so indispensable?

John Horne Tooke, whose work in philology reigned supreme in England until the 1830s, attempted to resolve this dilemma for Bentham.[12] The tension between the Lockian theory of meaning and the experiential epistemology required a program of linguistic reductionism. According to Tooke, abbreviation was the key to understanding language. Words are divisible into two groups: those that are immediately the signs of impressions and ideas; and those that "are merely abbreviations employed for dispatch, and are the signs of other words."[13] Hence, Tooke reasoned that one word could stand for a series of other words and thereby for an even greater series of ideas and impressions. Abbreviations were also present in parts of speech and in construction.[14] Since all meaningful words must stand for simple ideas and impressions, the only real parts of speech were nouns and verbs. All other parts of speech were derivative; they functioned to facilitate communication by "standing in" for a series of nouns and verbs.

An abbreviation in construction was a participle or an adjective once followed by a substantive word. But even though the substantive word had fallen away, the shortened expression still signified the same set of ideas and impressions that its longer parent phrase had done.[15] Here, as with the earlier cases of abbreviation, the theorist uncovered the true meaning of a word or phrase when he identified the particular ideas and sensations for which it stood. The etymologist reduced abbreviations to names explicitly linked to the relevant ideas and sensations. For example, terms like "from," "with," and "through" were not understood until

they were respectively linked by etymology to the terms "beginning," "join," and "door."[16] Etymology therefore had a philosophical purpose. It resolved the tension between the ideational
theory of meaning and Lockian epistemology by showing that
words having no real objects or ideas were derived from words
having definite objects, ideas, and sensations linked to them. For
example, Tooke derived "right" from *rect-um,* the past participle
of *regere* (to rule). Therefore, "when a man demands his right, he
asks only that which *it is ordered* he shall have."[17] He also derived
the term "law" from "that which is laid down."[18] The general
point is that etymology contributed to the philosophical clarification of language by reducing linguistic abbreviations to meaningful words, the immediate signs of simple ideas and impressions.

Bentham quite consciously followed Tooke's program of linguistic reductionism. Even though he introduced D'Alembert's
terminology of real and fictitious entities, Bentham followed
Tooke's advice, divided language in half, and reduced one half to
the other: "Throughout the whole field of language, two lan-
guages, as it were, run all along in a state of parallelism to each
other,—the one material, the other immaterial;—the material all
along the basis of the immaterial."[19] Consequently, the names of
fictitious entities that had neither ideas nor objects corresponding
to them were reducible to the names of real entities that were the
immediate signs of our ideas and impressions.

As in the case of all words, which have an immaterial as well as a material [sic], the root of the *immaterial* will be found in the *material import;* so,
to explain the nature and origin of the idea attached to the name of a
fictitious entity, it will be necessary to point out the *relation,* which the
import of that word bears to the import of one or more names of real
entities.[20]

But this procedure was none other than the paraphrastic method.

The *paraphrasis* consists in taking the word that requires to be expounded—viz. the name of a *fictitious entity*—and, after making it up into
a *phrase* [phraseoplerosis], applying to it another phrase, which, being of
the same import [signifying the same idea], shall have for its principal
and characteristic word the name of the corresponding real entity.[21]

Bentham admitted the difficulty of discerning the archetype of
obscure terms when "the origin of the psychological, in some

physical idea, is often, in a manner, lost;—its physical marks, being more or less obliterated."[22] But etymology could raise the proper image in the mind by uncovering the original real entity and its corresponding term. Hence even if difficult to identify, even if a proposition "has for its subject some fictitious entity . . . some sort of image—the image of some real action or state of things, in every instance, is presented to the mind."[23] In this way, Bentham's paraphrastic method, like Tooke's theory of abbreviations, resolved the tension between his ideational theory of meaning and his Lockian epistemology. Bentham himself recognized this clearly. He summed up the rationale for his paraphrastic method as follows: "In a word, our ideas coming, all of them, from our senses, from what other source can the signs of them—from what other source can our language come?"[24] The names of fictitious entities were reducible to those of real entities because only the ideas and impressions of real objects existed. Bentham's paraphrastic method was embedded in eighteenth-century linguistic theory. It cannot be understood apart from the Lockian assumptions underlying it.

This utilitarian philosophical method becomes clearer if we examine it at work; for an example, applied to their definition of law as a command of a sovereign. The primary methodological directive required clarification and definition of words in terms that raised "images either of substances perceived, or of emotions." The basic way to raise such images or emotions was to reduce names of fictitious entities to names of real ones. Here Bentham expanded upon Tooke's etymological definition of law as "that which was laid down." Indeed, Bentham himself stated the relationship between his philosophical method and his definition of law.

A law is a discourse . . . expressive of the *will* of some person or persons, to whom . . . the members of the community to which it is addressed are disposed to pay obedience.

This is the only plain and proper sense of the word: in this sense the object of which it is designative is *a real entity*. In every other sense, it is figurative and improper; the object of which it is designative is a mere *fictitious entity*.[25]

Clearly, this passage indicates Bentham's commitment to a certain philosophical method and shows how the substance of

Bentham's legal philosophy is explicable upon methodological grounds.

Austin's refinements of this definition of law are also relevant. He considers the term "command" inseparably connected to duty, sanction, and superiority because "each embraces the same ideas as the others, . . . each of the three terms *signifies* the same notion."[26] The term "command" directly signifies the "intimation of a wish," while "the evil to be incurred [the sanction], with the chance of incurring it [the obligation], are kept . . . in the background *of my picture.*"[27] Words ultimately signified mental pictures or archetypes. Therefore, vague words like law and sovereignty were best defined with concrete language, with the names of real entities that brought the proper image to the mind readily and assuredly.

The utilitarians' factual criteria for the concept of sovereignty arose from the same methodological assumptions. Austin had to reduce the term to an idea evolved from sense experience. Only real things that were "sensible" could have any ideas (those traces or images of sensation) correlated to them. But the only persons that we can experience are definite, assignable individuals. Hence the sovereign was definite and factual because our experience attested to no other type of person.

The same methodological principles operated in the utilitarian theories of legal obligation and legal liability. Obligation was one of a group of ethical fictitious entities including rights, powers, privileges, and so on. Bentham insisted that the "fictitious entities which compose this group have all of them, for their real *source,* one and the same sort of real entity, viz. *sensation.*" Not the sensation of mere perception, Bentham cautioned, "but of perception considered as productive of pain alone, of pleasure alone, or of both."[28] Later, Austin omitted the sensation of pleasure because he thought "talk of rewards [pleasures] as *obliging* or constraining to obedience . . . a wide departure from the established meaning of the terms."[29] But both Austin's and Bentham's methodological commitments forced them to define obligation in terms of a real entity, in terms of sensation. Consequently, their reduction of "having an obligation" to "being obliged" was hardly coincidental. What constituted an obligation had to be something factual, something that really existed, something that could be perceived or felt, something that could produce our idea of it. This is why utility was an index to God's commands for Austin, rather than an obligatory standard. An abstraction could not oblige us, but God could through threats of pleasure and pain.[30] Pain and pleasure were facts of our experience; they existed; only they, not utility, could produce our idea of obligation.

The utilitarians also derived their knowledge-based theory of legal liability from their philosophical method. The traditional theory of legal liability required a "free" and an "evil" will. Accordingly, the state punished illegal acts done maliciously with a free will. Obviously the utilitarians could not accept this conclusion because their methodology identified the will as a fictitious entity; they could not explain a person's liability by something which did not exist.

But, besides the antecedent desire (which I style a *volition*), and the consequent movement (which I style an *act*), it is commonly supposed that there is a certain "Will" which is the cause or author of both. The desire is commonly called an act of the *will;* or is supposed to be an effect of a *power or faculty of willing*, supposed to reside in the man.

That this same *"will"* is just simply nothing at all, has been proved (in my opinion) beyond controversy by the late Dr. Brown: Who also expelled from the region of entities, those fancied beings called "powers," of which this imaginary *"will"* is one . . . But the author . . . was (I believe) the first who understood what we would be at, when we talk about the *Will*, and the *power or faculty of willing.*

All that I am able to discover when I *will* a movement of my body, amounts to this: I *wish* the movement. The movement *immediately* follows my wish of the movement.[31]

Austin concluded that since the will was "simply nothing," it had no significant role to play in his theory of legal liability.

Bentham also rejected the will as a fictitious entity and reduced it to desiring or wishing. Indeed, he thought that any appetitive and perceptual faculty of the mind consists only of "the *operation* which, when called into exercise, it performs . . . or the impressions which . . . it receives."[32] Memory was nothing but its operation; the aesthetic sense, nothing more than a series of impressions received. The will received similar treatment. It was not an independent faculty, but only a different name for the appetitive faculty, for the "faculty in which desire, in all its several modifications, has place." But if, Bentham reasoned, "no act of will can take place but in consequence of a correspondent desire," and if "no desire can have place, unless the idea of pleasure and pain . . .

has place,"[33] then the act of willing is equivalent to acting under the influence of the desire for pleasure and of the avoidance of pain. Therefore, Bentham and Austin rejected the will as a criterion of legal liability for identical methodological reasons. They both recognized its fictitious character and therefore reduced it to the only real entities found in the appetitive faculty, to the desires or wishes for pleasure and the avoidance of pain.

But the reduction of will to desires or wishes does not ultimately explain why the utilitarians dismissed motives from their theory of legal liability. Desires and wishes were names of real entities, so why did some of them incur legal liability while others avoided it? The answer lies in utilitarian psychology. All desires held the same status; they were desires of pleasure and the avoidance of pain. Any superficial distinction drawn between types of desire collapsed before this basic uniformity. The serious purpose of a theory of legal liability demanded not only a real entity as the criterion, but a real entity that could distinguish between acts. Consequently, the utilitarian philosophical method and psychology necessitated a criterion of legal liability found elsewhere than in the appetitive faculty of the mind. Motives were irrelevant; they were invariably desires of pleasure and the avoidance of pain and therefore they could not distinguish between culpable and excusable acts.

Since the utilitarians divided the mind into active appetitive and passive perceptive parts, only one option remained. Fortunately, the perceptive faculty was composed of real entities not reducible to one uniform type, which could function to separate culpable from excusable acts. The different real entities of the perceptive faculty were the agent's beliefs, either about the circumstances of the act or about the act's consequences. Therefore, rather than motive, the utilitarians placed great emphasis upon intention. According to Austin, intention "is a precise state of mind, and cannot coalesce or commingle with a different state of the mind. 'To intend,' is to believe that a given act will follow a given volition, or that a given consequence will follow a given act ... Intention, therefore, is a state of consciousness."[34] A peculiar real entity, a certain state of consciousness, a distinctive belief about one's future acts and their consequences sufficed to incur liability for an illegal act.

Bentham too switched the criterion of legal liability from will to knowledge: "Upon the degree and bias of a man's intention, upon the absence or presence of consciousness or mis-supposal, depend a great part of the good and bad, more especially of the bad consequences of an act; and on this, as well as on other grounds, a great part of the demand for punishment."[35] Accordingly, Bentham and Austin concluded that certain real entities made an individual liable for his illegal acts. Their philosophical method demanded a real entity upon which to base legal liability; their psychology forced them to find that entity in the perceptive faculty of the mind. Rather than the will of the agent, his consciousness (his beliefs and expectations) became the crucial test.

Heedless, negligent, and rash acts also needed to fit within this theory even though they imply no positive state of consciousness. In these cases, either the agent was not cognizant of the possibility of the harmful consequences of his act or failure to act (heedlessness and negligence respectively), or he was aware of the possibility but discounted its probability (rashness). But the individual was punished despite his lack of awareness. However, here too the utilitarians thought knowledge the cental issue. What should the agent have known of the consequences of his act, but did not? What should the agent have known of his present circumstances, but did not? In Bentham's view, cases of unconsciousness (where the agent did not know that the tendency of his act was dangerous) and of mis-supposal (where the agent did not know that the circumstances made his act dangerous) were "unmeet for punishment" if the agent acted rationally and prudently. Austin also emphasized the knowledge that the agent should have had, but never explicitly endorsed the test of the rational, prudent man. In cases of heedlessness, negligence, and rashness, the particular laws of a legal system would identify those beliefs that the agent must have at his peril. But in any case, methodological principles underlay the utilitarian theory of legal liability. The utilitarians rejected the will in favor of knowledge or consciousness as the criterion of legal liability. Their philosophical method in conjunction with their psychology gave them no other choice.[36]

In every intellectual issue they examined, the utilitarians reduced all vague and ambiguous terms to the names of real entities. Conclusions could vary according to different ontological commitments. Bentham, for example, believed in the existence of matter and abstract ideas. The former was an inferential real entity; the latter a perceptible one.[37] Therefore Bentham denied

115

that the names of matter, objects, and abstract ideas necessarily had to undergo the paraphrastic method of elucidation. If they were names of existing ideas, their meanings were clear. But James Mill's psychology introduced a more radical ontology into the utilitarian tradition. John Stuart Mill unraveled the implications of this new psychology for the utilitarians' conception of reason and their philosophical method. A brief sketch of these developments follows. However, it should be emphasized that these developments did not constitute a change in the philosophical method. The method remained the same; only the ontology changed.

James Mill's foremost contribution to philosophy was the introduction of David Hume's associationist psychology into the utilitarian school of thought. The complex and abstract phenomena of the human mind were reduced to their simplest elements and explained by their association. Simple ideas, for example of colors or shapes (each of them a trace or copy of a sensation), and the sensations themselves were united upon a synchronous or successive order. Synchronous association explained the development of a complex idea—for example, the idea of a horse; successive association explained complex ideas involving time—for example, the idea of a falling star.[38] To what degree the simple ideas were united depended upon the vividness and the frequency of their association. At one extreme, the fancies of imagination united ideas only for a moment; while at the other, our beliefs in the existence of souls and external bodies were ideas "inseparably connected."[39]

But if the psychologist could explain the beliefs in souls and external bodies without appealing to the external world, then their independent ontological existence becomes questionable. Science demands the simplest explanation of the phenomena. If beliefs in the existence of souls and of matter were the inevitable effect (not the cause or presupposition) of a stream of sensations and simple ideas, then they have lost their status as real entities. The term "horse" would not be the name of a real entity, but rather a name for a cluster of sensations: "the names of what I call objects, I am referring, and can be referring, only to my own sensations."[40] So also the belief in a self independent of the stream of sensations and simple ideas was a fiction. As the term "horse" referred to a cluster of sensations in synchronous order, the term "self" or "soul" referred directly to the stream of simple ideas and sensations, not to some ulterior being experiencing this stream of perceptions. Simple ideas and sensations were the only real entities; every other phenomenon of the human mind was derivative. Consequently, the meanings of all terms were ultimately reducible to a cluster or succession of simple ideas and sensations.

James Mill's psychology therefore narrowed the ontology of the utilitarians. In effect, he threw out "inferential real entities" as psychologically induced fictions; only "perceptible real entities" existed. However, though ultimately all mental phenomena were reducible to simple ideas and sensations, Mill recognized collections of these simple ideas as distinct kinds of phenomena. A complex idea was something more than the sum of its parts. A complex idea, "however in reality complex, appears to be no less simple, than any of those of which it is compounded."[41] General abstract ideas—for example, the idea of "man"—received a similar explanation as a particular species of complex ideas, a very complex and therefore indistinct variety.

Thus, when the word man calls up the ideas of an indefinite number of individuals, not only of all those to whom I have individually given the name, but of all those to whom I have in imagination given it or imagine it will ever be given, and forms all those ideas into one—it is evidently a very complex idea, and, therefore, indistinct.[42]

Like Bentham before him, James Mill was a conceptualist. The meaning of an abstract general term was not a universal substance as the realists assumed, or nothing at all as the nominalists claimed. Their belief was that a general term could call "up an indefinite number of ideas, by the irresistible laws of association, and *forming* them into one very complex, and indistinct, but *not therefore unintelligible* idea."[43] Therefore, general ideas existed; they were real entities. Consequently, the names of general ideas were still names of real entities; they needed no special paraphrastic clarification.

But John Stuart Mill criticized his father's reasoning. Though the younger Mill adopted his father's laws of association as the ultimate laws of all mental phenomena, he did not grant to them the power to form abstract ideas. In fact, he thought his father's endorsement of the laws of association contradicted his belief in abstract ideas. "It is evident, indeed," J. S. Mill wrote, "that the existence of Abstract Ideas—the conception of the class qualities

by themselves, and not as embodied in an individual—is effectually precluded by the laws of inseparable association."[44] Ideas
were united so inseparably by the laws of association that the
mind could not abstract or separate attributes to form general
ideas. All ideas were individual.

The formation, therefore, of a Concept, does not consist in separating
the attributes which are said to compose it, from all other attributes of
the same object, and enabling us to conceive those attributes, disjoined
from any others. We neither conceive them, nor think them, nor cognize
them in any way, as a thing apart, but solely as forming, in combination
with numerous other attributes, the idea of an individual object.[45]

In J. S. Mill's opinion, the mind could not abstract attributes, but
only "fix our attention" on those attributes relevant to our current topic. But never was this attention so exclusive as to eliminate other elements of the concrete idea. Mill stated his
conclusion forcefully.

General concepts, therefore, we have, properly speaking, none; we have
only complex ideas of objects in the concrete: but we are able to attend
exclusively to certain parts of the concrete ideas: and by that exclusive
attention, we enable those parts to determine exclusively the course of
our thoughts as subsequently called up by association.[46]

Hence Mill rejected his father's and Bentham's conceptualism in
favor of the nominalist thesis that names alone were general.
Ideas were always individual. The mind consisted of a stream of
sensations, simple ideas (the traces of sensation), and complex
ideas (simple ideas inseparably connected). General ideas did not
exist. The reasoning of Berkeley and Hume finally won acceptance in the utilitarian tradition.

J. S. Mill saw clearly that these developments in psychology
had implications for the philosophical method of the utilitarians
and their conception of human rationality. General terms
(though an important class of seemingly meaningful words) occupied the embarrassing position of having no ideas to stand for. To
resolve this paradox, Mill abandoned the ideational theory of
meaning, which had claimed that meaning was inherent in a
word's function as the name of an idea. However, Mill's refinements did not destroy the utilitarian philosophical method;
rather, they preserved its essentials by reconciling it with associa-

tionist psychology. First, Mill rejected the Lockian view that meaning was a species of naming, that a word was the name of something in the mind. Common sense dictated that a word was the name of whatever it denoted, that is, the word was the name of whatever it was predicable of. Hence, the terms "white," "long," and "virtuous" were the names, not of ideas, but of all objects of which the terms were predicable, of all white, long, and virtuous objects respectively.[47]

In his second modification of the utilitarian philosophical method, Mill denied that the meaning of words was found in the ideas for which they stood. Advances in psychology gave Mill no other alternative. Even Hume had stated much earlier that some words stood not for ideas but for impressions; not for the faint images of impressions present in thinking, but for the more lively feelings that occur when sensations, passions, and emotions first appear in the soul.[48] But the denial of the existence of abstract ideas quickly eroded the popularity of the ideational theory of meaning. No one doubted that general terms meant something; the question was what could they mean if no general ideas existed. The utilitarians had assumed that the meanings of such words were clarified by reducing them to names of real entities. As associationist psychology reduced the mind to its simplest feelings, to the sensations, impressions, or perceptions that were the basic building blocks of all mental phenomena, the answer to the question of what general terms meant became obvious. Since these "sensory units" were the only real entities, the meanings of words were explicable through them.[49] J. S. Mill contributed to the utilitarian philosophical method by clarifying this new theory of meaning. He fashioned a "connotative" theory of meaning which held that the meaning of a word consisted of the attribute or attributes connoted by it. Hence, while the terms "white," "long," and "virtuous" were the names of the external objects denoted by them, they also con-noted certain attributes—"whiteness," "length," and "virtue" respectively. A word's meaning was the attribute or set of attributes connoted by it.

But Mill's emphasis upon attributes seems far from simple sensations, the only real entities that the associationist psychology recognized. The common view that attributes exist in external objects suggests that Mill found the meanings of terms in external qualities, rather than in internal sensations. But this is a radical misunderstanding of Mill's position. He gave the terms "property," "quality," and "attribute" an unusual subjective sense. An attribute which words connoted and meant was not "a real thing possessed of objective existence;" rather, it was "a particular mode of naming our sensations, or our expectations of sensation."[50] Mill stated the conclusion clearly.

For if we know not, and cannot know, anything of bodies but the sensations which they excite in us or in others, those sensations must be all that we can, at bottom, mean by their attributes; and the distinction which we verbally make between the properties of things and the sensations we receive from them, must originate in the convenience of discourse rather than in the nature of what is signified by the terms.[51]

The names of sensations, the names of attributes, were now the only names of real entities; the meanings of all other words were explicable through them.

Clearly, the class of names of real entities had shrunk considerably since Bentham. James Mill had rejected "inferential real entities" as fictitious beliefs; his son similarly dismissed abstract ideas, thereby reducing the mind to a stream of particular impressions and traces of impressions (ideas). But despite these developments in ontology, the basic utilitarian philosophical method remained. J. S. Mill modified the method to preserve its essentials. His connotative theory reconciled the core of the utilitarian philosophical method (clarify words by the names of real entities) with the ontology of associationist psychology (sensations and their traces were all that existed in the mind). Given the popularity of associationist psychology, Mill had no option but to modify the utilitarian philosophical method to preserve it.

Moreover, the implications of associationist psychology extended beyond the utilitarian philosophical method. Associationism also influenced Mill's understanding of the rational process and his opinion of the relative value of inductive versus deductive logic. If abstract general ideas were nonexistent, then what was the status of the major premise of a syllogism? Did the rational mind operate inductively or deductively? Traditional deductive logic had assigned the major premise an important role. A suitable general proposition conjoined to a particular one, like "Socrates is a man," could prove the mortality of Socrates. The basic assumption underlying this proof was the old principle *dictum de omni et nullo;* whatever can be affirmed or denied of a class may be affirmed or denied of everything in a class. However, Mill considered deductive logic a necessarily incomplete and inaccurate description of the rational process.[52] He thought it incomplete because it did not explain the discovery of new truth, the inference from the known to the unknown, which is the undeniable core of the rational process. If anyone was engaged in rational activity, it was the empirical scientist. But in this case, the formal logician admitted failure by his concession that the conclusion of a syllogism contained nothing not also found in its premises. Deductive logic, if it portrayed the rational process at all, portrayed it incompletely. Since the syllogism involved no movement to the unknown, it did not comprehensively describe the rational process. Science was every day acquiring new knowledge and putting it to use.[53] These new truths, Mill reasoned, were attained through induction, not deduction.

But the traditional view that syllogistic reasoning was an accurate characterization of rational activity was not only incomplete; it was also fundamentally wrong, according to Mill. The principle *dictum de omni et nullo* was at odds with psychology and any acceptable theory of meaning. Mill applied his connotative theory of meaning (which held that a word meant either an attribute or a set of attributes) to general propositions.[54] Propositions like "All men are mortal" meant that a set of attributes (all men) either possessed or constantly accompanied another attribute or set of attributes (mortality). Hence, the proposition "All men are mortal" did not mean that the class "man" was a subset of the class "mortal beings," because general ideas of "all men" or of "all mortal beings" were psychologically impossible. All that existed in the mind was a stream of sensations (attributes) and ideas (whether simple or complex) of particular objects, and therefore the rational pursuit of scientific truth involved only the inferring of one sensation or set of sensations from another sensation or set of sensations. True inference from the known to the unknown was a matter of inferring particulars from particulars, a matter of induction.

A fuller discussion of Mill's theory of propositions helps to clarify his psychological rejection of deductive logic as an accurate characterization of the rational process. The meaning of real and verbal propositions was always reducible to the attributes connoted, to the phenomenal facts of our experience. Verbal propositions concerned the meaning of words; definitions were the most important examples of them. But since these propositions told us nothing of the world, they were essentially arbitrary. A definition could conform to ordinary usage or convention, but it could not be true or false. Nonetheless, whether a definition conformed or not, it either specified the relevant attributes or (by use of another word) connoted the same set of attributes.[55]

Real propositions were assertions about things. With these, Mill believed

that whatever be the form of the proposition . . . the real subject of every proposition is some one or more facts or phenomena of consciousness, or some one or more of the hidden causes or powers to which we ascribe those facts; and that what is predicated or asserted . . . of those phenomena or powers, is always either Existence, Order in Place, Order in Time, Causation, or Resemblance.[56]

Hence the nature of sensation and the relationships possible between sensations limited the types of real propositions. Sensations could exist, coexist, succeed one another, cause one another, and resemble one another, and so the different types of fact were Existence, Coexistence, Succession, Causation, and Resemblance.[57] Consequently, all real propositions described some sensation or set of sensations in one of the above relationships with another sensation or set of sensations.

Mill suggested a different formulation of this theory of "the import of propositions" when applied to active reasoning. At this time, a proposition meant that a certain attribute or set of attributes marked another set of attributes. The proposition "All men are mortal" meant that a certain set of attributes, that of mankind, was a mark of another set, that of mortality.[58] But then the basic maxim of syllogistic reasoning, the *dictum de omni et nullo,* was fallacious. The mind did not work in classes or with ideas as subsets of more general ideas; it worked rather in "marks" of particulars. The mind reasoned "that whatever has any mark, has that which it is a mark of. Or, when the minor premise as well as the major is universal, we may state it thus: Whatever is a mark of any mark, is a mark of that which this last is a mark of."[59] Psychology was therefore the basis for Mill's theory of the import of propositions, and his conclusion was that the mind reasoned inductively.

The question then arose about the explicit value of the syllogism and general propositions. Mill responded as follows:

All inference is from particulars to particulars: General propositions are merely the registers of such inferences already made, and short formulae for making more: The major premise of a syllogism, consequently, is a formula of this description: and the conclusion is not an inference drawn from the formula, but an inference drawn according to the formula: the real logical antecedent, or premise, being the particular facts from which the general proposition was collected by induction.[60]

Hence one should avoid the error, Mill urged, "of overlooking the distinction between two parts of the [rational] process of philosophizing, the inferring part and the registering part; and ascribing to the latter the functions of the former. The mistake," he cautioned, was "of referring a person to his notes for the origin of his knowledge."[61] Mill considered general propositions merely as convenient shorthand notes serving communication and memory. But placing our knowledge into its shorthand, generalized form did not change its nature. All knowledge and inference were ultimately of particulars, and particular facts of experience were "the real premises of the [inductive] reasoning."[62]

Now, all which men can observe are individual cases. From these all general truths must be drawn, and into these they may be again resolved; for a general truth is but an aggregate of particular truths; a comprehensive expression, by which an indefinite number of individual facts are affirmed or denied at once.[63]

The syllogism and general propositions thus had little status for Mill. They were not the true basis of reasoning.

Though general propositions had no significance apart from the particular facts they contained, Mill thought generalization a convenient test of the validity of our inferences. "From instances which we have observed, we feel warranted in concluding, that what we found true in those instances, holds in all similar ones."[64] The essential movement of the rational process from the unknown to the known "lies in the act of generalization."[65] "What remains to be performed afterwards [any deductions from the major premise] is merely deciphering our own notes."[66] But even so, general propositions do not contribute to the validity of any conclusion. The major premise is only "an intermediate halting place for the mind, interposed by an artifice of language between the real premises and the conclusion."[67] The real premises consist of particular sensations or sets of sensations that people experience; they are the real entities composing the rational process to which all language is ultimately reducible.

It is reasonable to assume that the ontological commitments of later utilitarian psychology influenced not only the philosophical method and conception of the rational process, but also the utilitarian theory of judicial decision-making. We have already examined how the philosophical method shaped utilitarian theories of liability, sovereignty, law, and obligation. The utilitarians clarified these concepts by using names of real entities as the relevant criteria. But the aim of their theory of judicial decision-making was the description and explanation of phenomena, not merely the analysis of a term. The discussion in Chapter 3 showed how the utilitarians replaced the traditional deductive theory of judicial decision-making with an inductive one. Now all that is needed is to point out the resemblances between Austin's philosophical method and conception of reason and J. S. Mill's in order to explain how these assumptions form the foundation of Austin's theory of judicial decision-making. Once this is done, we can turn to the relationship of Holmes's methodology to his utilitarian antecedents.

Austin's methodological writings are few and far between. Moreover, since Austin was considerably older than J. S. Mill, it seems paradoxical to argue that Austin's theory of judicial decision-making rested upon methodological ideas clarified by J. S. Mill. However, despite their meagerness, the relevant writings clearly indicate that the two men shared the same critical attitude towards deductive logic. There was a difference in age, but J. S. Mill was a student and friend of John Austin.[68] Furthermore, in metaphysical matters Austin deferred to James Mill and Dr. Thomas Brown and accepted associationist psychology.[69] But it was the ontological implications of this psychology that forced J. S. Mill to adjust the utilitarian philosophical method and to modify his understanding of the rational process. Austin may have seen similar difficulties with deductive logic for reasons that were explicitly presented only later by J. S. Mill. Of course I do not mean that Austin anticipated Mill's inductive philosophy in all its detail. That would be absurd. However, I do believe that the origin of many of the central ideas of Mill's *A System of Logic* lies in the effect that associationist psychology had upon utilitarian ideas of reality, ideas, and language. In this sense, associationist psychology may have influenced Austin's theory of judicial decision-making by producing a hostile attitude toward deductive logic.

Austin's views on logic are found in fragments of an "Essay on Analogy" which his wife published, with some misgivings, after his death.[70] No doubt the unfinished nature of this work raises doubts of its value. Nevertheless, the similarities between Austin's and J. S. Mill's views are evident and rather striking. He agreed with Mill that in the rational acquisition of knowledge the key step was the inductive formation of the major premise. The syllogism's role was negligible.

Whatever there has been of reasoning, as meaning process from known to unknown, has been performed by an analogical argument (an induction), by which we obtained the major premise. . . .

Since then syllogism can give us no new truth, and since it may mislead, what is its use?

I incline to think that the important part is not syllogism. But terms, propositions, divisions . . . are all-important . . . From my friend John Mill, who is a metaphysician, I expect that these, and analogical reasoning and induction . . . will receive that light which none but a philosopher can give.[71]

Besides revealing their friendship, this quote shows Austin making the same connection that Mill did between inductive inference and the acquisition of knowledge and indicates also Austin's negative evaluation of the syllogism and of its use in legal reasoning.

Since Austin's views on reasoning were based on psychological grounds, then like Mill he could not but have thought legal reasoning inductive. The mind could not change its mode of operation when it moved from conducting a scientific experiment to deciding a legal case. That Austin's position rested upon psychology is evident: "But, in fact, we never syllogise, though we perform an analogous process. We run the mental eye along the analogous [particular] objects."[72] In sum, Austin thought that man reasoned by analogy, not by deduction. Likewise, a judge examined the cases similar to the one he must currently decide. If the case was very similar to a set of cases, then the judge merely applied the rule. But if the case did not resemble previous ones, then the judge legislated a new rule by inductively discovering the preferred policy of the public or sovereign, or by calculating the costs and benefits of conflicting policies.[73]

In either case, whether the judge applied a rule or created a new one, Austin thought syllogistic reasoning had no crucial role to play. In the application of law, inductive comparisons of cases were the crux of the judge's rational activity. The judge ran his mental eye from particular case to particular case noticing similarities and differences. In a difficult case he would find competing analogies: two or more sets of cases with separate rules competing for dominance over the case at hand. But even here the judge decided the case inductively, not deductively. Was the case more similar to set A requiring rule B, or to set X requiring rule Y? Once the judge decided this question, he had little else to do. Deducing the legal consequence of the rule was anticlimatic. In cases requiring judicial legislation, the judge's decisions involved even less syllogistic reasoning. Here the judge fashioned a new rule upon inductive calculations of facts, weighing the advantages and disadvantages of different policies that were reflected in the similar but not controlling precedents. Therefore here too the deduction of the legal consequence was something of an afterthought.

Austin therefore was the first to apply the utilitarian conceptions of the rational process and of general propositions to judicial decision-making. Judges reasoned inductively from particular case to particular case, from particular policy to particular policy. General legal propositions did not establish judicial decisions; they were only containers for analogous cases already decided. Associationist psychology, with its effect upon the utilitarian conception of the rational process, created a need for a new inductive theory of judicial decision-making. The essentials of this new theory were formulated by Austin. Later, once J. S. Mill had clarified and systematized the philosophical implications of associationist psychology, the necessity of an inductive theory of judicial decision-making became more obvious. I shall argue that Holmes adhered to this utilitarian conception of reason and philosophical method, and that his well-known and explicitly inductive theory of judicial decision-making is completely understandable only in this light.

However, it is necessary first to describe Holmes's general attitude toward reality, ideas, and language before methodologically explaining his substantive doctrines. Many commentators have noticed Holmes's skepticism, but no one has explored its utilitarian assumptions. Holmes believed that any world outlook rested upon an act of faith. The existence of an external world cannot be proved, but should nonetheless be accepted. The world was not a dream, nor were people little gods who had created it. Philosophy, which all too often "sinned through arrogance,"[74] had to admit the *ding an sich;* philosophers must realize that they were born inside a universe, not it inside of them.[75] But the existence of an objective world did not mean that we could attain absolute truth of it. Chauncey Wright had long ago convinced Holmes of absolute truth's impossibility.[76] No matter how clear is the "clang" behind the phenomena, Holmes cautions that "Certitude is not the test of certainty."[77] The only promising activity is "to make *my* universe coherent and livable, not to babble about *the* universe."[78] Despite faith in a noumenal world, Holmes confined man's knowledge to the phenomenal one.

Holmes's restriction of human knowledge to phenomena perfectly accorded with the utilitarian emphasis upon experience. Man's knowledge of reality consisted of ideas that first arose through sense impressions. But how did these ideas function? What laws governed their operation? Holmes and the post-Benthamite utilitarians responded that the key to man's intellectual and emotional life was the association of ideas: "property, friendship, and truth have a common root in time." Consequently, what "we must love and revere generally is determined by early associations."[79] Man does not choose his beliefs: "It is in the nature of man's mind. A thing which you have enjoyed and used as your own for a long time, whether property or an opinion, takes root in your being and cannot be torn away without your resenting the act and trying to defend yourself, however you came by it."[80]

The psychological laws of the human mind turn truth into a system of "can't helps" and therefore a set of intellectual limitations.[81] The associations of personal experience determined our opinions; they created those beliefs that we "couldn't help" but believe in. Each person was therefore trapped in the associations of his personal experience; what he believed revealed more concerning the limitations of his experience than the nature of reality. "Those of us who flatter ourselves that we have intellectual detachment only get one story lower in our personality."[82] Moreover, because our emotional and intellectual lives are governed by the same principles, Holmes finds it unsurprising that people "for the most part believe what they want to."[83] Holmes lamented this fact and the fallacies ("humbugs") preserved by it.[84] He believed that a rational person could avoid enslaving his intellect to his passions and criticized those who preached otherwise.[85] Man could not escape from the laws of association, but he could purify his beliefs from emotional corruption through the use of dispassionate reason operating with scientific procedures. Holmes admired reason and science as much as the early utilitarians had done; he considered reason operating with scientific procedures the best "bet" going.[86] Since there were no Archimedean points of view, it was impossible to be certain;[87] but every person had to take his chances. According to Holmes, man was inherently a "betabilitarian,"[88] and Holmes's money, like the utilitarians' before him, was on reason and science.

But reason and science need a closer definition. J. S. Mill reduced experience to phenomenal facts of existence, coexistence, sequence, resemblance, or causation. However, of these Mill assigned a special role in scientific investigations to facts of causation.

Now among all those uniformities in the succession of phenomena, which common observation is sufficient to bring to light, there are very few which have any, even apparent, pretension to this rigorous indefeasibility: and of those few, one only has been found capable of completely sustaining it. In that one, however, we recognize a law which is universal also in another sense; it is coextensive with the entire field of successive phenomena, all instances whatever of succession being examples of it. This law is the Law of Causation. The truth that every fact which has a beginning has a cause, is coextensive with human experience.[89]

Rational scientific analysis of successive phenomena concerned causes and their effects. Holmes agreed with Mill entirely:

The postulate on which we think about the universe is that there is a fixed quantitative relation between every phenomenon and its antecedents and consequents. If there is such a thing as a phenomenon without these fixed quantitative relations, it is a miracle. It is outside the law of cause and effect, and as such transcends our power of thought, or at least is something to or from which we cannot reason. The condition of our thinking about the universe is that it is capable of being thought about rationally, or, in other words, that every part of it is effect and cause in the same sense in which those parts are with which we are most familiar.[90]

Experience consists of facts; when they are rationally and scientifically examined, it must be assumed that these facts—our phenomenal universe—are causally tied together. "If the world is a subject for rational thought it is all of one piece; the same laws are found everywhere, and everything is connected with everything else."[91] Though Mill's language is different, their conceptions coincide. Mill described the causal relationships of the world as a web "composed of separate fibres."[92] A fiber (a fact) was a part of the web because every fact was connected with every other fact.

Holmes and Mill agreed that a theorist could therefore reduce general scientific knowledge to facts. Particular facts were the real premises of argument; general propositions, only their hollow containers. The thinker unifies these facts, "which lay scattered in an inorganic mass, when he shoots through them the magnetic current of his thought."[93] But this did not change the nature of scientific speculation. In the end it was only gossip.

Of course I know that ideas are merely shorthand for collections of the facts . . . It is the eternal seesaw of the universe. A fact taken in its isolation . . . is gossip. Philosophy is an end of life, yet philosophy is only cataloguing the universe and the universe is simply an arbitrary fact so that as gossip should lead to philosophy, philosophy ends in gossip.[94]

Since we know of no reason why the cosmos works thus and not otherwise, scientific theories are a form of "chatting about the universe." Therefore, as with gossip, the truth and validity of scientific theories depend upon the truth of the particular facts of which they are composed.

Hence Holmes's primary methodological directive was to recognize the facts. He described "looking the facts in the face" as the "first step toward improvement."[95] Consequently, the scientist should stalwartly refrain from criticizing unpleasant facts. Such futile whimperings, like complaints about the weather, only exhibited the immature, maladjusted nature of the commentator.[96] Moreover, to ignore distasteful facts was dangerous. It encouraged action contrary to the truth, and those who act ignorantly "take the chances that some day the sunken fact will rip the bottom out of their boat."[97] Hence science should not assume a benevolent universe; the social sciences should especially recognize the brutal facts of human society and explore their ramifications.

Holmes also had views of language similar to those of the utilitarians, but especially to those of J. S. Mill. He agreed with Mill that the only real entities were the phenomenal facts. Facts were all that were; if words meant not facts they meant nothing at all. Consequently, Holmes insists that we "think things not words, or at least ... translate our words into the facts for which they stand"; only then will we "keep to the real and true."[98] Language was dangerous. It attracted attention away from the "living thought" that ultimately gave it significance. "A word is not a crystal, transparent and unchanged, it is the skin of a living thought and may vary greatly in color and content according to the circumstances and the time in which it is used."[99] Dealing with a seemingly difficult case, Holmes followed his own advice to "think things not words." When he seized and pulled off the intimidating "lion skin" of legal language, he always discovered that the uncovered case was just another "old donkey of a question of law." In sum, once he "got hold of the language there was no such thing as a difficult case."[100]

Other academic disciplines also needed the benefits of concrete language, of the advantages of reducing language to things, to real entities, to the phenomenal facts of our universe. We must regret that Holmes never finished his book on legal philosophy; as he envisaged it, "a book of the law keeping to hard facts."[101] In economics, Holmes suggested dropping terms like "ownership, money, etc., and to think of the stream of products; of wheat and cloth and railway travel."[102] Throughout his life and in every subject, Holmes followed this utilitarian policy of linguistic reductionism. Words stood for real entities, things, the phenomenal facts of our experience. The psychology and ontology of Bentham had long since departed, but his philosophical method had survived.

This program of linguistic reductionism operated at all levels of language. No matter how abstract the concept or general the proposition, clarification required its reduction to things, to the particular facts of our experience. "A generalization is empty," in Holmes's words, "so far as it is general. Its value depends on the number of particulars which it calls up to the speaker and the hearer."[103] For this reason, Holmes qualified his opinion that the chief end of man was to form general propositions with the paradoxical assertion that "no proposition was worth a damn."[104] The general proposition, reducible to its particulars, functioned simply as "a string for the facts."[105] Abstractions received the same treatment; since abstract ideas did not exist, all abstract terms were reducible to particular facts. Holmes advised his intellectual protégé John Wu to "nourish your abstractions with the particulars that give them value."[106] In his own work, Holmes therefore gave legal and scientific concepts—for example, right and gravity—a factual orientation.

Then as we pretend to account for that mode of action by the hypothetical cause, the force of gravitation, which is merely the hypostasis of the prophesied fact and an empty phrase. So we get up the empty substratum, a right, to pretend to account for the fact that the courts will act in a certain way.[107]

Just as a general proposition was not worth a damn apart from particulars, so general terms were useless and misleading when separated from the phenomenal facts.

Holmes's rejection of abstract or general ideas also explains his hostility to deductive reasoning. He often cites "the danger of reasoning from generalizations unless you have the particulars in mind. A generalization is empty so far as it is general. Its value depends on the number of particulars," not the number of abstract ideas, "which it calls up to the speaker and the hearer."[108] Man's psychology enabled him to associate only particular ideas and impressions; all abstract concepts and general propositions were therefore reducible to these. Any one who thought otherwise deluded himself with language. Holmes's command "to think things not words" is understandable only in this light. Given Holmes's commitment to associationist psychology and his belief that the meaning of words was the "living thought" they stood for, Holmes had no choice but to reduce both reasoning and language to the phenomenal facts. In this he followed the fresh footprints of John Stuart Mill, who had recently adapted the utilitarian view of reality, ideas, and language to the psychology of his day. But it was still the same tradition of thought. Holmes had different ideas than Bentham concerning what constituted a real entity; but he insisted no less than Bentham did that all words and propositions were reducible to the names of real entities.

For Holmes, real entities were the phenomenal facts of our consciousness; conceptual clarification was dependent upon them. Holmes's specific substantive theories of law, obligation, and liability provide convenient examples of the utilitarian philosophical method in operation. An examination of the methodological foundation of these theories will not only clarify more deeply the substance of Holmes's legal philosophy, but also reaffirm the connection between the utilitarians' and Holmes's methodological opinions and their substantive doctrines. But a first step is to point out how Holmes's commitment to the utilitarian philosophical method explains his descriptive theoretical orientation. Since the universe consisted only of particular facts associated with one another, Holmes conceived of philosophy's task as empirical—to describe and explain. He saw no reason why any intellectual system "should disagree with the facts."[109] Even moral philosophy should stick to the facts and refrain from proselytizing. This attitude may seem incongruous with the early utilitarians' censorial and reformist attitude; but even Bentham based his new morality upon the facts. He avoided the errors of the moral-sense school and the natural-law school by recognizing that "Nature has placed mankind under the governance of two sovereign masters, *pain* and *pleasure*. It is for them alone to point out what we ought to do, as well as to determine what we shall do."[110] Utility was the standard of morality because of the facts of human psychology.

Holmes was much of Bentham's opinion. He chastised Laski (as Bentham had criticized natural-law moralists and the moral-sense school) for his morally superior attitude on issues of democracy, socialism, and equality. Holmes then confided to Laski that he did "accept a rough equation between isness and oughtness . . . You" continued Holmes, "respect the rights of man—I don't, except those things a given crowd will fight for—which vary from religion to the price of beer."[111] Hence, moral rules were "imperfect social generalizations expressed in terms of feeling . . . [To] make the generalization perfect we must wash out the emotion and get a cold head."[112] Holmes's attitude was to face these moral facts. The facts that Holmes found were different from those emphasized by the early utilitarians, but they were still facts. In his own sobering opinion, Holmes understood morality as a veneer of politeness that hid the ultimate fact of force.[113] Though now surely dated, Holmes's attitude towards sexual equality reveals his distinctive moral outlook: "With your belief in some apriorities like equality you may have difficulties. I who believe in force (mitigated by politeness) have no trouble—and if I were sincere and were asked certain *whys* by a woman should reply, 'Because

Ma'am I am the bull'."[114] Holmes's moral philosophy revolves around the above general idea; persons ought to be treated much as they are treated, much as the factual relationships of power and force permit.

The same factual descriptive and explanatory orientation extended to Holmes's jurisprudence: "The first call of a theory of law ... [was] that it should explain the facts."[115] His theories of law, sovereignty, obligation, and liability were all explanatory; the criteria used within them, factual. For example, Holmes disagreed with Bentham's and Austin's reduction of all laws to commands because, "Law also as well as sovereignty is a fact."[116] Holmes argued that by "whom a duty is imposed must be of less importance than the definiteness of its expression and the certainty of its being enforced."[117] If a custom is enforced, it is a fact of the empirical world and deserves recognition for what it is—a law.

In a contemporary context, Holmes's factual orientation led him also to claim that modern law was no "brooding onmipresence in the sky but the articulate voice of some sovereign."[118] The facts of enforcement had changed from a customary age to the present age of centralized states. If the state enforced a law, it existed; if not, then not. Moreover, since courts had become the primary means of law enforcement, Holmes thought law equivalent to what the courts enforced. "The prophecies of what the courts will do in fact, and nothing more pretentious, are what I mean by the law."[119] A law's existence was not a mystery; it was an empirical fact. The question was whether the courts of an articulate sovereign were going to enforce a rule or not.[120]

Not only was law itself an external fact, but the law addressed itself only to external facts. Legal philosophy should therefore resolve legal concepts into certain external facts and the legal consequences attached to them. Legal possession was Holmes's favorite example, but any legal compound required the same analysis.

The word "possession" denotes such a group of facts. Hence, when we say of a man that he has possession, we affirm directly that all the facts of a certain group are true of him, and we convey indirectly or by implication that the law will give him the advantage of the situation. Contract, or property, or any other substantive notion of the law, may be analyzed in the same way, and should be treated in the same order.[121]

Holmes thought every legal concept could "be analyzed into fact and right, antecedent and consequent."[122] All "rules of law presuppose a certain state of facts to which they are applicable."[123] Here again Holmes's methodological assumptions explain his factual orientation to law. Not only must a court enforce a law for it to exist, but the law itself had to address these same external facts and attach legal consequences only to them, not to anything else.

Holmes derived his psychological theory of legal obligation from the same methodological sources. If a person was obliged to act by the threat of coercion, then an obligation existed; if not, then not. The term "legal right" received an identical analysis; legal duty meant "nothing but a prediction that if a man does or omits certain things he will be made to suffer in this or that way by judgment of the court; and so of a legal right."[124] Holmes sometimes added another condition to distinguish a legal obligation from a tax: a sovereign's absolute wish. But the requirement of a sovereign's absolute wish that his subjects refrain from or do the relevant act was itself a matter of fact. The existence of such a wish depended upon whether the sovereign enforced contracts to perform the illegal act or whether the sovereign granted the subject any legal alternative but obedience. In both cases, the question was one of fact. If the sovereign neither enforced the contracts nor permitted any legal alternative, then a legal obligation existed; if he did, then the sanction was only tax. Therefore, whether Holmes added the requirement of an absolute wish or not, his theory of legal obligation was factual.

The concept of sovereignty endured a similar analysis. The sovereign's identity was "a question of fact equivalent to the question who has the sum of the political powers of a state in his hands."[125] Because of the factual nature of the sovereign, Holmes thought that its power could vary from region to region, that observation (not a constitutional law book) provided the only true indication of a sovereign's limits.[126] "The only limit that I can see to the power of the lawmaker is the limit of power as a question of fact ... It seems to me all fact—and this endless jaw the blowing of soap bubbles."[127] Holmes's criteria of sovereignty implied that the sovereign of a society could change without any change in the formal constitutional rules. In such a situation, the courts must yield to the powers that be, not the powers that were.[128] Often courts would have trouble assessing the facts of power. Political instability would render the sovereign unknown. But even if the sovereign was hard to identify, the court had no excuse to ignore the empirical facts upon which the question depended. The legal theorist should follow the judge's example. He too should clarify his concepts by reducing them to names of real entities. For Holmes, this meant that the sovereign's existence and identity were decided according to hard empirical facts.

A theory of legal liability had to fulfill two requirements; it had to fit the facts in two different senses. First, the theory must explain the general tendency of the common law;[129] and second, the theory's criteria of legal liability had to be factual. An individual's liability was a question no different from one concerning his height. The phenomenal facts of Holmes's universe had to contain the criterion of his theory of legal liability. Holmes thought his scientific external theory of legal liability fulfilled both requirements. It is of course impossible in this space to evaluate Holmes's claim that his theory of liability explained the vast majority of cases at common law. But an examination of the factual character of Holmes's theory of legal liability is feasible and will reveal the methodological presuppositions underlying his theory.

A scientific theory of legal liability had to base liability upon a real entity, a knowable something that existed in the world. Consequently, as Bentham and Austin had done earlier, Holmes rejected a free will or an evil will as necessary conditions of legal liability. First, Holmes was a determinist. For Holmes, as we saw above, thinking of the world rationally consisted in considering particular facts causally related to one another. A theory basing liability upon a free will therefore demanded a miracle: an uncaused cause. But Holmes saw no incompatibility between his determinism and legal responsibility. If he had a philosophical talk with a condemned convict, he would say "I don't doubt that your act was inevitable for you but to make it more avoidable by others we propose to sacrifice you to the common good."[130] A free will was not a real entity, and Holmes therefore excluded it from his theory of liability.

An evil motive was also discarded as a condition of legal liability. The external utilitarian purpose of law justified punishment of acts even if done from beneficial motives. But there was another methodological reason for their rejection. Since the utilitarians adhered to an objective moral standard that reduced morality to a matter of fact, they were able to say whether the motive of a particular act was good or bad. Holmes could not and did not.

For him, morality was in the eye of the beholder, not in the external factual world. Moreover, it was perceived with the heart (emotions) rather than with the mind. Holmes even doubted "if the intellect accepts or recognizes that classification of good and bad."[131] The scientific intellect dealt only with phenomenal facts and their causal relationships. Therefore, a scientific theory of legal liability must base liability upon the presence or absence of a fact, not upon a fact's goodness or badness. Quantitative judgements must replace qualitative ones. The goodness or badness of a will could have no place in a scientific theory of legal liability.

Holmes finally chose as the criterion of liability foresight of harmful consequences. Foresight did exist; it was a fact. Holmes described it as "a picture of a future state of things called up by knowledge of the present state of things, the future being viewed as standing to the present in the relation of effect to cause."[132] However, liability did not require the individual to foresee the harmful consequences. Holmes adopted an external standard of liability. Would a man of reasonable prudence have foreseen the harmful consequences? If so, then the person was liable even if he failed to foresee the harm. Holmes justified this criterion upon utilitarian grounds; but methodological commitments also had their bearing upon the issue. For instance, the internal fact of foresight (did that man foresee the harm?) was not a part of any court's phenomenal experience. Since one cannot experience another person's foresight, Holmes reasoned that legal liability could not depend upon it. The law "does not attempt to see men as God sees them, for more than one sufficient reason. It might be said that the investigation and just appreciation of the actual [internal] facts is beyond the power of any human tribunal."[133] Consequently, the methodological rationale for an external test of liability has become clear. A scientific theory of legal liability would not use as the crucial condition a fact beyond human experience. The theory of legal liability had to be external.

Moreover, the fact that Holmes usually measured what a rational man would foresee by the agent's actual knowledge of the circumstances does not detract from the external factual nature of Holmes's test. If in "most cases, the question of knowledge is a question of the actual condition of the defendant's consciousness, the question of what he might have foreseen is determined by the standard of the prudent man, that is, by general experience."[134] But there are cases in which the law "requires a man to find out present facts, as well as to foresee future harm, at his peril, although they are not such as would necessarily be inferred from the facts known."[135] Holmes's example was an English statute prohibiting the abduction of girls under sixteen from persons having lawful charge over them. If a man knowingly abducted a girl from her parents, he must find out her age at his peril. The law did not accept the fact that he had every reason to think her over sixteen as an acceptable excuse.[136] The agent incurred liability despite the lack of knowledge; the state punished because the defendant failed to know facts that a legislature would have him know, not because he failed to foresee the harm that a prudent man would have foreseen. Such cases of strict liability were perfectly acceptable to Holmes. Though Holmes objected to the old common-law doctrine that a man was responsible for all the harm he caused, he did endorse specific rules of strict liability. "It is the coarseness, not the nature, of the standard which is objected to." Therefore, Holmes was "by no means opposed to the doctrine that he [the agent] does certain particular acts at his peril."[137] The trouble with the old common-law standard was that it placed men in peril whatever the time, place, or activity. It encouraged sedentary lives (when activity was the only means of improving the general welfare) and unfairly gave a person no chance to avoid the harm.[138] It was therefore bad policy and an unjust rule.

But when experience had shown that a particular act (shooting a gun) was dangerous, Holmes preferred specific rules. Then their violators were liable whatever their "internal facts" of knowledge.

There is no longer any need to refer to the prudent man, or general experience. The facts have taught their lesson, and have generated a concrete and external rule of liability. He who snaps a cap upon a gun pointed in the direction of another person, known by him to be present, is answerable for the consequences.[139]

Even if the person had every reason to believe the gun defective or empty, the law held him liable for the act. Holmes thought this process of "specification" the culmination of legal development; it was the final advancement from moral to external legal standards.[140] Since Holmes's conception of legal liability was perfectly compatible with these specific rules of strict liability, his theory did not always require the examination of the knowledge of the agent. Internal facts were not a necessary condition of legal liability. In cases of strict liability, the external fact of the act sufficed.

However, even if in the future the law may consist of specific rules of strict liability, its current standard is the foresight of the rational prudent man. And if the actual knowledge of the agent is used to measure what a rational man would foresee, one could argue that Holmes's theory of legal liability contradicts his methodology. In fact, it would seem that Holmes's crucial condition of liability was usually the actual knowledge of the defendant, a set of internal facts beyond the court's experience that only God could know. But the way out of this paradox is to note how Holmes thought the court ascertained internal facts. The question of means was all important.

It is further to be noticed that there is no question of the defendant's knowledge of the nature of tigers, although without that knowledge he cannot be said to have intelligently chosen to subject the community to danger. Here again even in the domain of knowledge the law applies its principle of averages. The fact that tigers and bears are dangerous is so generally known, that a man who keeps them is presumed to know their peculiarities. In other words, he does actually know that he has an animal with certain teeth, claws, and so forth, and he must find out the rest of what an average member of the community would know, at his peril.[141]

The solution to Holmes's dilemma was therefore presumption. Since the court could not experience the internal facts of an agent, it presumed that he acted with the knowledge of an average member of the community. The crucial test of legal liability was still external. Would the average member of a community know enough of the circumstances of an act for a reasonably prudent man to have foreseen the harmful consequences that in fact ensued? If so, then the agent was liable; if not, then not.

The question now is whether this criterion can still be considered factual. Holmes's universe consisted of particular facts; but the abstract rational and prudent man hardly seems related to the facts of the world. Nevertheless, in order to understand Holmes's theory of legal liability completely, it is necessary to recognize that the standard of the rational and prudent man was a test to see if certain facts existed. Holmes considered the abstract rational man as a convenient device to clarify the teachings of experience concerning the factual dangerousness of various forms of conduct.

The question what a prudent man would do under given circumstances is then equivalent to the question what are the teachings of experience as to the dangerous character of this or that conduct under these or those circumstances; and as the teachings of experience are matters of fact, it is easy to see why the jury should be consulted with regard to them.[142]

The jury decided controversial cases because liability amounted to a matter of fact. Was the conduct sufficiently dangerous to make the agent liable? Did the defendant fire the gun? Holmes saw no essential difference between these questions; in his judgment, both were factual. Consequently, Holmes's scientific theory of legal liability made the jury substitute quantitative measurements for qualitative judgments in controversial cases.[143] The line separating punishable from nonpunishable conduct was therefore no different from the one separating crows from black birds in zoology. In both cases only particular facts were involved, and differences were therefore ultimately only of degree. Hence, it was the presence or absence of *external facts of danger* that Holmes chose as his fundamental criterion of legal liability. His methodological opinions necessitated an external fact; the utilitarian purpose of law necessitated that the external fact be the one of dangerous acts.

The last topic under consideration is Holmes's theory of judicial decision-making and the extent to which it was shaped by his utilitarian methodology. Earlier I showed how the utilitarians' conception of reason and their philosophical method formed the basis for Austin's understanding of judicial decision-making. The syllogism was subordinated to inductive analogical reasoning. The judge's job was either to decide if the present case was more like one or another set of cases, or to legislate by comparing the costs and benefits of various policies. The deduction of the legal consequence was anticlimatic.

Holmes's views on the nature of human reason and his philosophical method were also found to have affinities with utilitarian doctrines, especially with those of J. S. Mill. Holmes accepted J. S. Mill's associationist psychology and the implication that abstract or general ideas did not exist. For this reason, he reduced general propositions to the particular facts that composed the universe. Holmes thought that to make "a general principle worth anything you must give it a body; you must show in what way and how far it would be applied actually in an actual system; you must show how it has gradually emerged as the felt reconciliation of concrete instances no one of which established it in terms."[144] General legal propositions did not decide concrete cases; they were only the receptacles of particular decisions. They could not have been the major premises of legal deductions because they came into existence only after the fact. Principles of law emerged from cases, not vice versa. Here Holmes cited Mill's example of Lord Mansfield's advice to a businessman recently appointed judge: "Lord Mansfield knew that if any reason were assigned it would be necessarily an afterthought, the judge being in fact guided by impressions from past experience."[145] Holmes agreed, but added that Mansfield's caution was also good advice for more educated courts because legal principles arise "only after a series of determinations on the same subject matter."

> In cases of first impression Lord Mansfield's often-quoted advice to the business man who was suddenly appointed judge, that he should state his conclusions and not give his reasons, as his judgment would probably be right and the reasons certainly wrong, is not without its application to more educated courts. It is only after a series of determinations on the same subject-matter, that it becomes necessary to "reconcile the cases" as it is called, that is, by a true induction to state the principle which has until then been obscurely felt.[146]

General propositions did not decide concrete cases because they had no content, no meaning, no significance, and no existence until particular analogous cases were decided. Only through the induction of particulars was a legal principle established. And even then it was just a container, a string for the facts. An easy case was only easily resolvable, not because the case involved an easy deduction, but because the facts of the case clearly indicated into which receptacle the case should be placed.

To decide cases properly, the judge had to follow an inductive method. If a case similar to those grouped under a legal principle or a statute arose, then the judge inferred the appropriate legal consequence. But the crux of the decision concerned the issue of similarity. Was this case similar enough to those of set A or set B? Here the judge patiently and inductively examined the facts and circumstances of the particular case; the finer the similarities were, the more difficult the case. As cases "begin to approach each other, the distinction becomes more difficult to trace; the determinations are made one way or the other on a very slight preponderance of feeling, rather than articulate reason."[147] But once the judge had a "feel" for the case, the legal consequence would follow as a matter of course. Moreover, in cases of judicial legislation, the judge also used inductive rather than deductive reasoning. He extended one of two or more rules to a case because he believed that the policy underlying the rule covered the present case and that this particular policy would better serve society's interests. "Behind the logical form lies a judgment as to the relative worth and importance of competing legislative grounds, often an inarticulate and unconscious judgment, it is true, and yet the very root and nerve of the whole proceeding."[148]

Holmes endorsed this inductive approach to judicial decision-making because it was the only method that was psychologically possible. As Austin thought before him, Holmes believed the "mental eye" could only run along particular analogous cases. Therefore Holmes was not sketching out a new theory of how judges should decide cases. His deterministic outlook did not permit alternatives, and his method (equating "isness" with "oughtness") forced him "to stick to the facts." His theory was thus descriptive and explanatory, not critical or prescriptive; it was not meant to change the nature of our rational process, but only our delusions concerning it. The possibility that prejudiced understandings of the facts should have their weight in an unconscious form is what repelled Holmes.[149] The time for unconscious legal development was over. Law "has become a conscious reaction upon itself of organized society knowingly seeking to determine its own destinies."[150] Hence, Holmes supported an inductive and utilitarian method of judicial legislation for methodological reasons. It was a call to recognize the *facts*, not to change them.

With these conclusions in mind, Holmes's famous aphorism that "the life of the law has not been logic but experience" takes on a deeper meaning.

The life of the law has not been logic: it has been experience. The felt necessities of the time, the prevalent moral and political theories, intuitions of public policy, avowed or unconscious, even the prejudices which judges share with their fellow-men, have had a good deal more to do than the syllogism in determining the rules by which men should be governed.[151]

In this passage, Holmes did not deny reason an important role in legal development. Though formal deductive logic was excluded, inductive reasoning had an esteemed part to play. By "experience," by "felt necessities," by "intuitions of policy" Holmes meant the "can't helps" of the legislating judge. The judge decided cases according to policies that he could not help but believe in. A judge's "prejudices" were more important than the syllogism in legal development because the principles of association that formed the judge's intellectual beliefs also shaped his emotions. Not only property and friendship, but also truth (an assessment of what the law is or ought to be) had a common root in time, and so a judge's prejudices accordingly shaped his decisions.

Holmes did not favor this type of judicial legislation, preferring a scientific weighing of the costs and benefits. In his view, there were few qualities more admirable in a judge "than this accuracy of thought, and the habit of keeping one's eye on the things for which words stand."[152] Of course, the things the judge was to eye were the facts of how proposed policies would affect the individuals in the case and society at large. Consequently, Holmes not only thought it a fact that judges decided cases inductively, but he advised them to pay attention to the facts. The utilitarian end of law required judges to be scientific, to keep their eyes on the facts, and to ignore their own prejudices. Both Holmes's theory and his advice are in line with his methodological presuppositions.

But Holmes did not believe his theory of judicial legislation would secure unanimity. Since disagreements existed in the past and since his theory was primarily descriptive, Holmes made no suggestion that it would secure harmonious legal development. Conceptions of policy were informed by various interests, and as long as men's interests were opposed, their policies would conflict. Moreover, judges were not omniscient. When the judge faced conflicting options from which he had to choose a rule, he should not always follow his own judgment. If the interests supporting the different policies were roughly equal, then the judge had no choice. He placed the bet for society. But if there was a dominant interest and opinion on the issue, the judge must defer to the wishes of the community. Even if the judge is certain that the dominant policy will send the country to hell, he should doubt his own opinion and defer to society's beliefs. Submission is requisite because law was a practical thing.[153] However, even here the judge should look to external facts. The judge first ascertains the fact of any dominant opinion on the issue. If there is one, he decides the case accordingly. If not, then he examines the facts of how different policies will affect the individuals of the case and society in general. In either case, the deduction of the legal consequence is anticlimatic.

In conclusion, Holmes's methodological assumptions have had their impact upon his theory of judicial decision-making, just as they had influenced his theories of law, sovereignty, obligation, and legal liability. Holmes's substantive doctrines become clearer in the light of his methodological assumptions about reality, ideas, and language. These methodological ideas form the thread that unites Holmes's jurisprudence into a consistent whole. If we ignore them, we can never grasp the complexity, unity, and subtlety of Holmes's legal thought. Of course the same holds true for utilitarian jurisprudence. Even though there were important differences in how the utilitarians conceived reality, ideas, and language, they adhered to a common philosophical method. Methodology not only clarifies the substantive doctrines of utilitarian jurisprudence, but also unites the different theorists into a single school. We shall never fully understand their doctrines until we appreciate their peculiar methodological outlook. In this chapter, I have examined the similarities of Holmes's methodological assumptions to those of the utilitarians. Clearly his views of reality, ideas, and language more closely resembled J. S. Mill's than those of the early utilitarian thinkers. But Mill's ideas developed within the utilitarian tradition, and Holmes's methodology ought to be perceived in the same way. Of course there were subtle changes and terminological differences, but they pale before the broad areas of agreement. Consequently, Holmes's method was similar to utilitarian methodology, and his substantive doctrines resembled those of the utilitarians because he agreed with their understanding of the interrelationships of reality, ideas, and language.

VI

CONCLUSIONS AND COMMENTARY

The discussion at this point has reached two general and related conclusions: that the central core of Holmes's legal philosophy was utilitarian in origin and, by implication, that utilitarian ideas have seeped into American jurisprudence. The result should be a better understanding of the complexity, subtlety, and unity of Holmes's legal thought and a more ready appreciation of the historical importance of utilitarian jurisprudence. This does not mean that utilitarian ideas have become commonplace. Indeed, if they were commonplace, then my thesis that they explain the distinctive elements of Holmes's legal philosophy would be undermined. Though utilitarian ideas were preserved in Holmes's jurisprudence, and though many of these insights flowered into the school of American legal realism, contemporary legal philosophy has followed its own lights. Following the example of political theory, which has recently adopted a normative and prescriptive orientation, legal philosophy has abandoned the realistic orientation inherited from the utilitarians and Holmes. Holmes's and the utilitarians' legal theories are of special interest because they conflict, rather than agree, with current modes of thought. They offer a perspective from which to appraise critically the methods and assumptions of contemporary jurisprudence.

But first, I wish to emphasize the originality of O. W. Holmes. Despite the similarities of substance and method, which justify my conclusion that any differences between Holmes's legal thought and the utilitarians' are minor relative to the broad areas of agreement, these theoretical resemblances in no way detract from the significance of Holmes's contributions. Though they

144

were refinements within a utilitarian tradition of jurisprudence, Holmes's insights into our understanding of legal liability, a legal system, legal obligation, law, and finally judicial decision-making were original. The fact that his starting point was utilitarian does not lessen the distance Holmes traveled or the importance of his modifications of utilitarian doctrine. Therefore Holmes's legal writings surely deserve their special place within American jurisprudence.

But notwithstanding Holmes's originality, my conclusion that the core of his jurisprudence was utilitarian in origin should in some way affect orthodox interpretations of Holmes's legal philosophy. The utilitarian perspective permits a better understanding of the content, the subtlety, and the unity of Holmes's legal theory. Though I have refrained throughout this investigation from commenting upon the overwhelming body of Holmesian literature, the purpose of my restraint was to provide a readable book; it was not for lack of criticisms. Indeed, as I suggested in the first chapter, the greatest part of this *corpus* is entangled in anachronisms, panegyrics, and obloquies. Was Holmes a fascist? a civil libertarian? a liberal? Much of the commentary addresses such questions and is of little intellectual value.

But the serious expositions of Holmes's legal thought that do exist are a different matter. My examination of the utilitarian origin of Holmes's jurisprudence should help us evaluate these interpretations. For instance, in the case of Holmes's theory of legal liability, everyone is sure that there is something radically distinctive about it, but there are disagreements about what this distinctive element is and why Holmes found it attractive. Grant Gilmore has argued that Holmes narrowed the existing sphere of liability by adopting an external and objective theory. In his interpretation, Holmes believed that ideally losses should lie where they fall and that everyone should escape liability.[1] Holmes favored this theory for two reasons: first, it made the Langdellian view of law respectable by reducing liability to a "single continuous series." Consequently, judges could (as C. C. Langdell had encouraged) decide cases as mathematicians solve equations— without knowing anything of the real world.[2] Gilmore's second reason why Holmes liked external and objective standards of legal liability was more practical.

On a deeper level the legal theorists who preached the doctrines of limited liability—the loss must lie where it falls—and of the lowest possible damages shared a community of interest with their economic counter-parts who preached the religion of *laissez-faire.*[3]

Though Justice Holmes would defer to the legislature's will and not invalidate social and economic legislation that redistributed losses, he did so only because he believed that law must reflect the community's values. But if Holmes had had his way, his theory of legal liability would have served the interests of the capitalist class in the Darwinian struggle for life. Gilmore closes with the asser-tion that Holmes's "philosophically continuous" theory of legal li-ability was unprecedented since it covered every facet of law.[4]

Gilmore's interpretation of Holmes's theory of legal liability re-veals how far a sincere analysis can go wrong because its author ignores the historical origins of Holmes's ideas. The only thing right about this interpetation is that Holmes did formulate a comprehensive theory of legal liability. But this was not, as Gil-more asserts, unprecedented in legal literature; we have seen and examined previous utilitarian attempts to formulate such a com-prehensive theory. However, the more important issue is Gil-more's assertion that Holmes's external theory of legal liability served the interests of early capitalism by narrowing legal liability.

First of all, Gilmore presumably does not mean that Holmes's theory narrowed criminal liability. We have seen above how Holmes rejected as conditions for criminal liability an evil will or a moral fault. Therefore, compared to his contemporaries or pred-ecessors, there is no question that Holmes widened criminal liabil-ity.[5] Holmes thought that if the objective act was sufficiently dangerous (considered as a matter of fact) according to the com-munity's standard, then the agent was criminally liable. It is then clear that Holmes's external standard did not serve every interest of the early capitalist. If the employer acted in ways that were un-reasonably dangerous to his employees or customers, Holmes thought that the state could hold him criminally liable. Of course, late nineteenth-century Americans did not usually find the em-ployer's acts sufficiently dangerous to justify criminal punish-ment. But this state of events hardly proves that Holmes's theory was a shield for capitalist interests. Neither Holmes nor his theory of liability was responsible for the values current in the late nine-teenth century.

However, even if we ignore the tendency of Holmes's theory to widen criminal liability, there are other problems with Gilmore's

146

claim that Holmes's standards of *civil* liability aided capitalists by narrowing contractual liability. Morton Horwitz has already shown a number of fallacies in Gilmore's argument.[6] First, Gilmore gives us no clear reason why making it more difficult to enter and to withdraw from a contract (assuming that Holmes's theory narrows contractual liability) serves capitalist values. The orthodox (and more commonsensical) view is that capitalists preferred easy access to contracts since they had faith in their own ability to predict and shape the future and to understand the "fine print" of the contracts they signed. Narrow contractual liability would rather seem to serve the interests of the weak, poor, and ignorant. The state would narrow their contractual liability to the shrewd and grasping capitalist.

But this first objection to Gilmore's argument is moot since there is no reason to think that external standards necessarily narrowed contractual liability. Horwitz's example is that of unilateral mistake.[7] The earlier "will" theory had denied contractual liability if one of the parties could show mistake, could prove that their "minds had not met." Objectivists thought that this requirement of a "meeting of the minds" was too severe. Contractees could too easily avoid their promises. Therefore, Holmes's objective theory of contract—which required only the conventional acceptance of a conventional inducement and not an actual meeting of minds—widened at least one aspect of contractual liability.

But even if (in some other area of contract law) external standards narrowed contractual liability, this could be explained as a consequence of the social, political, and economic circumstances of the late nineteenth century. How a theory is applied—whether it widens or narrows contractual liability—depends in large part upon the values and policies of the individuals involved. Of course the circumstances, values, and policies of the late nineteenth century encouraged a system of contractual liability that served capitalism. This should not surprise us. What is wrong is either to explain this trend by pointing exclusively to a particular person and his theory, or to hold a particular person and his theory morally responsible for the circumstances, values, and policies of his age. I believe Gilmore comes very close to making this mistake with his characterization of Holmes.

The most plausible aspect of Gilmore's argument is that Holmes's external standards narrowed *tort* liability. Indeed, Morton Horwitz seems to find this argument convincing.[8] Since earlier common-law tort liability was strict, the argument seems to have much merit. While the earlier view (at least in certain forms of action) was that the agent was liable for any damage he caused, Holmes insisted that before an agent incurred liability the act that caused the damage had also to be unreasonably dangerous in the eyes of the rational and prudent man. Thus the very rationale of Holmes's theory of tort liability was apparently meant to serve capitalism. Under his theory the entrepreneur would escape liability for damages that he caused if he could convince a jury of the reasonableness and utility of his action.

But plausible though it may be, I believe the above conclusion must be qualified in important ways if we are to remain true to the spirit of Holmes's legal thought. First, at the most important level, I have no doubt that Holmes's reason for narrowing civil liability was to fashion a comprehensive theory of legal liability. If judges were to apply the same criteria of legal liability in civil and criminal cases, then the old common-law notion that causation of damage sufficed for civil liability had to go. Therefore, Holmes's basic rationale for narrowing civil liability was philosophical and jurisprudential; it was not meant to serve the interests of capitalism. Holmes wanted to make the law consistent with itself; he spent his entire life at this enterprise.

Moreover, Holmes believed that the current criterion of legal liability had to be external and general because political power had grown enormously in the age of the nation-state and because modern secularization had slowly rooted out from the law many moral and religious prejudices, taboos, and illusions.[9] Therefore, Holmes's view that standards of liability must inevitably become external and general depended upon his judgments that the modern state has the power to draw the line of liability where it wills and that the modern secular and scientific attitude encouraged the state to draw the line where it served utility, that is, it encouraged external general standards. Even in a socialist state, Holmes was convinced that the standard of liability would become external and general if the state became strong enough to enforce such a high standard and if the socialism was based upon modern scientific secular thought rather than upon religion. The conclusion is that Holmes's external and general theory of legal liability was based on his conception of the modern nation-state and modern secularism, not on the interests of early American capitalism. Consequently, any community of interests that existed between Holmes's theory of tort liability and capitalism was a contingent fact and an unintended consequence.[10] However, if the relationship was contingent, then neither Holmes nor his theory of legal liability is responsible for the economic dislocations of early American capitalism. As every historian knows, adherents or followers have used ideas, principles, or theories in ways directly contrary to the author's or founder's intentions.

But even the question of whether Holmes's theory of tort liability was contingently related to the interests of capitalism is not as easily answered as Gilmore supposes. It all depends upon the degree to which Holmes's theory narrowed legal liability. If it narrowed tort liability to a great degree, then it may make some sense to speak of a community of interests between Holmes's theory and capitalism. Gilmore argues that Holmes reduced liability to the point "that, ideally, no one should be liable to anyone for anything," and that the "loss . . . must lie where it falls."[11] I find this description of Holmes's views odd beyond all measure. There is no question that Holmes conceived of these principles—"that the loss must lie where it falls" and (more paradoxically) "that, ideally, no one should be liable to anyone for anything"—as defeasible assumptions. Holmes's substantive standard was the rational and prudent man. Losses should not lie where they fall nor should every person escape liability if the act that caused damage was unreasonably dangerous in the eyes of the prudent man. Consequently, Gilmore's characterization of a community of interests existing between Holmes and early American capitalism may rest upon a misunderstanding of Holmes's theory of liability. It is true that Holmes narrowed tort liability by adding the requirement of unreasonable danger to the traditional one of causation, but the resulting degree of liability was a far cry from "let the loss lie where it falls" or "let no one be liable to anyone for anything."

Although Holmes added to the traditional criterion of causation the requirement of unreasonably dangerous action, this is not the whole story. Holmes also rejected the established view that the act causing harm had to violate the explicit legal rights of some individual. While the orthodox theory insisted that the agent was only liable for the damage he caused if his act violated someone's legal rights, Holmes's theory of liability reduced the conditions of legal liability to one—unreasonably dangerous action. If the agent acted dangerously, caused damage, but violated no one's rights, the state could still hold him liable according to Holmes's theory, but not according to the orthodox approach. Consequently, Holmes's theory of legal liability not only widened *criminal* liability, but it also (in an important sense) significantly increased *tort* liability. So even in tort liability, where Gilmore's argument has some plausibility, there are aspects of Holmes's thought (which heretofore have been ignored) that cast doubt upon Gilmore's argument.

Of course the real extent of tort liability under Holmes's theory would depend upon how many acts judges conceived as unreasonably dangerous. Holmes's advice to judges was to defer to the legislature's or the community's wishes or, if neither of these alternatives were possible, to impose liability according to the rule that best served society's interests. Consequently, it is absurd to link Holmes's theory of legal liability to Langdell's prescription that judges should decide cases apart from the real world. Holmes's own theory of judicial decision-making is an insurmountable barrier to this conclusion. In every instance, the Holmesian judge decided the case before him according to the facts of the real world, whether the relevant fact was the existence of a statute, a popular common belief, or a beneficial social policy. For example, there is plenty of evidence to show that Holmes applied the relevant statute even if the law conflicted with the interests of capitalists. Holmes's dissents to the Supreme Court opinions that invalidated social-economic legislation reflect his attitude that the legislature (and in other contexts the jury) embodied the standard of the rational prudent man and thereby defined unreasonably dangerous activity.

Moreover, if the legislature wanted to set the standard higher than the rational prudent man for some special reason of policy, Holmes had no objection. The legislature could make certain agents in certain situations strictly liable for knowing certain facts or for foreseeing and preventing certain evils. Holmes opposed strict liability only when its demands were too high; he approved of it when it was necessary or beneficial to society. Therefore, though Holmes may have personally doubted the wisdom of such a law, a statute that made employers liable for harms that no reasonable man could have foreseen was perfectly consistent with his theory of liability. Even if a legislature clearly extended liability beyond the criterion of unreasonably dangerous acts, the judge's job was not to decide cases apart from the real world, but to obey the legislature.

In cases when the legislature had not spoken, Holmes still does not advise the judge to decide the case apart from the real world. If there is a general consensus within the society that the agent should bear the liability in the circumstances, if it is agreed that his act was unreasonably dangerous, then the judge decides the case accordingly. If there is no consensus, then the judge must place "the bet" for society; he must decide (by a comparison of the case to analogous precedents) whether holding the agent liable serves society's interest. In neither case, of course, can the judge decide the case as mathematicians solve equations. The judge, with the help of the jury, distinguishes culpable dangerous acts from nonculpable, nondangerous acts according to the legislature's dictates, the general consensus of society, or the utilitarian standard of utility—a standard workable only with a consideration of a society's circumstances. In each case, Holmes's advice to the judge is directly contrary to what Gilmore claims it to have been. Holmes's ideal judge was neither a mathematician nor an idealist, but an empirical social scientist whose feet were firmly planted in reality.

The short answer to Gilmore's argument that Holmes's theory of legal liability was an "attempt to make Langdellianism intellectually respectable" is that this is impossible given Holmes's inductive and empirical theory of judicial decision-making. Since no sensible person would claim that Holmes's theory of judicial decision-making has any similarity to the theory of the "legal theologian" Langdell, and since Holmes's theory of legal liability walks hand in hand with his inductive theory of judicial decision-making, there is no connection between Holmes's endorsements of external and general standards of legal liability and Langdell's intellectual pursuits. And there is little to the argument that Holmes's theory of liability is explicable as a shield for early American capitalism. Even if we exclude criminal and contractual liability, even if we ignore the fact that Holmes's theory did not require an explicit violation of legal rights before an agent incurred tort liability, Holmes's theory would let employers escape liability for harms to employees and customers only if the legislature, the society, and the judge believed that liability was detrimental to the public welfare. Of course, in the days of classical liberalism, relatively few believed that liability would serve any beneficial purpose. But here again, neither Holmes nor his theory was responsible for the values and beliefs of the era.

The relationships that Gilmore has drawn among Holmes's

"positivism," his theory of liability, Langdell's formalism, and nineteenth-century liberalism are regrettable not only because they are wrong, but also because they have encouraged other commentators to find either radical contradictions in or transformations of Holmes's legal thought. These commentators can see clearly that if Gilmore's characterization of Holmes's theory of liability is true, then it conflicts with other elements of Holmes's thought. Consequently, depending upon whether the commentator tries to push the discordant elements of Holmes's thought into different chronological periods, Holmes is described as a contradictory legal theorist or as a jurist who underwent a major transformation in his thinking. An example from the first group is Robert Gordon, who has argued that it is impossible to derive from the historical context "any single thread of ideas that unifies and integrates [Holmes's book] *The Common Law*. One will discover, rather, that it contains multiple and contradictory strands of thought."[12] Hence, not only are Holmes's writings (presumably) inconsistent with one another, but even Holmes's chief work is self-contradictory. The evidence for this surprising conclusion is that Holmes's positivism, which is the basis of his theory of legal liability, served the ends of "formalism, classical-legal, or liberal thought."[13] The upshot was that Holmes's external standard of liability was "a brilliant technical apparatus for putting into effect liberal legal ideas."[14] But though Gordon accepts Gilmore's depiction of Holmes's theory of legal liability, he sees that the formalism ascribed to Holmes conflicts with Holmes's historical orientation to law,[15] his *de facto* theory of sovereignty,[16] his definition of legal duty,[17] and his social Darwinism.[18] Therefore, Gordon argues that Holmes "was a pioneer in breaking up this system [of formalism] at the same time that he was engaged [by endorsing external standards of liability] in furthering its development."[19] Gordon's conclusion is that *The Common Law* "is a book at war with itself."[20]

I find this characterization of Holmes and his book too extreme. Though there are no doubt tensions and inconsistencies in *The Common Law* and in Holmes's legal thought generally, it is too much to say that Holmes's ideas are contradictory or that they are at war with one another. The principal evidence underlying Gordon's characterization of Holmes as a contradictory theorist has been discredited above. Holmes was not a formalist, and his theory of legal liability had no significant relationship to classical liberalism. Once we reject these ideas popularized by Gilmore, we can see how Holmes's philosophical method (decribed in Chapter 5) unites his substantive theories of liability, law, and judicial decision-making into a consistent whole. While tensions and inconsistencies in this legal philosophy may exist, no one has uncovered any valid evidence of significant substantive contradictions.

Both G. Edward White and Saul Touster have claimed that Holmes underwent a radical transformation in his thought during the late nineteenth century. White argues that Holmes's disappointing experience as a Massachusetts judge fundamentally changed his orientation, while Touster claims that Holmes's endorsement of the new case method marked a deep change in his intellectual commitments. The surprising fact about these two articles—a fact that helps us assess their merits—is that they directly contradict one another. White thinks that at the time of the publication of *The Common Law* Holmes endorsed "activist judging in pursuit of broad general principles of law." Judges were "to help arrange legal subjects in what Holmes called a philosophically continuous series."[21] However, the "experience of a Massachusetts judgeship tansformed Holmes' thought from its expansive, conceptualist, reformist early form to its cryptic, skeptical later variety."[22] The conclusion is that Holmes's thought moved from a Langdellian view of law and judicial activity to something else.

But according to Touster, the transformation of Holmes's thought went the other way. In an 1880 review of Langdell's book on contracts, in which Holmes called Langdell "a legal theologian," Holmes "made a devastating attack not only on Langdell but upon the case method generally."[23] But in a few years following this review, Holmes is lavishly praising Langdell and A. V. Dicey is paradoxically referring to Holmes as "a legal theologian." Touster therefore argues that "in the midst of writing *The Common Law*, Holmes made a critical intellectual choice leaning *toward* Langdell and not away from him."[24] The author believes that Holmes came to his warmer appraisal of Langdell because he adopted the case method and therefore came to admire the "narrow view of law that limited its vision to the judicial process."[25] The conclusion of course is directly contrary to White's opinion.

My belief is that both accounts can be dismissed because no radical transformation of Holmes's thought occurred. In the pre-

vious chapters I examined the central doctrines of Holmes's jurisprudence that remained stable throughout his life, even if some of
his ideas underwent certain developments and refinements.
White's thesis that Holmes moved away from a conceptualistic
Langdellian theory is wrong because his chronological compart-
mentalization of the evidence is completely arbitrary. He claims
that only after Holmes came to the Massachusetts bench did he
discover that legal distinctions were arbitrary, that judicial opinions were instinctive policy preferences cloaked with logic, that
law must reflect the community's wishes, that survivals exist in
the common law, and that judges should defer to the legislature.[26]
But the fact is that these ideas were a part of Holmes's repertoire
from the 1870s, and one needs only to turn to Holmes's early articles to refute White's thesis.

For example, a mere glance at a passage from Holmes's article
"The Theory of Torts," which was published in 1873, will show
how early he came to his view that legal distinctions were ultimately matters of degree:

The growth of law is very apt to take place in this way: Two widely different cases suggest a general distinction, which is a clear one when
stated broadly. But as new cases cluster around the opposite poles, and
begin to approach each other, the distinction becomes more difficult to
trace; the determinations are made one way or the other on a very slight
preponderance of feeling, rather than articulate reason.[27]

There is also no reason to doubt that by 1879 Holmes understood
judicial reasoning as a facade for policy decisions. He expressed
many of these ideas in a review of the second edition of Langdell's
book on contracts. Here again, a passage we have seen before, is
quite to the point.

The life of the law has not been logic: it has been experience. The seed of
every new growth within its sphere has been a felt necessity. The form of
continuity has been kept up by [judicial] reasoning purporting to reduce
every thing to a logical sequence; but that form is nothing but the evening dress which the new-comer puts on to make itself presentable according to conventional requirements. The important phenomenon is
the man underneath it, not the coat; the justice and reasonableness of a
decision, not its consistency with previously held views.[28]

In contradiction to White's claim that until Holmes became a
judge he was ignorant of the survivals in modern law, the very

title of a two-part article published by Holmes during 1876–77—
"Primitive Notions in Modern Law"[29]—suggests otherwise.
Holmes's well-known analogy between precedents and the clavi-
cle of the cat is also quite relevant to White's contention.

> But as precedents survive like the clavicle in the cat, long after the use
> they once served is at an end, and the reason for them has been forgot-
> ten, the result of following them must often be failure and confusion
> from the merely logical point of view. It is easy for the scholar to show
> that reasons have been misapprehended and precedents misapplied.[30]

Many citations could prove how early Holmes came to his opinion that law must reflect the existing values of the community.
His critical response to the 1872 English prosecution of the leaders
of the London gas-stokers' strike is one of the most explicit: "All
that can be expected from modern improvements is that legislation should easily and quickly, yet not too quickly, modify itself in
accordance with the will of the *de facto* supreme power in the community."[31] In the same vein, the judge's task was to adapt the law
to the needs and wishes of the sovereign power represented in the
legislature. Holmes consistently and early endorsed the utilitarian
doctrine of judicial deference to the sovereign. In 1871, when
North Carolina judges were considering the legal validity of an
unconstitutional change of their constitution, Holmes advised
abiding with the old constitution, unless the intent and power of
the sovereign became "irresistible." But "if the will of the majority is unmistakable, and the majority is strong enough to have a
clear power to enforce its will, and intends to do so, the courts
must yield . . . because the foundation of sovereignty is power, real
or supposed."[32] So even when the sovereign acted unconstitution-
ally, Holmes preached submission. It is then obviously wrong to
say that Holmes was a judge before he endorsed the doctrine of
judicial deference to the legislature, the representative of the sovereign.

The passages that I have cited clearly refute White's argument.
The simple fact is that Holmes adhered to these beliefs and opinions all along. Moreover, the evidence for the other side of White's
argument, supposedly proving that Holmes left behind his early
love of generalizations and his early belief that judges should reform the law, is also false. Few knowledgeable commentators on
Holmes's thought could doubt that Holmes always believed that
judges did and should make law according to the community's

wishes and needs. White himself agrees that Holmes was something of an activist on the Supreme Court, and this admission does much to discredit his own argument.[33] There is also plenty of evidence (especially from his letters and speeches) that Holmes throughout his life thought the chief end of man was to form general propositions. At the mature age of sixty, Holmes regretted that he had only had the opportunity to decide a thousand cases,

when one would have liked to study to the bottom and to say his say on every question which the law ever has presented, and then to go on and invent new problems which should be the test of doctrine, and then to generalize it all and write it in continuous, logical, philosophic exposition, setting forth the whole corpus with its roots in history and its justifications of expedience real or supposed![34]

Just as Holmes believed, before he rose to the Massachusetts bench, that judges should defer to the sovereign legislature, that law reflected the community's wishes, that judicial opinions were instinctive policy preferences cloaked with logic, and that historical survivals existed in modern law, so also did he keep faith with his early views that judges do and must adapt the law according to the community's wishes and that the urge to generalize was an admirable characteristic of human intellectual life. Consequently, White's argument has not accomplished its purpose of undermining the integrity of Holmes's jurisprudence.

The same can be said for Saul Touster's claim that Holmes's legal philosophy developed into Langdellianism, presumably because Holmes adopted the case method and the correspondingly narrow, judicial-process view of law. Touster's evidence is that Holmes praised Langdell publicly and that A. V. Dicey referred to Holmes as a "legal theologian"—the term once used by Holmes to condemn Langell's formalism.[35] This argument is plainly insufficient. First, the fact that Holmes praised Dean Langdell at a Harvard commencement is hardly evidence for an intellectual transformation. Nineteenth-century politeness, the nature of the occasion, or Holmes's hopes for an academic appointment at Harvard Law School can each singly explain why Holmes would publicly praise Langdell's contributions. Moreover, many academics may be found admiring the intellectual achievements of those who are completely foreign to their own intellectual outlook. Indeed, the letter Touster cites, which Holmes wrote only three months before the commencement, describing Langdell as representing "the powers of darkness," is in fact more complimentary than Touster suggests.

A more misspent piece of marvellous ingenuity I never read, yet it is most suggestive and instructive. I have referred to Langdell several times in dealing with contracts because to my mind he represents the powers of darkness. He is all for logic and hates any reference to anything outside of it, and his explanations and reconciliations of the cases would have astonished the judges who decided them. But he is a noble old swell whose knowledge ability and idealistic devotion to his work I revere and love.[36]

Holmes's later public praise of Langdell is not therefore evidence for any change in Holmes's intellectual orientation, since he had always admired certain traits of Langdell's personality. On the other hand, his admiration was always tempered with the awareness that they were in fundamental opposition on substantive issues.

The fact that A. V. Dicey described Holmes as a legal theologian is an interesting bit of historical irony, but it hardly proves that Holmes endorsed Langdell's substantive doctrines. Indeed (as Touster himself realizes), Mark DeWolfe Howe has shown that Holmes and Dicey used this term in two different senses.[37] Holmes criticized Langdell as a "legal theologian" because in the law he sacrificed expediency and justice to logical consistency, while Dicey called Holmes a "legal theologian" because he justified contemporary substantive doctrines on ancient precedents— "a mass of texts which, to impartial readers, seem to have but a remote bearing on the matter in hand."[38] But Touster, after acknowledging that Dicey meant something very "un-Langdellian" by the term "legal theologian,"[39] argues that to distinguish the two different senses of the term "is to ignore the natural tendency of theology, whether scriptural (in the case of Holmes) or sophistical (in the case of Langdell) to live within a common church and embrace a common underlying orthodoxy."[40] According to Touster, we should ignore the fact that Holmes and Dicey meant different things by the term "legal theologian" because Holmes and Langdell shared a "common underlying orthodoxy."

This common underlying orthodoxy was the case method. In fact, it was Holmes's commitment to the case method that explains "the want of breadth of *The Common Law,* and its failings."[41] The book was only a "theory of the judiciary alone, limited to the special conditions of common law development during a period before legislation became the dominant mode of lawmaking."[42] Indeed, since he had accepted the virtues of the case method, Holmes looked upon the law as a closed system, and therefore when he edited *The Common Law*, besides ignoring legislation, he threw out all references to "feelings," "justice," "the reasonableness of judicial decision," and "human needs."[43] So Touster's conclusion is that Gilmore is right to a limited extent. Holmes did make Langdellianism respectable by treating the common law as a closed system of logically related principles.

However, there are a number of objections to Touster's argument. First, since there is no assurance that Dicey would accept Touster's characterization of an underlying case-method orthodoxy between Holmes and Langdell, Dicey's use of the term "legal theologian" cannot serve as evidence for Holmes's Langdellian transformation. Indeed, since Dicey in the same review links Holmes's methodology and substantive doctrines to the historical school of Maine and the analytical school of Bentham and Austin,[44] it is clear that he ascribed to Holmes an intellectual orientation totally foreign to Langdellian formalism. Therefore, Touster's argument consists of his claim that Holmes's endorsement of the case method and the peculiar qualities of *The Common Law* suffice to prove Holmes's Langdellianism.

Touster's interpretation of *The Common Law* must be evaluated against the book itself. Does Holmes ignore everything but judicially created law? Does he treat law as a closed logical system? I do not think so. In Holmes's text and notes there are references to the Bible, Plato's *Laws*, Gaius's *Institutes*, Justinian's *Pandects*, Bracton's *Tractatus de Legibus*, Savigny's *Besitzes*, Puchta's *Institutes*, Tylor's *Primitive Culture*, and to many other scholarly legal, historical, and anthropological works. Moreover, though of course legal cases were emphasized, Holmes was familiar with the statutes relevant to the common law. He cites Bigelow's *Placita Anglo-Normannica*, Merkel's *Lex Salica*, Thorpe's *Ancient Laws*, the Laws of Alfred, the Statutes of Gloucester, and many other ancient laws and documents. Therefore, Touster's argument that *The Common Law*—a book that begins with the idea "the life of the law has not been logic but experience"—treats law as a closed system is not easily understandable, much less substantiated.[45]

But since scholars have generally conceived of the common law as a judicially created body of law, it should not surprise us that much of Holmes's book is a close analysis of cases. One could say that given the nature of the common law, it was the only way for Holmes to write his book. But that is certainly not enough to make him into a Langdellian. Many nineteenth-century commentators used close analysis of cases in their expositions of the common law; few modern critics could believe (unless the term is vacuous) that they were all conceptualists.

Whether Holmes in *The Common Law* referred to "justice," "feelings," and "human needs" as many times as he had referred to them in earlier works is undetermined.[46] But assuming that it was less often, many alternative explanations are possible. Perhaps Holmes changed his writing style; perhaps he found such references platitudinous or repetitious and therefore unnecessary; perhaps, in an exposition of positive law, he wanted to guard against confusing law with either morals or law as it ought to be. But in any case, there is no question that throughout the book Holmes referred to forces outside of the law—for example, to vengeance, to utility, to experience and to intuitions of public policy.[47] Indeed, this is the way that *The Common Law* was understood at its inception (for example, by A. V. Dicey) and for much of the last one hundred years. Touster has not done enough to show how this traditional interpretation is wrong.

Of course, much of *The Common Law* is a logical exposition of common-law doctrines. But Holmes wrote it for that reason. As a jurist, his purpose was "to make known the content of the law; that is, to work upon it from within, or logically, arranging and distributing it, in order, from its *summum genus* to its *infirma species,* so far as practicable."[48] It is small wonder that the emphasis is upon the logical exposition of the law rather than the outside forces that shape the law. Touster's conclusion that Holmes's purpose in writing *The Common Law* "sounds like a Langdellian project"[49] is just an assumption. For example, many lawyers today write books or conduct classes that consist of logical expositions of the law. On this basis alone, we would not say that these lawyers are therefore necessarily insensitive to the outside forces that shape the law; we would not, without more information, call them Langdellians. We owe the same consideration to Holmes.

In the end, Touster's argument is reducible to the fact that Holmes admired the case method. But it seems clear that this fact hardly makes Holmes a Langdellian. There were many who have supported and who still support the case approach who do not have a narrow view of law, who do not reduce all law to judicially created law, and who have nothing whatsoever in common with Langdellianism. There is more than enough evidence to say that Holmes was one of this group.

The reasons why Holmes and Langdell favored the case method are opposite and show why they had little in common intellectually. Langdell liked cases because through them the student could see abstract general principles in operation. As the student became conversant with the cases, Langdell hoped that he would see how the various principles of a certain branch of law fit together into a system. In time, when the student became sufficiently aware of how the principles logically hung together, he could ignore the cases through which he had gained this insight. The judge or the (legal theologian) theorist applied these independently existing, logically related principles directly to the case at hand. The justice of the decision, its reasonableness, and its effect upon society were irrelevant.

Holmes condemned this formalistic understanding of law. General propositions do not and should not decide concrete cases. Rather, the judge should decide the case according to how close it is to opposing precedents. This decision will depend upon a utilitarian assessment of the similarities and differences that the case at hand has to those already decided. But to make a meaningful assessment, the judge has to know the cases. Holmes did not perceive cases as means to the end of appreciating independent abstract legal principles, but rather as the particulars that give a body and a meaning to the general principles of the law. While Langdell encouraged the use of the case method for formalistic reasons, Holmes advised students, lawyers, and judges to pay attention to cases to discourage undue emphasis upon logical legal reasoning. The link that Touster tries to establish between Holmes's preference for the case method and Langdellianism is fallacious. Likewise, the Gilmore thesis—that we should understand some or all of Holmes's intellectual activity as "an attempt to make Langdellianism intellectually respectable"—has no merit.

The dispute concerning the relationship of Holmes's theory of legal liability to conceptualism is not the only controversial interpretation of his theory of liability that deserves comment. For example, Mark DeWolfe Howe has claimed that Holmes was committed to external standards because he admired legal certainty.[50] The more we restrict, as Holmes encouraged, the legislative role of the jury, the more the law will develop into specific concrete rules of strict liability. The end result is a more predictable and certain system of law. But our study of the utilitarian origins of Holmes's thought reveals his belief that law was in a continual state of adaptation to society's changing needs.

> The truth is, that law hitherto has been and it would seem by the necessity of its being is always approaching and never reaching consistency. It is for ever adopting new principles from life at one end, and it always retains old ones from history at the other which have not yet been absorbed or sloughed off. It will become entirely consistent only when it ceases to grow.[51]

Holmes thought that legal "certainty generally is illusion"[52] and "delusive exactness is a source of fallacy throughout the law."[53] Moreover, even if Holmes did admire legal certainty more than the evidence indicates, it is puzzling how that would explain his commitment to external and objective standards of liability. Legal certainty is a formal value; it insists that whatever their content, the rules ought to be unambiguously worded, widely promulgated, and strictly enforced. So the greatest admirer of legal certainty could still favor an internal theory of legal liability. He would only want the law strictly enforced according to known, precisely worded requirements. But theories of liability are substantive; they widen or narrow the necessary conditions for punishment. Consequently, Holmes's theory of legal liability cannot be derived from any special commitment to legal certainty.

Yosal Rogat argues that Holmes favored an external theory of legal liability because he believed that law should be separated from morality.[54] Now Holmes no doubt was a positivist. To prevent any confusion of law with morality, Holmes advised the student to look upon law as a "bad man." But can this fact explain Holmes's endorsement of an external standard of liability? I think not. Holmes himself believed that his theory based liability upon moral blameworthiness; not, it is true, upon a personal failing, but upon what is blameworthy in the average member of the community: "It is not intended to deny that criminal liability, as well as civil, is founded on blameworthiness. Such a denial would shock the moral sense of any civilized community."[55] Hence,

Holmes understood his standard of liability as a moral standard. He knew that a theorist having a morality radically different from his own would propose a different standard of liability. Consequently, Rogat's claim that Holmes's positivism explains his theory of legal liability is unsupported. After all, there are many contemporary legal theorists who describe themselves as legal positivists and insist that a law's validity is an issue separate from its morality. But to my knowledge none of these theorists admire Holmes's theory of legal liability. The conclusion is that Holmes's separation (for educational purposes) of law from morality does not explain his theory of legal liability.

The correct explanation of Holmes's adherence to his relatively radical theory of legal liability is implicit in the utilitarian origins of Holmes's legal philosophy. For example, Holmes's theory was not as distinctive as many reviewers have thought. Both Bentham and Austin endorsed external and objective standards of liability, because they believed in a secular theory of punishment and responsibility. The conditions of punishment should be those that serve utility in the modern state. In their opinion, the utilitarian external purpose of law required, and the power of the modern state permitted, an external and objective theory of legal liability that ignored the motives and the intellectual shortcomings of the agent. Holmes agreed to this formulation:

Considering this external purpose of the law together with the fact that it is ready [and able] to sacrifice the individual so far as necessary in order to accomplish that purpose, we can see more readily than before that the actual degree of personal guilt involved in any particular transgression cannot be the only element, if it is an element at all, in the liability incurred.[56]

Since the early utilitarians came to an identical conclusion for similar reasons, there is no need to look for a deeper rationale for Holmes's commitment to an objective and external theory of legal liability.

H. L. A. Hart has claimed that Holmes's argument involves a *non sequitur:* "Even if the general justification of punishment is the utilitarian aim of preventing harm . . . it is still perfectly intelligible that we should defer to principles of justice or fairness to individuals, and not punish those who lack the capacity or fair opportunity to obey."[57] Perhaps for a theorist who believed in independent principles of justice or fairness, this criticism would make sense. But a utilitarian would obviously object to this reasoning because in his opinion any principles of justice or fairness were dependent upon utility. Mankind has no source of moral validity other than the experience of beneficial rules and practices. So even if a utilitarian distinguished between the general aim of punishment and distributive principles of punishment,[58] he would still subordinate the latter to the principle of utility. In the opinions of Holmes, Bentham, and Austin, this subordination of distributive principles of punishment to utility required in modern circumstances an external and objective theory of legal liability. Whether they were right or not, whether utility is best served by an external and objective theory, is a debatable factual question. While the utilitarians' and Holmes's factual assessment may not strike us as plausible, their argument is not one of logical deduction. Therefore, it is misleading to charge the utilitarians with a *non sequitur*.

In the same way that tracing the utilitarian origins of Holmes's legal philosophy has improved our understanding of his theory of legal liability and the reasons for his adherence to it, similar insights are thereby gained into Holmes's theory of law. All too often Holmes's pragmatism is cited to explain his "predictive" theory of law.[59] But in fact Holmes never described himself as a pragmatist. He even told Laski that "judging the law by its effects and results did not have to wait for W[illiam] J[ames]."[60] In another place, Holmes described James's *Will to Believe* as "an attractive piece of pleading which neglected every scientific canon of evidence."[61] Holmes believed fervently in a scientific understanding of the world and interpreted James's philosophy as a call to "turn down the gas lights" (reason) so that mankind could enjoy the miracle of a free will.[62] Holmes would have none of it. Regardless of the intellectual discomfort which resulted from living in a "bleak" scientific world, Holmes preferred the bright light of reason.

The other founder of American pragmatism, Charles Peirce, fared no better in Holmes's estimation. He thought Peirce's work "was overrated especially allowing for what he owed to Chauncey Wright," the philosopher who had taught Holmes that you could not "affirm necessity of the universe."[63] Holmes's basic objection to Peirce was that he "thinks his ultimates are cosmic ultimates, whereas I think they couldn't be assumed to be more than his intellectual limitations."[64] Holmes was a skeptic; in his view, philosophy all too often sinned through arrogance. Peirce and the pragmatists in general had too high an assessment of man's intellectual and moral capabilities. Man's will could not alter the truth; nor could man ever be certain of his truth.

But even if one could squeeze some pragmatism out of Holmes's skepticism and relativism, it is difficult to see how that could explain Holmes's definition of law as "the prediction of what the courts will do in fact." Even Morton White has conceded that "philosophies other than pragmatism have seen the value of prediction, and that it is questionable whether the concern with prediction of itself makes Holmes a pragmatist."[65] But evidently, in White's opinion, one can come very close to this conclusion, especially considering that Holmes in his youth belonged to a Metaphysical Club that included among its members Charles Peirce and William James. But clearly this evidence is very weak. If there are important concrete similarities between Holmes and the pragmatists that indicate Holmes's commitment to pragmatism and explain his predictive theory of law, then why not describe them?[66] But whether they exist or not, Holmes's membership in the Metaphysical Club is not to the point. The biographical fact alone clearly cannot bear the weight of the argument.

But my explanation of the utilitarian origins of Holmes's legal philosophy shows that there is no mystery to Holmes's predictive definition of law. It refined the "practical" Austinian definition of law as a "command of a sovereign." For both Austin and Holmes, the underlying rationale for their respective definitions of law was to identify the boundaries of jurisprudence, the limits of the lawyer's subject matter. Holmes's alteration of the Austinian definition depended upon the fact that contemporary sovereigns enforced their rules in courts. But Austin was aware of this fact. In the case of customs and constitutional norms, he used judical enforcement as the criterion of the sovereign's commands. Hence Holmes's definition of law was not only meant to further the utilitarian method of legal education, but it also closely resembled the utilitarian definition.

My second general conclusion, that utilitarian ideas seeped into American jurisprudence, rests upon the assumption that Holmes's legal philosophy was crucial to the growth of American legal realism. Few theorists would doubt this relationship.[67] Most legal realists have paid their respects to Holmes as their intellectual mentor, and few commentators have disagreed. The result is that Holmes has occupied a preeminent position in American jurisprudence. On the other hand, twentieth-century American legal philosophers have looked upon the utilitarian jurists with cold, ungrateful eyes.[68] But if the ideas expounded in this study have any validity, then the utilitarian jurists deserve some credit. Some of the central insights of American legal realism were undoubtedly first established by early nineteenth-century Englishmen, and no American intellectual insularity should prevent us from recognizing this fact.

A few examples will help to justify this conclusion: Holmes's theory of judicial decision-making, for one. The essentials of a realistic understanding of the judge's activity were all included in utilitarian jurisprudence: a recognition that judges made law; a sensitivity to a judge's policy-making functions; an awareness of the fictitious quality of logical legal continuity; an insight into the effects of a judge's prejudices upon legal development. For these insights, Holmes was apotheosized. In the meantime the intellectual antecedents of Holmes's theory of judicial decision-making were ignored. But the utilitarians knew that judges made law and that the logical form hid law's ever-changing substance. They encouraged judges to legislate according to utility and decried the effects of prejudice on the law. Consequently, American jurisprudence should look upon the utilitarians with a more kindly eye.

Holmes's legal philosophy transmitted other utilitarian ideas into the twentieth century. For example, Holmes preserved the ideal of a unified theory of legal liability. Of course, twentieth-century legal developments have radically departed from Holmes's ideal. Statutes and judicial legislation have weakened civil law requirements of legal liability while at the same time they have tightened criminal law requirements. For example, the growth of insurance has let judges impose civil liability upon defendants who were not in any sense at fault. Many criminal laws, on the other hand, require before liability is incurred more than unreasonably dangerous activity on the part of the defendant; the defendant must also have a specific internal mental state, for example, an intent to kill. Therefore, Holmes's unified theory of legal liability seems to be more of a dream than an ideal. It departs so widely from current practices—and there is no way to turn this clock back—that commentators on the law are insensitive to any redeeming value that a comprehensive theory may have.

However, insight may be gained by probing the assumptions underlying our current bifurcated system of legal liability from a Holmesian perspective. Since it is clear that a civil judgment can hurt as much as a fine or even (in some cases) as much as a prison sentence, one may ask why our civil law requirements of liability are so much weaker than those used in criminal law. Insurance will ease our conscience in the great majority of cases, but there is the anomalous case where the uninsured person must pay for a harm that he had no reasonable chance to avoid. Can we avoid the moral dilemma by claiming that the uninsured are at fault for not having insurance? Is such a fictionalized account good enough, or should we face the moral dilemma squarely? Even if the state's motives are purely compensatory in civil cases and punitive in criminal ones, does this alone justify inflicting serious civil sanctions more readily than criminal ones? Would a father feel comfortable compensating the son who lost an ice cream cone (because of his elder brother's act) by giving him his brother's cone, when (let us assume) his brother was not at fault in any way? Could the father make it clear to his older son how our compensatory notions explain and justify why he must suffer though he could not have avoided the damage?

This example is, of course, a little farfetched and probably more than a little trivial (since we cannot ignore a century of civil law development). Indeed, in all likelihood there are theories that can explain why civil liability is properly far weaker than criminal liability. On the other hand, Holmes's and the utilitarians' unified theory of liability at least provides the perspective to probe contemporary assumptions and thereby to justify modern practices. For that end, the legal writings of Holmes and the utilitarians deserve study. Though it is no longer an ideal, the unified theory of liability is worthy of our consideration.

Even stronger conclusions concerning the value of the Holmesian and utilitarian theory of a legal system are appropriate. Although today few legal thinkers subscribe to it, the Holmesian-utilitarian formulation of a legal system has clear advantages over the contemporary approach. Formerly a legal system was understood as a hierarchy of persons, with a determinate and factual sovereign enforcing with sanctions obligatory rules upon his subjects; today a legal system is described as a hierarchy of rules, with the obligatory character of the subordinate rules deduced from their logical relationship to superior ones. A hierarchy of norms has replaced a hierarchy of persons; a valid logical relationship of one norm to another has replaced an "obliging" sanction. Though it is not possible here to point out all the merits and difficulties of either approach, I can at least show what Holmes's and the utilitarians' position has to offer.

If one uses H. L. A. Hart's theory of a legal system as an example of current thinking, then a legal system exists only if secondary rules (rules of recognition, change, and adjudication) that define and constitute the legal authority of the state are accepted.

There are therefore two minimum conditions necessary and sufficient for the existence of a legal system. On the one hand, those rules of behaviour which are valid according to the system's ultimate criteria of validity must be generally obeyed, and, on the other hand, its rules of recognition specifying the criteria of legal validity and its rules of change and adjudication must be effectively accepted as common public standards of official behaviour by its officials.[69]

But what about a tyrannical legal regime, such as Hart's example of Rex I, wherein no secondary rules defining Rex I as the legal authority exist? Here we have a hierarchy of power and coercion, but no secondary rules. According to Hart's theory, a pure tyrannical legal system is a contradiction in terms. But it is conceivable that in such a regime external peace and harmony exist, that crime is relatively unknown and people walk the streets at night without fear. Under these conditions might a legal system be said to exist no matter what the subjects thought of Rex I? If so, then Hart's theory is wrong by requiring secondary rules for a legal system's existence.

Moreover, this objection applies against regimes other than tyrannies. Any regime not defined by or constituted upon secondary rules is not a legal system according to Hart's theory. The constitutive role of secondary rules is an especially severe requirement. The term "constitutive rule" is an elliptical expression. When one describes a rule as constitutive this does not mean that some metaphysical rule establishes a legal authority. People constitute authority; rules do not. Therefore, a constitutive rule exists only when people consciously rest their legal authority upon their acceptance of a conventional norm or set of norms. Many West-

ern legal systems have such constitutions and the relevant societies understand their legal authorities accordingly.

The only problem is that many societies do not have such constitutive rules. The people of charismatic, religious, and traditional regimes may or may not accept customary rules that define
who is the legal authority. But in such societies, the people do not
believe that a human convention consciously adopted by them
has solved the problem of authority. Under a charismatic regime,
followers obey their leader because they believe him god-like, not
because they believe in some human rule about what charismatic
persons are entitled to. That is why, for example, the followers of
Jimmy Jones took cyanide. Furthermore, in a religious regime,
the subjects obey "the Lord's anointed" because they believe that
God has so commanded, not because they believe in a human rule
about God. For example, the followers of the Ayatollah Khomeini
go into battle because the Imam has ordered it, not because some
human constitutive rule has given the Ayatollah the authority to
issue such commands. In a traditional society, the subjects obey as
their forefathers have done because they believe it is holy to do so,
not because they believe that they have adopted the rule "obey as
thy forefathers have done" as a conventional contrivance to solve
the problem of authority. The provincial members of a traditional society are not even aware that there is a problem of authority that the members of a society can resolve. They have no
sense of the possibility of things being different than they are.
Therefore they cannot "constitute" legal authority upon the rule
"obey as thy forefathers have done" because they have no awareness that human beings can solve the problem of authority
through the use of human conventions. The point is that the internal facts necessary for a constitutive rule's existence do not
exist in these kinds of societies. But clearly charismatic, religious,
and customary legal systems are possible. And so Hart's theory
errs by claiming that every legal system has constitutive rules.

One problem with Hart's theory of a legal system is that there
are examples that do not fulfill the definition's criteria. Perhaps a
better way to appreciate this problem is to note the analogies that
Hart himself uses to elucidate the function of secondary constitutive rules. Hart finds secondary power-conferring rules to be
much like the rules that define and constitute a game.[70] Officials
of the game, like the officials of a legal system, are empowered by
the rules to make authoritative decisions and valid judgments.

Constitutive rules are also said to resemble rules of private law that empower persons to marry, to contract, and to write a will.[71] The law grants to persons the capacity to consciously and deliberately alter their legal relations. Elsewhere, Hart describes constitutive rules as "recipes for creating duties."[72] A constitutive rule tells an authorized person what to do to create a legal duty. By these analogies, Hart suggests that constitutive rules only exist when the members of a society regard the relevant rule as a "recipe," a game-like method of resolving the problem of human authority, an "artificial contrivance" by means of which they can alter their legal relations. But clearly, if Hart means to say that these "internal facts" must exist before a legal system is established, then charismatic, religious, and traditional societies fail the test.

On the other hand, in other parts of his book Hart suggests that the officials of a legal system need not state or even be able to state the secondary rule: "For the most part the [constitutive] rule of recognition is not stated, but its existence is *shown* in the way in which particular rules are identified, either by courts or other officials or private persons or their advisors."[73] But a set of rules cannot be "a recipe," "directions for a game," or "a contrivance to alter legal relations" and at the same time not be "stateable." Hart never resolves this problem. He only dogmatically asserts that the constitutive rules that confer power upon the ruler's authority are shown to exist by the practice of how rules are identified. But this is clearly a fiction required by a misguided theory of a legal system. If a gang of terrorists were able to blackmail an entire country by the threat of exploding strategically placed atomic bombs, and if the officials, courts, lawyers, and private persons started to identify laws according to the terrorists' ideology and whims, then Hart's criteria would force us to say that the power-conferring rule, "obey the terrorists," was shown to exist by the practice of the courts, other officials, private persons, and their advisors. But clearly this goes too far. There are too many conceptual links between "constitutive," "constitutional," "constitution," and "constitute" to permit this gross extension of the term.

However, my objection to Hart's criteria of a legal system is more than a quibble about which sense of "constitute" is more in accord with general usage. The real problem with Hart's claim that constitutive rules can be shown to exist by the way particular rules are identified is that it is incompatible with the function that these rules play in Hart's theory. Constitutive rules, as the analogies discussed above suggest, are the source of all legal validity and obligation. Throughout his discussion, Hart has tried to establish the validity and the obligatory nature of laws from their logical relationship to independently identifiable secondary rules. But when examples are considered, Hart infers the existence of constitutive rules from the fact that laws are being identified and enforced. No doubt the circularity of the argument vitiates the integrity of Hart's validity-oriented theory of legal obligation. The tension between the important function that Hart assigns to constitutive rules and the loose criteria used to ascertain their existence is the crux of the problem. Laws are valid and therefore obligatory if enacted in accordance with constitutive rules. But if secondary rules are shown to exist by the fact that laws are being identified, then subjects or citizens have an obligation to do X whenever they are obliged to do it. Even though this conclusion is contrary to what Hart explicitly says about legal obligation, it seems that this is what he implies. Therefore, Hart's theory of a legal system is defective not only because it denies legal status to societies that are usually believed to have legal systems, but also because it is internally inconsistent. Hart's criteria of a constitutive rule undermine his own theory of legal obligation.

But these are not the only faults with the popular normative theory of a legal system. The theory also mischaracterizes regimes whose de facto and de jure constitutions diverge. In these cases, the formal institutions of state are merely nominal "rubber stamps" subject to the control of a private institution, clique, or individual. Since the secondary constitutional rules have become the convenient means by which the legal officials of the regime implement the ideologies, policies, and even prejudices of persons who either have no legal authority or act beyond it, the factual origin of legislation, of judicial decisions, and of executive policies is neither defined nor constituted upon secondary rules.

The normative theory has two options for describing these cases. First, it can deny that the habitual obedience of the legal officials to the de facto power-center has any relevance to the identity of the legal system. The second argument may claim that the de facto power is in fact constituted upon "informal" secondary rules existing apart from the formal constitution. The first option is very unattractive. If we followed it, we could no longer consider the Nazi Party a part of Nazi Germany's legal system, nor take cognizance of the Communist Party's influence in the day-to-day activities of the Soviet state's institutions (because the Party goes beyond its formal mandate to guide the state).[74] Since no Nazi or Russian lawyer would suffer from such a delusion, neither should any legal philosopher.

The second option is also defective. It misleadingly claims that "informal" secondary rules exist in all cases where legal officials are subordinate to a de facto power. But certainly such legal officials might obey a de facto military power only out of fear and not out of any respect for a constitutive rule. In such a hidden military despotism, clearly no secondary rules exist; but the de facto junta, not the powerless president, would be the very center of the relevant legal system. Moreover, in some cases informal rules justifying the de facto power's role might exist, but not satisfy other requirements of secondary rules. For example, Nazi and U.S.S.R. officials generally accept the role of their respective parties, but according to Hart's criteria we still could not say that secondary rules exist in these cases. As Hart has clarified them, a secondary rule must "be regarded from the internal point of view as a public, common standard of correct judicial decision."[75] But often in these societies where de facto and de jure constitutions diverge, the informal rules are neither public nor common. The constitution functions as a facade behind which actual power exists elsewhere. In order to keep up appearances, the legal officials would not cite the informal rule to justify their actions. If they do not, then the rule is not constitutive according to Hart's own sense of the term.

The point is that the contemporary definition of a legal system as a hierarchy of norms denies legal status to regimes that have traditionally been considered legal systems and mischaracterizes legal systems whose de facto and de jure constitutions diverge. Modern theory does so because it makes the existence and the identity of a legal system depend upon a set of internal facts. According to Hart, a legal system exists only if the legal officials accept a constitutive rule with a "critical reflective attitude" and use it to justify their official acts; the identity of a legal system is ascertained by these same rules even though they may conflict with the actual facts of political subordination. Maybe there are considerations that would justify this popular normative definition of a legal system despite the fact that it departs from our ordinary habits of speech and thought. Perhaps the attractiveness of the validity-oriented theory of legal obligation that is wedded to this theory of a legal system would be reason enough to overlook its inaccurate and misleading characteristics. According to this contemporary theory of obligation, a law is valid and therefore obligatory only because its validity is derived from deeper, more fundamental secondary rules. I have discussed above, however, why the beauty of this theory is only skin deep. In the end, Hart also comes close to saying that if laws are being identified (presumably meaning if they are being enforced), then legal obligations exist. Consequently, it is very doubtful whether Hart's theory of legal obligation can justify his inaccurate and misleading theory of a legal system. If we reconcile ourselves to the drawbacks of Hart's theory of a legal system for the sake of his theory of legal obligation, we lose much and gain little. The price is too high.

On the other hand, Holmes's and the utilitarians' understanding of a legal system as a modicum of peace and stability achieved through a coercive hierarchy of persons is free from the flaws of the contemporary theory of a legal system. If the external facts of peace and stability exist, then (assuming a sufficient number of people) a coercive hierarchy of persons qualifies as a legal system regardless of the internal facts. This formulation would not deny legal status to tyrannical, charismatic, religious, or traditional regimes; nor would it misleadingly characterize societies whose de facto and de jure constitutions diverge. If a de facto superior power gives the orders, it is the center of the legal system. With this "external" definition of a legal system goes a more humble theory of legal obligation. If a rule is enforced with a sanction by someone who has the sum of political powers, then a legal obligation exists. "Being obliged" is equal to "having an obligation." Many legal theorists tremble at this step. However, if legal obligations in tyrannies are reducible to what the sovereign power obliges his subjects to do with the threat of coercion, then perhaps obligations in Western, rule-based legal systems are correspondingly reducible. Hart's superficially attractive theory of legal obligation does not lead (at least not immediately) to this conclusion, but only at the price of a theory of a legal system that is divorced from the way we ordinarily think. If we follow the more realistic view of Holmes and the utilitarians, then we must stoically accept the humble theory of legal obligation that equates obligations with being obliged. Our choice (given the peculiar mesh of the concept of legal obligation with that of a legal system) is rather Machiavellian—one of the lesser of two evils. But the wiser choice is the approach that coincides with ordinary language and avoids misleading characterizations of many legal systems that populate our planet.

However, the more fundamental point is whether or not the legal philosophy of Holmes and the utilitarians may be used to probe the validity of contemporary legal thinking. Regardless of any acceptance of Holmes's utilitarian view of a legal system and obligation, it is certainly true that his ideas form a convenient perspective from which to examine contemporary legal philosophy. Another example of how the Holmesian-utilitarian views on certain theoretical issues are still valuable is their theory of judicial decision-making. Contemporary theories of judicial decision-making emphasize heavily the role of "principled justification." Herbert Wechsler, perhaps the most persuasive theorist of this perspective, claims that "the main constituent of the judicial process is precisely that it must be genuinely principled."[76] Mere justification is not enough; the justification must be "principled," meaning that it "is one that rests on reasons with respect to *all* the issues in the case, reasons that in their *generality* and their *neutrality* transcend any immediate result that is involved."[77] The test of neutrality requires that the judge be willing to apply the reason to all other similar cases. Wechsler's example of judicial reasoning that fails this test is the decision in Shelley v. Kramer. Here the Supreme Court held that judicial enforcement of private covenants that discriminated against blacks in housing was unconstitutional state action under the Fourteenth Amendment. According to Wechsler, this reasoning does not pass the test of neutrality,

unless it is affirmed that a private discrimination becomes discrimination by the state whenever it is legally enforced. But such a proposition is absurd and would destroy the law of wills and a good portion of the law of property, which is concerned precisely with supporting owners' rights to make discriminations that the state would not be free to make on the initiative of individuals. Hence, I suggest that this was not a principled decision in the sense that is demanded of the courts.[78]

In Wechsler's view, judges must use neutral decisions in the justifications of their legal decisions.

Wechsler's condition of "generality" is apparently an additional requirement. The reasoning must extend beyond the facts of the case; judges cannot tailor principles for the case at hand. Therefore, narrow principles, even if the judge were willing to apply them neutrally to similar cases, are not appropriate in principled judicial decision-making. Also, a principle cannot be vague; a general principle must indicate the class of related cases to which the rule would be applied. Whether the neutrality and generality of judicial reasoning are not two sides of the same coin is a subtle question. If a principle is neutral, the judge must apply it to a set of similar cases. So then any neutral principle is also general, at least to a degree. Consequently, the only feature added by the requirement of generality is that the set of similar cases cannot be too small. But for our purposes, the important point concerning Wechsler's theory of judicial decision-making is its emphasis upon principled justification: before a judge can decide a case, he must be able to justify it with general legal principles.

Though in the past a few legal philosophers have criticized Wechsler's theory,[79] the great majority of contemporary theorists have accepted this prescriptive approach to judicial decision-making.[80] Indeed, perhaps because the court became more conservative during the 1970s, or because prescriptive political theory (which experienced something of a revival during the same period) gave them an example to follow, legal philosophers have even established substantive guidelines that monitor and restrict the way courts can properly decide cases. While Wechsler's requirements were purely formal,[81] the current view is that judges must abide by substantive guidelines. Now it is true that judges may not act as these theories require, but the increasingly popular assumption is that they ought to do so. It is even more surprising to find that some of these theories contain extra-constitutional *moral* standards that require courts to decide very controversial political issues in a certain way. In my view, this trend is intellectually indefensible and politically unjustified. Philosophers have no special insight into moral issues nor (in this country at any rate) any special political authority. Academic jurists likewise presume too much when they use their professional position to offer moral advice to judges. As Holmes cautioned throughout his life, philosophy is especially susceptible to arrogance. The politicization of philosophy is the height of intellectual *hubris* regardless of political orientation.

In any case, the normative orientation in recent theories of judicial decision-making reveals how far we have departed from Holmes and the utilitarians. Their orientation was descriptive and explanatory—how judges decide cases, not how judges ought to decide cases. From the Holmesian-utilitarian perspective, the basic question is how relevant are the above (moral) standards to a judge whose intellectual training perhaps is not extensive, whose intellectual capacity perhaps is only mediocre, and whose interests may be more practical than theoretical. Can we expect him even to attempt to follow the guidelines to judicial decision-making found in contemporary literature? Ronald Dworkin is honest enough to give the name of Hercules to the judge able to follow his theory of how judges ought to decide cases.[82] But there is no point in having ideals of judicial decision-making that are so far beyond the capacities of ordinary judges. Holmes and the utilitarians thought that legal philosophy should respect the limits of the feasible. Any reforms of the law they proposed or supported they clearly saw within the realm of the possible. If we wanted to, could we say the same?

But even if one considers the contemporary approach to judicial decision-making on its own terms, ignoring the more controversial moral prescriptivism, it is not clear that the ideal of principled justificiation is preferable. Perhaps in high appellate courts, after the relevant arguments and counterarguments have been considered and reconsidered over a number of years, principled justification is not only possible but also preferable. But in the courts of original jurisidiction where most litigation occurs, should a judge have ready a consistent theoretical justification applicable to a set of cases before he decides the first case of the set, or should he be a bit more humble, decide the hard case on the given facts, and keep the amount of *obiter dicta* in the *ratio decidendi* down to a minimum?

Here again utilitarian theories of judicial decision-making provide a convenient perspective to evaluate our current practices. According to Holmes and the utilitarians, legal principles were identified, interpreted, and established by a method of induction and abstraction. Legal principles, including constitutional ones, had no meaning or existence until a number of cases were decided; they arose only when the judge reconciled a number of analogous precedents. Holmes's underlying insight is that a "well settled legal doctrine embodies the work of many minds,"[83] and

175

therefore, that "just in proportion as a case is new and therefore valuable, no one, not even judges, can be trusted to state the *ratio decidendi.*"[84]

In a difficult case especially, Holmes did not want the presiding judge to formulate general neutral principles applicable to all future similar cases. The judge had enough to do to decide the tough case before him; there was no need for him to try to decide future cases as well. Holmes advised judges to leave that task to those who inevitably had to decide the future cases anyway—the judges of the future. How judicial successors will receive a judge's rationale for a controversial decision is a question no one can control or predict. They may ignore or overrule it, accept it in part, or establish it as a controlling precedent. Therefore, since the presiding judge can neither control nor predict the future, there is no point in giving principled justifications for hard cases. If the case is an easy one, having clear resemblances to a set of decided cases, citation of the relevant rule would of course be appropriate. But in difficult cases, which are the only ones likely to go far in appellate courts, Holmes would prefer not to confuse the legal landscape with poorly considered principles merely for the sake of principled justification. Because a legal doctrine or a principle is the work of many minds, Holmes's advice—advice that recognizes the limited human capabilities of judges—is that when necessary judges should forego principled justification. Judges, like other people, "frequently see well enough how they ought to decide on a given state of facts without being very clear as to the *ratio decidendi.*"[85] When judges see farther than they are able to justify, they should not rationalize their decision merely to have the comfort of a rationalization. Nothing is gained by introducing misguided legal principles into the law.

Though I have made my preference for the older perspective of Holmes clear, my basic purpose is only to show that the outlook shared by Holmes and the utilitarians makes a convenient lens for examining our contemporary assumptions and attitudes. Along the way, I have argued that a grasp of the utilitarian origins of Holmes's thought enables us to correct serious flaws in our current understanding of Holmes's ideas and reveals the influence that utilitarian jurisprudence has had upon twentieth-century American legal realism. However, my hope is that this study will encourage reappraisals of the normativism and the prescriptivism that are now so popular in legal academic circles. Legal philosophy is at something of a crossroads, and the writings of Holmes and the utilitarians can help us evaluate recent trends in jurisprudence. In emphasizing the utilitarian origins of Holmes's legal thought, I do not wish to tarnish his reputation. Indeed, by placing his thought within the context of utilitarian jurisprudence, I aim to give it added status and security. It would be imprudent to discard ideas that have satisfied the intellectual needs of jurists for one hundred and fifty years. Seen as the culmination of the utilitarian school of jurisprudence, Holmes's legal philosophy gives us an understanding of law that has served admirably well. We should discard it, if at all, knowing what it has to offer and what our contemporary outlook costs.

NOTES

1. THE PROBLEM WITH HOLMESIAN SCHOLARSHIP

1. G. Edward White has already described this anachronistic tendency in Holmesian scholarship. He shows how Holmes's reputation has ebbed and flowed depending upon what philosophical issue, from progressivism to fascism, was the primary focus of attention. He concludes: "The ambiguities and controversy surrounding Holmes have emerged as his image has changed in the eyes of the American intellectual community. Commentators have woven his thoughts and attitudes into their own social, political, or intellectual preoccupations. As those preoccupations have shifted, the image of Holmes has changed accordingly." "Rise and Fall of Justice Holmes," *University of Chicago Law Review* 39 (Fall 1971), 54. Overly partial biographies were often written by Holmes's close friends, former clerks, or distant admirers. Examples include: Francis Biddle, *Mr. Justice Holmes* (New York: Scribner, 1942); *Justice Holmes, Natural Law, and the Supreme Court* (New York: Macmillan and Co., 1961); Catherine Bowen, *Yankee from Olympus: Justice Holmes and His Family* (Boston: Little, Brown, 1944); Felix Frankfurter, *Mr. Justice Holmes and the Supreme Court,* 2nd ed. (Cambridge: Harvard University Press, 1961); Frankfurter, ed., *Mr. Justice Holmes* (New York: Coward-McCann, 1931); Samuel Konefsky, *The Legacy of Holmes and Brandeis: A Study in the Influence of Ideas* (New York: MacMillan, 1956); Edith P. Meyer, *That Remarkable Man: Justice Oliver Wendell Holmes* (Boston: Little, Brown, 1967). And even Mark DeWolfe Howe's valuable but incomplete biography has a tendency to wax eloquent in praise of its subject. *Justice Oliver Wendell Holmes: The Shaping Years* (Cambridge: Harvard University Press, 1957); *Justice Oliver Wendell Holmes: The Proving Years* (Cambridge: Harvard University Press, 1963).

179

2. Howe's Introduction to O. W. Holmes, *The Common Law* (Cambridge: Belknap Press of Harvard University Press, 1963), p. xiv.
3. Howe, *The Proving Years,* chap. 3.
4. Ibid., p. 161.
5. Morton White, *Social Thought in America: The Revolt Against Formalism* (New York: Viking Press, 1949).
6. Ibid., chap. 5.
7. "Holmes's Jurisprudence: Aspects of Its Development and Continuity," *Social Theory and Practice* 5 (Spring 1979), 183–207.
8. Ibid., pp. 189, 191.
9. Other studies of note include the following: G. Edward White, "The Integrity of Holmes' Jurisprudence," *Hofstra Law Review* 10 (Spring 1982), 633–671; Robert Gordon, "Holmes' *Common Law* as Legal and Social Science," *Hofstra Law Review* 10 (Spring 1982), 719–746; Saul Touster, "Holmes a Hundred Years Ago: The *Common Law* and Legal Theory," *Hofstra Law Review* 10 (Spring 1982), 673–708; Mark Tushnett, "The Logic of Experience: Oliver Wendell Holmes on the Supreme Judicial Court," *Virginia Law Review* 63 (Oct. 1977), 975–1052; Grant Gilmore, *Ages of American Law* (New Haven: Yale University Press, 1977), pp. 41–67; *The Death of Contract* (Columbus: Ohio State University Press, 1974), pp. 5–34; Yosal Rogat, "The Judge as Spectator," *University of Chicago Law Review* 31 (Winter 1964), 213–256; Samuel Krislow, "O. W. Holmes: The Ebb and Flow of Judiciary Legendry," *Northwestern University Law Review* 52 (Sept.–Oct. 1957), 514–525; M. D. Howe, "The Positivism of Mr. Justice Holmes," *Harvard Law Review* 64 (Feb. 1951), 529–546; Irving Bernstein, "The Conservative Mr. Justice Holmes," *New England Quarterly* 23 (Dec. 1950), pp. 435–452; Daniel J. Boorstein, "The Elusiveness of Mr. Justice Holmes," *New England Quarterly* 14 (Sept. 1941), 478–487; Walton H. Hamilton, "On Dating Mr. Justice Holmes," *University of Chicago Law Review* 9 (Dec. 1941), 1–29; Morris Cohen, "Holmes and the Nature of Law," *Columbia Law Review* 31 (March 1931), 352–367; Harold J. Laski, "The Political Philosophy of Mr. Justice Holmes," *Yale Law Journal* 40 (March 1931), 683–695.
10. *Holmes-Pollock Letters,* ed. M. D. Howe, 2 vols. (Cambridge: Harvard University Press, 1961), I, 58; 31.
11. "Under the influence of Germany, science is gradually drawing legal history into its sphere." *The Occasional Speeches of Justice Oliver Wendell Holmes,* ed. M. D. Howe (Cambridge: Harvard University Press, 1962), p. 40.
12. "Some Definitions and Questions on Jurisprudence," *Harvard Law Review* 6 (April 1892), 22.
13. *Harvard Law Review* 44 (March 1931), 725–737; reprinted from *American Law Review* 5 (1870).

14. O. W. Holmes, *Collected Legal Papers* (New York: Peter Smith, 1952), p. 225; "Law in Science and Science in Law," *Harvard Law Review* 12 (Feb. 1899), 452.

15. Holmes, *Collected Legal Papers*, p. 157; "The Bar as a Profession," *The Youth's Companion* 70 (Feb. 1896), 92.

16. O. W. Holmes, "A Summary of Events," *American Law Review* 7 (1873), 579.

17. Holmes, *Collected Legal Papers*, p. 157; "The Bar as a Profession," p. 92. Also see *Holmes-Laski Letters*, ed. M. D. Howe, 2 vols. (Cambridge: Harvard University Press, 1953), I, 182; II, 891.

18. Howe, *The Proving Years*, pp. 62–63.

19. "Codes, and the Arrangement of the Law," pp. 726–727. Also see *Justice O. W. Holmes: His Book Notices and Uncollected Letters and Papers*, ed. Harry Shriver (New York: Central Book, 1936), pp. 50, 65–66.

20. "I always say that the chief end of man is to frame them and that no general proposition is worth a damn." *Holmes-Pollock Letters* (Harvard University Press), I, 118.

21. Holmes, *Collected Legal Papers*, p. 245; from a speech given at a dinner to Chief Justice Holmes by the Bar Association of Boston on March 7, 1900. In other words, Holmes believed that "Theory is the most important part of the dogma of the law, as the architect is the most important man who takes part in the building of a house." Ibid., p. 200; Holmes, "The Path of the Law," *Harvard Law Review* 10 (March 1897), 477.

22. Holmes, *Collected Legal Papers*, p. 157; "The Bar as a Profession," p. 92.

23. T. E. Holland, quoted by Holmes in a book notice, *American Law Review* 5 (1870), 114.

24. O. W. Holmes, "A Book Notice," *American Law Review* 7 (1873), 319.

25. O. W. Holmes, "A Book Notice," *American Law Review* 5 (1870), 115.

26. Ibid.

27. "Codes, and the Arrangement of the Law," p. 726.

28. Ibid.

29. See *Holmes-Laski Letters*, I, 122, 165, 272, 385, 431, 597, 658–659; II, 950.

30. Holmes, *Collected Legal Papers*, pp. 196–197; "The Path of the Law," p. 475.

31. John Austin, *Lectures on Jurisprudence*, ed. R. Campbell, 4th ed. (London: John Murray, 1873), I, 45.

32. *Holmes-Pollock Letters* (Harvard University Press), I, 20–21.

33. Holmes, *Collected Legal Papers*, p. 313; "Natural Law," *Harvard Law Review* 32 (Nov. 1918), 42.

34. *Holmes-Pollock Letters* (Harvard University Press), II, 212. See also p. 200.

35. Ibid., p. 307: "I can imagine a book on the law, getting rid of all talk of duties and rights."
36. Ibid., p. 213.

2. UTILITY, MORALITY, AND LIABILITY

1. See generally Jeremy Bentham's *Principles of Morals and Legislation* (Darien: Hafner Publishing Co., 1948), pp. 2, 24, 70, 170, 178; John Austin, *Province of Jurisprudence Determined* (New York: Noonday Press, 1954), lectures 2, 3, 4.
2. O. W. Holmes, *Collected Legal Papers* (New York: Peter Smith, 1952), p. 186; Holmes, "The Path of the Law," *Harvard Law Review* 10 (March 1897), 469.
3. Holmes, *Collected Legal Papers*, p. 195; "The Path of the Law," p. 474.
4. Bentham, *Principles, chap. 4.*
5. *Holmes, Collected Legal Papers*, p. 231; "Law in Science and Science in Law," *Harvard Law Review*, 12 (Feb. 1899), 456.
6. Holmes, *Collected Legal Papers*, pp. 225–226; "Law in Science and Science in Law, p. 452. See generally, *Collected Legal Papers*, pp. 210–243.
7. Bentham, *Principles,* chap. 1; Austin, *Province,* lectures 2, 3, 4.
8. Holmes, *Collected Legal Papers,* p. 312; "Natural Law," *Harvard Law Review,* 32 (Nov. 1918), 41.
9. See generally, Holmes, *Collected Legal Papers,* pp. 310–316.
10. See J. S. Mill, *Utilitarianism,* in *The Philosophy of John Stuart Mill,* ed. Marshall Cohen (New York: Modern Library 1961), chap. 3.
11. Holmes, *Collected Legal Papers,* p. 314; "Natural Law," p. 42.
12. Bentham, *Principles,* chap. 17, especially pp. 309–323.
13. Holmes, *Collected Legal Papers,* p. 170; "The Path of the Law," p. 459.
14. Those who believe that Holmes's concern with positive law is evidence that his intellectual interests diverged from the utilitarians should take note of the character of Austin's jurisprudence. No doubt Austin was more concerned with the ordering of positive law than with any ideal system. Hence, if such evidence can drive a wedge between Holmes and the utilitarian jurists, it also destroys the existence of the analytical school of utilitarian jurisprudence by opposing the positive-theorist Austin against the scientist-of-legislation Bentham. The more reasonable conclusion is to admit that utilitarian jurisprudence was both normative and descriptive.
15. For Bentham's distinction between law as it is and law as it ought to be, between "expository" and "censorial" jurisprudence, see his Preface to the *Fragment on Government* (London: Oxford Univ. Press,

1951), pp. 98–99; and *Principles,* chap. 17. The educational purpose of the distinction is emphasized in Austin's work. As a teacher of positive law, he necessarily had to determine the province of jurisprudence. "But positive law (or law, simply and strictly so called) is often confounded with objects to which it is related by *resemblance,* and with objects to which it is related in the way of *analogy:* with objects which are *also* signified, *properly* and *improperly,* by the large and vague expression *law.* To obviate the difficulties springing from that confusion, I begin my projected Course with determining the province of jurisprudence, or with distinguishing the matter of jurisprudence from those various related objects; trying to define the subject of which I intend to treat, before I endeavor to analyze its numerous and complicated parts." (*Province,* pp. 9–10.) The first ten lectures of Austin's course on positive law were meant to accomplish this task. These lectures were later published separately as six lectures in *The Province of Jurisprudence Determined.* See also "Uses of the Study of Jurisprudence" in *Province,* pp. 369–372.

16. Holmes, *Collected Legal Papers,* pp. 170–171; "The Path of the Law," p. 459. "It is on this account that the province of jurisprudence has to be so carefully determined." "Codes, and the Arrangement of the Law," *Harvard Law Review* 44 (March 1931), 729; *American Law Review* 5 (1870).

17. Holmes, *Collected Legal Papers,* p. 171; "The Path of the Law," p. 459.

18. Holmes, *Collected Legal Papers,* p. 170; "The Path of the Law," p. 459.

19. Holmes, *Collected Legal Papers,* p. 177; "The Path of the Law," p. 463.

20. Bentham, *Principles,* p. 70: "The general tendency of an act is more or less pernicious, according to the sum total of its consequences . . . Now among the consequences of an act, be they what they may, such only, by one who views them in the capacity of a legislator, can be said to be material, as either consist of pain or pleasure, or have an influence in the production of pain or pleasure."

21. O. W. Holmes, *The Common Law* (Cambridge: Belknap Press of Harvard University Press, 1963), p. 42. See also p. 88.

22. O. W. Holmes, "Trespass and Negligence," *American Law Review* 1 (Jan. 1880), 21. The methodological and epistemological principles shared by the utilitarians and Holmes that were responsible for their restriction of human knowledge to the phenomenal world will be discussed thoroughly in Chapter 5 below.

23. See Howe's citation of Holmes's marginal note in *The Common Law,* p. 36; "Accord. the discussion of the purpose of pun. will lead directly into the discussion of the principles of liab. wh. are the main object. I shall try to show that the purp. is prev. & that in acc. with this standard are general."

24. Ibid., pp. 6–7.

25. H. L. A. Hart has clarified this connection between the utilitarian justification of punishment and their principles of liability. He criticizes this approach, however, because it fails to take seriously the distinction between the general aim of punishment and distributive principles of punishment. In Hart's opinion, the aim and the distributive principles are logically distinct and the utilitarian attempt to rest distributive principles of punishment upon utilitarianism involves a *non sequitur*. Even if, Hart argues, at first sight it makes no sense from a utilitarian point of view to punish persons who cannot be deterred, it may make perfect sense if their punishment deters responsible agents from violating laws because they hope to escape liability by feigning insanity, ignorance, or some other condition that is excused. Hart concludes that utilitarianism is unable to explain why we excuse people and is for that reason an unacceptable theory of the distributive principles of punishment. But the fallacy in this argument is relatively obvious. Just because some (perhaps overlooked) consequential implications of a practice are imaginable neither makes them significant nor as weighty as the consequences that led to the establishment of the practice in the first place. As Hart admits, utilitarians would have to reject excuses unless they "believed that the terror or insecurity or misery produced by the operation of laws so Draconic was worse than the lower measure of obedience to law secured by the law which admits excuses": *Punishment and Responsibility* (New York: Oxford University Press, 1968), p. 19. But since it is clear that the great majority of utilitarians would find such a Draconic code pernicious, it seems misleading to claim that their support for the practice of excuses rests upon a *non sequitur*. But Hart rightly emphasizes the connection that the utilitarians made between punishment and liability. See also Bentham's *Principles,* chap. 13; *Works,* ed. J. Bowring, 11 vols. (Edinburgh: William Tait, 1843), I, 397.

26. The existence of "survivals" accounts for Holmes's belief that his theory of legal liability was only a general tendency of the common law; and, to some degree, for his imperturbable attitude towards details of the law that fit unhappily with his theory; and, lastly, for his quotation of Lehüerou in the Preface to *The Common Law: "Nous faisons une théorie et non un spicilege."*

27. Sir William Blackstone, *Commentaries on the Laws of England,* ed. W. P. Lewis, 19th ed., 2 vols. (Philadelphia: Geo. T. Bisel, 1922), II, 1437-1438.

28. Blackstone, *Commentaries,* II, 1438.

29. Sir Frederic Pollock and Frederic William Maitland, *The History of English Law,* 2nd ed. (Cambridge: Cambridge University Press, 1903), II, 470-472; Sir William Holdsworth, *A History of English Law,* 17 vols. (London: Methuen and Co., 1903-1972), II, 50-54;

Naomi D. Hunard, *The King's Pardon for Homicide: Before A.D. 1307* (Oxford: Clarendon Press, 1969), pp. vii–xiv.

30. Holdsworth, *A History*, II, 43.
31. For a contrary view, see Hunard, *The King's Pardon*, p. 1.
32. Pollock and Maitland, *The History*, II, 451–452; Holdsworth, *A History*, II, 48.
33. Holdsworth, *A History*, II, 48; Hunard, *The King's Pardon*, p. 1.
34. Holdsworth, *A History*, II, 54; Hunard, *The King's Pardon*, chap. 13.
35. Hunard, *The King's Pardon*, chap. 3; Pollock and Maitland, *The History*, II, 476–478.
36. Holdsworth, *A History*, II, 358–359; Hunard, *The King's Pardon*, p. 156.
37. Holdsworth, *A History*, III, 258–259.
38. Before the fifteenth century, imprisonment was used to exact fines rather than to punish. Also, it is not exactly true that the pardoned reckless or negligent agent got off scot-free. He forfeited his chattel to the king. Forfeiture was at one time the penalty for having fled from the king's justice, but in time the sanction was applied whether one stayed or ran. In turn, the infliction of the sanction became the evidence for moral culpability on the part of the agent no matter how accidental the act. See Hunard, *The King's Pardon*, p. x.
39. J. M. Kaye, "The Early History of Murder and Manslaughter," *The Law Quarterly Review* 83 (July 1967; Oct. 1967), 569–570.
40. Ibid.
41. Ibid., p. 582.
42. However, those convicted of manslaughter were branded to insure that if they culpably but unintentionally killed again, the judge would impose death.
43. Kaye, "The Early History of Murder and Manslaughter," pp. 587–601.
44. Holdsworth, *A History*, IV, 512.
45. Ibid., V, 216.
46. Ibid., IV, 281.
47. Ibid., V, 216.
48. Ibid., 273.
49. I am not suggesting that a vicious will or a guilty mind sufficed for legal liability nor that the vicious-will theory of criminal law rendered all sins into crimes. The English law has always required an act, and until the sixteenth century the act usually had also to harm persons or property. But in the sixteenth century, it became customary to punish acts that did not harm but only expressed a vicious will. Also, it is obvious that the state neither could nor wanted to punish all sins; it had enough to punish those that were detrimental to the public safety and interest.
50. Kaye, "The Early History of Murder and Manslaughter," pp. 590–594.

51. R. v. Mawgride (1707), cited by Holdsworth, *A History*, VIII, 435. Holdsworth also quotes there Coke's principle that "if it be voluntary the law implieth malice."

52. Kaye, "The Early History of Murder and Manslaughter," p. 593.

53. Bentham, *The Limits of Jurisprudence Defined*, ed. C. W. Everett (New York: Columbia University Press, 1945), p. 53. See also *Works*, I, 299; III, 160; Dumont's Introduction to Bentham's *Theory of Legislation*, ed. C. W. Everett (New York: Harcourt, Brace, 1931), pp. 88–92, and *Principles*, p. 333, notes.

54. Austin, *Lectures on Jurisprudence*, 4th ed., 2 vols. (London: John Murray, 1873), I, 417. See also pp. 517–524.

55. Holdsworth, *A History*, XII, 588–605.

56. Austin, *Lectures*, II, 635–636. For Bentham's similar views, see *Works*, VII, 300–305.

57. For the substantive nature of Bentham's codes, see his *Principles of the Civil Code* and *Principles of the Penal Code* in *Works*, I, 299–364; 367–580.

58. Bentham, *Works*, II, 6.

59. Austin, *Lectures*, II, 751.

60. E. C. Clark, *Analysis of Criminal Liability* (Cambridge: Cambridge University Press, 1880), p. 3.

61. James Stephen, *General View of Criminal Law* (London: MacMillan, 1863), chap. 3; *History of Criminal Law*, 3 vols. (London: MacMillan, 1883), II.

62. William Markby, *Elements of Law* (Oxford: Clarendon Press, 1871), p. 123.

63. Holmes, *The Common Law*, p. 6. Also see *Justice O. W. Holmes: His Book Notices and Uncollected Letters and Papers*, ed. Harry C. Shriver (New York: Central Book, 1936), p. 58.

64. Holmes, *Collected Legal Papers*, p. 175; "The Path of the Law," p. 462. See also *Holmes-Pollock Letters*, ed. M. D. Howe, 2 vols. (Cambridge: Harvard University Press, 1961), I, 177; II, 233.

65. Holmes, *The Common Law*, p. 40.

66. Ibid., p. 43.

67. Ibid., p. 41.

68. Ibid., p. 42.

69. Bentham, *Principles*, chaps. 7–14.

70. Ibid., p. 102.

71. Ibid.

72. Ibid., p. 120. The above quotation may seem to contradict what Bentham had said in an earlier passage: "Strictly speaking, nothing can be said to be good or bad, but either in itself; which is the case only with pain or pleasure: or on account of its effects; which is the case only with things that are the causes or preventives of pain and

pleasure. But in a figurative and less proper way of speech, a thing may also be styled good or bad, in consideration of its cause. Now the effects of an intention to do such or such an act, are the same objects which we have been speaking of under the appellation of its consequences: and the causes of intention are styled motives. A man's intention then on any occasion may be styled good or bad, with reference either to the consequences of the act, or with reference to his motives." (Pp. 87-88.) But this quote is from Bentham's general introductory discussion; in a later more precise analysis of motive (from which the quote in the text was taken), Bentham corrected this "improper" manner of speech. There he made it clear that the sole conclusion compatible with his assumptions was that motives could only be assessed on an individual basis *ex post facto;* only after the intentional material consequences of the act were known.

73. A thorough analysis of the external nature of Austin's theory of legal liability would be tedious and superfluous. No one doubts that he also rejected any distinctive motive as a necessary condition for legal liability. He repeated familiar instances of offenses committed with good motives, and discussed particularly the irrelevance of the motive of malice, a position often repeated by Holmes. "It having been assumed inconsiderately that malice or criminal design is of the essence of every crime, the term is extended abusively to negligence (or criminal inattention), and to criminal knowledge short of criminal design. E.g. Murder is styled malicious, or the law (it is said) implies it to be malicious, although, in truth, it proceeded from negligence." Austin, "Notes on Criminal Law," *Lectures,* II, 1093. Also see lecture XIX. Holmes agreed: "He [a mistaken judge] took malice in the moral sense, as importing a malevolent motive. But nowadays no one doubts that a man may be liable, without any malevolent motive at all." See his *Collected Legal Papers,* pp. 176-177; "The Path of the Law," p. 463. Also see *The Common Law,* p. 44.

74. Bentham, *Principles,* pp. 89-90, 92.

75. Holmes, *The Common Law,* p. 67. See also M. D. Howe, *Justice O. W. Holmes: The Proving Years* (Cambridge: Harvard University Press, 1963), pp. 80-82.

76. It may seem paradoxical to claim that Holmes misinterpreted one of the jurists of the tradition to which (I am arguing) he was indebted. But it is not uncommon for a theorist to ignore the ideas of those who differ widely from him or to criticize them only generally. He believes their assumptions so wide of the mark that he sees little advantage in close analysis. On the other hand, it is often the case that a theorist will expend a large amount of energy distinguishing himself from his intellectual neighbors. The misinterpretations that may

arise from the endeavor to find one's own intellectual groove may explain why Holmes misinterpreted Austin's specific views on the need for personal fault in legal liability, even though he was indebted to him generally on the same subject. See *The Common Law*, p. 85 where Holmes only claims that personal moral fault "practically results" from Austin's teaching.

77. Austin, *Lectures*, I, lectures 20, 24, 25. These are the same lectures cited by Holmes to substantiate his claim that Austin adhered to a personal standard of legal liability. See Holmes, *The Common Law*, p. 67, note.

78. Austin, *Lectures*, I, 492.

79. Thomas Aquinas, *Summa Theologica* (Cambridge: Blackfriars; New York: McGraw-Hill, 1964), LXXVI, section 2.

80. Austin, *Lectures*, I, 495–496.

81. Holdsworth, *A History*, VIII, 449. See also John H. Wigmore, "Responsibility for Tortious Acts," in *Select Essays in Anglo-American Legal History*, ed. E. Freund, W. E. Mikell, and John H. Wigmore, 3 vols. (Boston: Little, Brown, 1907–1909), III, 474–537. For a contrary view, see Percy H. Winfield, "The Myth of Absolute Liability," *Law Quarterly Review* 42 (Jan. 1926), 37–51; Winfield, "The History of Negligence in the Law of Tort," *Law Quarterly Review* 42 (April 1926), 184–201.

82. Holdsworth, *A History*, VIII, 450.

83. Ibid.

84. See Austin, *Lectures*, I, 485.

85. Austin was of course unsuccessful. The medieval doctrine of absolute civil liability was not overturned entirely until 1891. See Stanley v. Powell [1891] 1 Q.B. 86. See also Holdsworth, *A History*, VIII, 466.

86. Austin, *Lectures*, I, 498–499. For Austin's views on the inevitable character of legal ignorance, see p. 497.

87. Ibid., p. 499.

88. Ibid., p. 506.

89. Ibid., pp. 507–508. According to Austin, there were three types of legal presumptions: *praesumptiones hominis* were inconclusive presumptions made at the discretion of the court to which contrary evidence was admissible; *praesumptiones juris* were defeasible presumptions drawn by law to which contrary evidence was admissible; *praesumptiones juris et de jure* were conclusive presumptions of law to which contrary evidence was prohibited. The two latter kinds of legal presumptions are those that are relevant to the issue of the general nature of Austin's standard of legal liability.

90. Ibid., p. 500. Also see p. 509, where Austin describes the inference of an infant's incapacity as a *praesumptio juris et de jure* made by both

Roman and English law even if the facts were different. In other words, the presumption held against the actual facts of the case. The personal capacities of the child, even if they were so extensive that he knew his act was in violation of the law, were ignored. The child's knowledge was presumed by a general standard.

91. Ibid., p. 512.

92. "A party is exempt, either because he is clear in fact from unlawful intention or inadvertence, or because, (which generally amounts to the same thing), he is presumed to be clear of both." Ibid., p. 504. Holmes also knew that negligence could be described in terms of presumed foresight; *The Common Law*, p. 117.

93. Austin, *Lectures*, I, 512–513.

94. Ibid., p. 513.

95. Holmes, *The Common Law*, p. 46.

96. Bentham, *Principles*, p. 174. However, note that to escape legal liability negligence, heedlessness, or rashness must have had no part in producing the unintentionality, the unconsciousness, or the missupposal.

97. Austin, *Lectures*, I, 485.

98. Ibid., I, 295. Also see Austin, "Notes on Criminal Law," *Lectures*, II, 1092–1093.

99. Holmes, *The Common Law*, pp. 44–46; *Collected Legal Papers*, pp. 176–177; "The Path of the Law," p. 463.

100. Austin, *Lectures*, I, 433; Holmes, *The Common Law*, p. 45. Bentham's opinions are not so explicit as Holmes's or Austin's because he never distinguished between a theory of legal liability and the factors relevant to assessing the proper amount of punishment. But in the end he too reduced "intention" to "knowledge of the circumstances." "Acts, with their consequences, are objects of the will as well as of the understanding: circumstances, as such, are objects of the understanding only. All he can do with these, as such, is to know or not to know them: in other words, to be conscious of them, or not conscious. To the title of Consciousness belongs what is to be said of the goodness or badness of a man's intention, as resulting from the consequences of the act: and to the head of Motives, what is to be said of his intention, as resulting from the motive." (*Principles*, p. 88.) But if my analysis is correct, then Bentham dismissed motive as irrelevant to responsibility, and therefore his theory of liability also ultimately emphasized the agent's knowledge of the circumstances.

101. Austin, *Lectures*, I, 442–443.

102. Again, Bentham's views are not as clear as those of Holmes and Austin. But the following indicates that he is in the same tradition: "Upon the degree and bias of a man's intention, upon the *absence* or *presence* of consciousness or missupposal, depend a great part of the

good and bad, more especially of the bad consequences of an act; and on this, as well as other grounds, a great part of the demand for punishment." *Principles,* p. 95.

103. "On the other hand, there must be actual present knowledge of the present facts which make an act dangerous . . . But there is this practical difference, that whereas, in most cases, the question of knowledge is a question of the actual condition of the defendant's consciousness, the question of what he might have foreseen is determined by the standard of the prudent man, that is, by general experience." Holmes, *The Common Law,* pp. 45, 47. Also see p. 117.

104. Ibid., p. 48.

105. Ibid., p. 49.

106. Ibid., pp. 42, 48.

107. Ibid., p. 90. See generally pp. 90–103 and p. 33.

108. See Holmes, *Collected Legal Papers,* pp. 49–115, especially pp. 114–115; "Agency," *Harvard Law Review* 4, 5 (March 1891; April 1891), 345–364; 1–23, especially pp. 22–23.

109. Holmes, *The Common Law,* p. 117.

110. Bentham, *Principles,* p. 70. Also see p. 2.

111. Holmes, *The Common Law,* p. 129. Also see p. 54.

112. Holmes, *Collected Legal Papers,* p. 190; "The Path of the Law," p. 471.

113. Ibid.

114. Ibid., p. 191; "The Path of the Law," pp. 471–472.

3. LAW, SOVEREIGNTY, AND LEGAL OBLIGATION

1. Mark DeWolfe Howe, *Justice Oliver Wendell Holmes: The Shaping Years* (Cambridge: Harvard University Press, 1959); Howe, *Justice Oliver Wendell Holmes: The Proving Years* (Cambridge: Harvard University Press, 1963); Martin P. Golding, "Holmes's Jurisprudence: Aspects of Its Development and Continuity," *Social Theory and Practice* 5 (Spring 1979), 183–207.

2. As I pointed out earlier, most commentators do not even consider Holmes's relationship to utilitarian jurisprudence. They rather pursue anachronistic questions: Was Holmes a civil libertarian? a liberal? a fascist? a progressive? But the few who do consider Holmes's historical antecedents describe him as a follower of historical or pragmatic jurisprudence and therefore as a critic of utilitarian legal philosophy. See preceding footnote and Morton White's *Social Thought in America: Revolt Against Formalism,* rev. ed. (Boston: Beacon Press, 1957), chap. 5.

3. John Austin, *Province of Jurisprudence Determined* (New York: Noonday

Press, 1954), p. 13. This section explores Austin's theory of law, sovereignty, and obligation rather than Bentham's because Austin addressed these issues explicitly and thoroughly, while Bentham's analyses are found in footnotes and rough drafts of writings published, if at all, only after his death. Also, Austin's ideas about law, sovereignty, and obligation were the ones that reigned supreme in English jurisprudence until they came under heavy criticism later in the century. Any comparison of the ideas of the later historical and utilitarian jurists with the opinions of the early utilitarians therefore requires the context of Austin's theories.

4. Ibid., p. 193.

5. Ibid., p. 14.

6. For Austin, these terms were inseparably connected because they were all names of the same ideas. "It appears from what has been premised, that *command, duty* and *sanction* are inseparably connected terms: that each embraces the same ideas as the others, though each denotes those ideas in a peculiar order or series." Ibid., pp. 17–18.

7. Ibid., pp. 193–194.

8. Ibid., p. 145.

9. Ibid., p. 14.

10. A specific description was singular; Augustus was sovereign because he was Augustus. A generic description was general; the members of Parliament were sovereign because individually they were either the king, peers, or representatives of the commons.

11. Austin understood the Roman empire in this fashion. The emperors acquired power "by a mode of acquisition which was purely anomalous or accidental: which had not been predetermined by any law or custom, or by any positive law or rule of positive morality." (*Province,* p. 152.) Of course Austin never doubted the existence of a Roman legal system.

12. Austin admitted that the criterion of a "habit" was vague. See ibid., pp. 202–203.

13. Ibid., pp. 253–268.

14. Ibid., pp. 245–246. For the same interpretation of Austin, see H. L. A. Hart, "Bentham on Sovereignty," in *Jeremy Bentham,* ed. Bhikhu Parekh (London: Frank Case, 1974), pp. 146–147.

15. Ibid., p. 249.

16. Ibid., p. 261.

17. Ibid., p. 263: "In case it be clothed with a legal sanction, or the means of enforcing it judicially be provided by its author [the sovereign], a law set by the body to any of its own members is properly a positive law ... If the means of enforcing it judicially be not provided by its author, it is rather a rule of positive morality than a rule of positive law." For Dicey's opinion, see his *Lectures Introductory to the*

Study of the Law of the Constitution (London: MacMillan, 1885), lecture 1.

18. Hart, "Bentham on Sovereignty," in *Jeremy Bentham,* pp. 145–153.
19. Ibid., p. 150.
20. See Bentham, *Fragment on Government* (London: Oxford University Press, 1951), chaps. 4–5.
21. Ibid., chap. 4, para. 24.
22. Austin, *Province,* p. 25.
23. Ibid., p. 161; p. 185, note.
24. See D. Hume, "Of the First Principles of Government," in Hume's *Moral and Political Philosophy,* ed. H. D. Aiken (New York: Hafner,1972), pp. 307–310.
25. Austin, *Province,* p. 220, note.
26. Ibid., p. 221.
27. For Austin's understanding of sovereignty in the United States and the German Empire, see respectively, ibid., pp. 250–251, 253.
28. Maine's objections to utilitarian doctrine flowed mainly from his belief that man was more a historical creature of inheritance than one of pleasure and pain. See his "The Effects of Observation of India on Modern European Thought," in *Village Communities of the East and West,* 3rd ed. (New York: Henry Holt, 1880), pp. 230–233; and *Lectures on the Early History of Institutions,* 7th ed. (1875; rpt. Port Washington: Kennikat Press, 1966), pp. 368–370. For this reason, Maine objected to utility as a standard of legislative reform. Though he conceded that it was fast becoming "the regulative principle of all legislation," he believed that following it would lead to disaster. Maine preferred a program of reform based upon his comparative method (*Village Communities,* pp. 4–6). From his historical analysis of the different branches of the Indo-European race, Maine concluded that all progressive societies were developing from tightly controlled status societies to the freedom of contract societies. See his *Ancient Law* (London: John Murray, 1861). Given this general movement from status to contract, Maine's program of reform for any country, though adapted to its stage of development, was to follow the precedents of presently or previously existing progressive societies. But since this progressive society's peculiar genius was expressed in law, Maine's comparative method in practice held that all legislative roads of reform ended in Roman law: "It is not because our own jurisprudence and that of Rome were once alike that they ought to be studied together—it is because they will be alike. It is because all laws however dissimilar in their infancy tend to resemble each other in their maturity; and because we in England are slowly, and perhaps unconsciously or unwillingly, but still steadily and certainly accustoming ourselves to the same modes of legal principle to which

the Roman jurisconsults had attained after centuries of accumulated experience and unwearied cultivation." See "Roman Law and Legal Education," in *Village Communities,* pp. 332–333. For those who believe that Holmes was a close follower of Maine, this endorsement of Roman law as an ideal is troubling. Holmes despised Roman law and dreaded its influence upon the common law.

29. See Maine, *Early History of Institutions,* chaps. 7 and 8, especially pp. 377–385.

30. Ibid., p. 346.

31. Ibid., p. 358.

32. Ibid., p. 398.

33. Ibid., p. 374.

34. Ibid., p. 366.

35. Maine, "The Conception of Sovereignty and its Importance in International Law," *Papers Read Before the Juridical Society of London* 1 (April 1855), 26.

36. Holmes, "Codes, and the Arrangement of the Law," *Harvard Law Review* 44 (March 1931), 728; reprinted from *American Law Review* 5 (Oct. 1870).

37. Ibid., p. 729. But there was a subtle difference between Maine's criticism of Austin's definition of law and Holmes's. Maine had claimed that not all laws were commands because customs were valid laws; Holmes believed all laws were commands, but not necessarily the commands of a definite political superior. The commands of indefinite bodies were laws if their form was definite enough and their enforcement relatively certain. This subtle difference of opinion had an important impact upon their respective attitudes toward the status of contemporary customs. Maine, who denied that the general public could command in a progressive society, was content to subsume all modern customs under the concept of command by the Austinian formula "whatever the sovereign permits, is his command." Holmes, on the other hand, thought that if a rule was definite enough and enforced regularly (though informally), then that rule was a law even in a contemporary state and even if the sovereign had commanded the contrary. See Holmes's review of "Law and Command," by F. Pollock, in *Harvard Law Review* 44 (March 1931), 788–789; reprinted from *American Law Review* 6 (1872) hereafter cited as "Review of Pollock's 'Law and Command' "). Maine's discussion of this issue can be found in *Early History of Institutions,* pp. 362–366.

38. For Markby's discussion of custom and his endorsement of an Austinian definition of law, see his *Elements of Law* (Oxford: Clarendon Press, 1871), pp. 32–35 and p. 3. For his admission that Austinian categories were vulnerable to criticism, see the 6th ed. (1905), p. 12.

39. Thomas Erskine Holland, *The Elements of Jurisprudence*, 2nd ed. (Oxford: Clarendon Press, 1882), pp. 43, 48.
40. Holmes, "Codes, and the Arrangement of the Law," p. 728. For Holmes's imaginary society of "jobbists," see *Justice O. W. Holmes: His Book Notices and Uncollected Letters and Papers*, ed. Harry Shriver (New York: Central Book, 1936), p. 178; *Holmes-Laski Letters*, ed. M. D. Howe, 2 vols. (Cambridge: Harvard University Press, 1953), I, pp. 385, 723.
41. Holmes, "Codes, and the Arrangement of the Law," p. 729.
42. Holmes, "Review of Pollock's 'Law and Command'," p. 789.
43. Holmes, *Collected Legal Papers*, p. 173; "The Path of the Law," *Harvard Law Review* 10 (March 1897), 461.
44. Holmes, "Review of Pollock's 'Law and Command'," p. 789.
45. For these examples, see Austin, *Province*, pp. 30, 262–264.
46. Dicey, *Lectures Introductory to the Study of the Law of the Constitution*, pp. 24–26.
47. Hyde and Schneider v. the U.S., 225 U.S. 347, 386–391 (1912).
48. Maine, "The Conception of Sovereignty," especially pp. 26, 29, 30–32.
49. Maine, *Early History of Institutions*, p. 357: "in every independent community of men, there resides the power of acting with irresistible force on the several members of that community." Moreover, Maine made it quite clear that by "irresistible power" he did not mean that the power was uncontrolled. Though the sovereign was not subject to the power of any determinate person, Maine agreed with Austin that most if not all sovereigns were controlled by public opinion. See pp. 359, 367.
50. Maine, "The Conception of Sovereignty," p. 31.
51. H. Maine, *Popular Government*, 3rd ed. (London: John Murray, 1866), essay 2.
52. Ibid., pp. 88–89. See also pp. 201–202, 210.
53. Austin, *Province*, pp. 216–217.
54. Ibid.
55. See John Austin's *Plea for the Constitution*, 2nd ed. (London: John Murray, 1859).
56. Austin, *Province*, p. 216.
57. Maine, *Early History of Institutions*, p. 351.
58. Southern Pacific Co. v. Jensen, 224 U.S. 205, 222 (1917). Also see Black and White Taxicab Co. v. Brown and Yellow Taxicab Co., 267 U.S. 518, 532–536 (1928); *Holmes-Laski Letters*, II, 822–823, 896, 1101.
59. *Holmes-Laski Letters*, I, 183. See also pp. 189–190.
60. Kawananakoa v. Polyblank, 205 U.S. 349, 353 (1907).
61. Carino v. Insular Government of the Philippine Islands, 212 U.S. 449, 458 (1909).

62. The Western Maid, 257 U.S. 419, 432 (1922): "Sovereignty is a question of power, and no human power is unlimited."

63. *Holmes-Laski Letters,* I, 115. See also p. 21.

64. Holmes, *Collected Legal Papers,* p. 172; *Holmes-Laski Letters,* I, 115.

65. Holmes's review of *Treatise on Constitutional Limitations,* by T. Cooley, in *American Law Review* 6 (Oct. 1871), p. 141.

66. There may seem to be tension between Holmes's belief that customary law can exist in a society and his insistence that law in contemporary society has an identifiable source. The distinction, however, between Holmes's philosophical definition of law and his practical definition dissolves this apparent contradiction. Since his interest in a philosophical definition of law was minimal, Holmes's insistence that law must have an identifiable source was the more important tenet of his theory of law.

67. Holmes, "Review of Pollock's 'Law and Command'," p. 788.

68. For a brief sketch of the German conception of law and the state, see Otto Gierke's "Conception of Law," in *Natural Law and the Theory of Society,* ed. Ernest Barker (Boston: Beacon Press, 1957), Appendix II.

69. Jurists who took this option usually emphasized the role and power of public opinion, the original source of customary law that still controlled legislation. Austin of course had also recognized that a sovereign habitually defers to public opinion. But these later theorists thought the facts of power and obedience sufficed to describe the people as sovereign despite their indeterminate nature. For example, Pollock, commenting on the English government's inability to alter the ancient customs of India, claims therefore that England is "not really sovereign: it is not the ultimate political superior to whose command everything is to be referred. Where then is the true sovereignty and fountain of law? It must be in the organized government of the conquering people taken jointly with unorganized general opinions of the subject people. But this indefinite element makes the total combination too indeterminate to fulfill the conditions of true political supremacy required by Bentham's school." Hence, Pollock quite deliberately rejected the English theory of law, sovereignty, and the state in favor of the Germanic perspective. See his "Law and Command," *Law Magazine and Review* n.s. 1 (Feb. 1872), 196. William Hearn, however, did not come to his conclusion about the sovereignty of the people by way of recognizing the force and power of public opinion. He was willing to deny customs legal status until judicially enforced. His peculiar problem with Austin's theory of sovereignty was its dualist character. The sovereign was conceived as something above the community. This was incompatible with Hearn's organic understanding of society derived again from German sources. Consequently, to reflect the organic unity of society, the state had to be the sovereign. But who was

the state? In the end, Hearn concluded "that the power of every government is simply the power of the people itself, and the State means nothing more than the organized community." See his *The Theory of Legal Duties and Rights*, 2 vols. (London: Trubner and Co., 1883), I, p. 17, and generally chap. 2.

70. Bryce explicitly criticized Bentham's and Austin's theory of sovereignty on the ground that their factual criteria of sovereignty were inapplicable to most primitive and modern states having constitutional laws that limit and divide the sovereign. But no doubt Bryce's approach, with its emphasis on the legal sovereign as the lawyer's sole concern, also has its difficulties. According to Bryce, if Austin's and Bentham's theory of sovereignty "means that every Sovereign *de facto* is also sovereign *de iure*, or the converse, it is untrue . . . Bentham and Austin have not this reason, for they are in the sphere of law, and law is not concerned with obedience as a fact. The right of the sovereign to be obeyed does not rest on Force, for he [the lawyer] assumes that whenever law exists it will make itself prevail." See James Bryce, *Studies in History and Jurisprudence*, (New York: Oxford University Press, 1901), pp. 540–541. See also chap. 10. The fictions and dogmatism found in this early quote are clues to the problems of our own contemporary understanding of the nature of a legal system.

71. Dicey, *Lectures Introductory to the Study of the Law of the Constitution*, pp. 64–70.

72. James F. Stephen, "Sovereignty," in *Horae Sabbaticae*, 3 vols. (London: MacMillan, 1892), II, 63: "sovereignty is a question of fact. He is the sovereign who actually is supreme, and by whose consent the laws are actually enforced, not he whom some one or other, at some time or other, has agreed to consider supreme."

73. John Salmond, *Jurisprudence or the Theory of the Law*, 2nd ed. (London: Steven and Haynes, 1907), p. 105.

74. Ibid., p. 106.

75. Ibid., p. 107.

76. Ibid.

77. Ibid., Appendix II, p. 480.

78. Bentham also thought rewards could be used by the sovereign to influence conduct. But the term obligation was reserved for the more efficacious sanction of punishment. See his *The Principles of Morals and Legislation* (Darien: Hafner, 1970), chap. 3. For Austin's ideas, see *Province*, pp. 14–17.

79. Austin's language is quite specific: "The truth is, that the magnitude of the eventual evil, and the magnitude of the chance of incurring it, are foreign to the matter in question . . . But where there is the smallest chance of incurring the smallest evil, the expression of a

wish amounts to a command, and, therefore, imposes a duty." (*Province*, p. 16.)

80. Holmes, "Review of Pollock's 'Law and Command'," p. 790.
81. Ibid.
82. Ibid.
83. Holmes, "Review of Pollock's 'Law and Command'," p. 791.
84. Holmes, *Collected Legal Papers*, p. 175; "The Path of the Law," p. 462.
85. *Holmes-Pollock Letters*, ed. M. D. Howe, 2 vols. (Cambridge: Harvard University Press, 1941), I, 233. Also see I, 3, 4–5, 21, 79–80, 119–120, 177; II, 55, 200–202, 233–235.
86. Holmes, *Collected Legal Papers*, p. 176; "The Path of the Law," p. 462.
87. Holmes, *Collected Legal Papers*, p. 173; "The Path of the Law," p. 461. For Holmes's insistence upon the need to purge all moral ideas from the law, see also pp. 168–179.
88. Holmes, *Collected Legal Papers*, p. 174; "The Path of the Law," p. 461.
89. In the early editions of their works, these two utilitarian jurists followed the Austinian line closely. Both of them insisted that legal validity flowed from the sovereign and that an obligatory law required a sanction. Markby, *Elements of Law*, pp. 19–20, 50. Also see chap. 2 where Markby reduced the different sources of law to the direct or indirect commands of the sovereign. For Holland's opinion, see *Elements of Jurisprudence*, p. 45: "The sole source of laws, in the sense of that which impresses upon them their legal character is their recognition by the state." For the necessity of a sanction, see p. 66: "when the state will compel B . . . we may . . . [say] that B is under a legal duty." But Austin's theory of legal obligation was under attack; and the criticisms eventually led the later utilitarians to weaken their endorsement of Austin's theory. Students of Maine thought it especially ridiculous to derive the validity of customs from the sovereign. F. Pollock, E. C. Clark, and James Bryce disputed this contention, arguing forcefully that the validity of custom was derived (as the German jurists had taught them) from the assent of the people, not from the assent of the sovereign. See Pollock, "Law and Command," pp. 196–199; E. C. Clark, *Practical Jurisprudence* (Cambridge: Cambridge University Press, 1883), pp. 165–168; and Bryce's Icelandic example of customary laws existing apart from a sovereign in *Studies in History and Jurisprudence*, pp. 671–674.
90. William Markby, *Elements of Law*, 6th ed. (Oxford: Clarendon Press, 1905), pp. 13–21.
91. Salmond, *Jurisprudence*, p. 125.
92. Ibid., p. 181.
93. Hans Kelsen, *General Theory of Law and State* (Cambridge: Harvard University Press, 1945); H. L. A. Hart, *The Concept of Law* (Oxford: Clarendon Press, 1961); J. Raz, *The Concept of a Legal System* (Oxford:

Clarendon Press, 1970). There might be some opposition to lumping Kelsen with Hart and Raz because he always emphasized the coercive element in law. Yet this is not to the point. It is correct that Kelsen understood law as the "primary norm which stipulates the sanction." The question is whether he required a sanction for the breach of every law. Here the answer is negative. Kelsen considered law as the set of orders to officials to apply sanctions. But an official could violate his legal duty by failing to apply the sanction, even if his act was not punished with a corresponding sanction. All legal duties were not enforced by sanctions. See chaps. 1–4.

94. Hart, *Concept of Law,* p. 113.

4. JUDICIAL IDENTIFICATION, INTERPRETATION, AND LEGISLATION

1. William Blackstone, *Commentaries on the Laws of England,* ed. W. D. Lewis, 2 vols. (Philadelphia: George T. Bisel, 1922), I, 38. For the sovereignty of Parliament, see p. 43. Blackstone adhered generally to the Lockian conception of the British Constitution. See Locke's *Second Treatise of Government* (New York: Mentor, 1965), chaps. 9, 12.
2. Blackstone, *Commentaries,* I, 80.
3. Ibid., p. 58.
4. Ibid., pp. 58–59.
5. For discussions of this "mouthpiece" or "slot-machine theory" of constitutional adjudication, see A. H. Kelly and W. A. Harbison, *The American Constitution: Its Origins and Development* (New York: W. W. Norton, 1948), chaps. 19–20, esp. pp. 537–542; William F. Swindler, *The Court and Constitution in the Twentieth Century: The Old Legality, 1889–1932* (New York: Bobbs-Merril, 1969), chaps. 1–4; Arnold M. Paul, *Conservative Crisis and the Rule of Law: Attitudes of Bench and Bar, 1887–1895* (Ithaca: Cornell University Press, 1960), chaps. 1–5; G. Edward White, *The American Judicial Tradition* (New York: Oxford University Press, 1976), chap. 4.
6. For a discussion of C. C. Langdell's conception of law, see Grant Gilmore, *Ages of American Law* (New Haven: Yale University Press, 1977), chap. 3; Lawrence M. Friedmann, *A History of American Law* (New York: Simon and Schuster, 1973), pp. 530–536; M. D. Howe, *Justice O. W. Holmes: The Proving Years* (Cambridge: Harvard University Press, 1963), pp. 155–159; 250–252.
7. Holmes's review of C. C. Langdell, *A Selection of Cases on the Law of Contracts,* 2nd ed., in *American Law Review* 14 (March 1880), 234 (hereafter cited as "Review of Langdell's *Contracts*"). See also *Holmes-Pollock Letters,* ed. M. D. Howe, 2 vols. (Cambridge: Harvard University Press, 1941), I, 17.

8. Blackstone, *Commentaries,* I, pp. 49–53.
9. Holmes, "Review of Langdell's *Contracts,*" pp. 233–234.
10. Holmes, "Common Carriers and the Common Law," *American Law Review* 13 (July 1879), 631; *The Common Law* (Cambridge: Belknap Press of Harvard University Press, 1963), p. 32.
11. John Austin, *Province of Jurisprudence Determined* (New York: Noonday Press, 1954), p. 235. For Holmes's opinion, see Springer v. Philippine I., 277 U.S. 189, 211 (1928).
12. Austin, *Lectures on Jurisprudence,* ed. R. Campbell, 4th ed., 2 vols. (London: John Murray, 1873), II, 652.
13. Southern Pacific Co. v. Jensen, 244 U.S. 205, 221 (1917).
14. *Holmes-Laski Letters,* ed. M. D. Howe, 2 vols. (Cambridge: Harvard University Press, 1953), I, 249.
15. Truax v. Corrigan, 257 U.S. 312, 344 (1921).
16. Lochner v. New York, 198 U.S. 45, 76 (1905).
17. Holmes, *The Common Law,* p. 168.
18. Austin, *Lectures,* II, 1023–1024.
19. Ibid., p. 645.
20. Ibid.
21. Holmes, *Collected Legal Papers* (New York: Peter Smith, 1952), pp. 207–208; "The Theory of Legal Interpretation," *Harvard Law Review* 12 (Jan. 1899), 419–420.
22. Johnson v. U.S., 163 U.S. 30, 32 (1908). See also Northern Securities Co. v. U.S., 193 U.S. 197, 400 (1904).
23. Austin, *Lectures,* II, 649.
24. Holmes, *Collected Legal Papers,* p. 239; "Law in Science and Science in Law," *Harvard Law Review* 12 (Feb. 1899), 460. See also *Holmes: His Book Notices and Uncollected Letters and Papers,* ed. H. Shriver (New York: Central Book, 1936), pp. 34–35.
25. Austin, *Lectures,* II, 651.
26. Ibid., p. 642.
27. Ibid., p. 647.
28. Ibid., p. 646.
29. Ibid., p. 647.
30. However, Austin did believe it possible to establish a precedent inductively from one case, just as in physical science the validity of a conclusion can rest upon a single experiment. But this type of induction was unusual; the normal kind would consist of an induction of a principle from a number of cases. See ibid., pp. 678–679.
31. Ibid., II, 643.
32. Holmes, "Codes, and Arrangement of the Law," *Harvard Law Review* 44 (March 1931), 725; reprinted from *American Law Review* 5 (1870).
33. Ibid.
34. Holmes's review of *A Digest of the Decisions of the Federal Courts,* by F. Brightly, in *American Law Review,* 5 (April 1871), 539.

35. Holmes, *Collected Legal Papers*, p. 42; from a speech before the Harvard Law School Association, November 5, 1886, on the 250th anniversary of Harvard University.
36. Holmes, "Codes, and the Arrangement of the Law," p. 725.
37. Jeremy Bentham, *Comment on the Commentaries* (Oxford: Clarendon Press, 1928), p. 213.
38. Austin, *Lectures*, II, 537.
39. Ibid., I, 36–37; II, 547–549, 637.
40. Ibid., II, 655.
41. Bentham, *Comment on the Commentaries*, p. 187. Holdsworth informs us that Bentham was mistaken about the liability of reporters to punishment. See *A History of English Law*, 17 vols. (London: Methuen and Co., 1903–1972), XIII, 80, n3.
42. Bentham, *Works*, ed. Bowring, 11 vols. (Edinburgh: William Tait, 1843), V, 235.
43. Bentham, *The Principles of Morals and Legislation* (Darien: Hafner, 1970), pp. 172–173.
44. Austin, *Lectures*, II, 673–674. Holmes agreed with the *ex post facto* characterization; see Kuhn v. Fairmont Coal Co., 215 U.S. 349, 370–372 (1910).
45. Austin, *Province*, p. 191.
46. Austin, *Lectures*, II, 702.
47. Bentham, *Works*, IX, 504–508.
48. Austin, *Lectures*, II, 697.
49. Ibid., p. 650. For the description of it as "spurious" and as a "bastard" type of interpretation, see pp. 597–598.
50. Ibid., p. 1025.
51. Ibid., p. 1026.
52. Ibid., p. 1025; see generally lectures XXXVIII, XXXIX.
53. Ibid., p. 599.
54. Ibid., pp. 547–548.
55. Holmes, "Review of Langdell's *Contracts*," p. 234.
56. Holmes, *Collected Legal Papers*, p. 137; "Privilege, Malice, and Intent," *Harvard Law Review* 8 (April 1894), 14.
57. Holmes, *Collected Legal Papers*, pp. 129–130; "Privilege, Malice, and Intent," p. 9.
58. Holmes, *Collected Legal Papers*, p. 181; "The Path of the Law," *Harvard Law Review* 10 (March 1897), 466.
59. Holmes, *Collected Legal Papers*, p. 184; "The Path of the Law," p. 467.
60. Holmes, *The Common Law*, pp. 31–32. See also *Collected Legal Papers*, p. 181; "The Path of the Law," pp. 465–466.
61. Holmes, *Collected Legal Papers*, p. 195; "The Path of the Law," p. 474.
62. Austin, *Lectures*, II, 652.
63. Holmes, *The Common Law*, p. 31.

64. See "Agency" in Holmes, *Collected Legal Papers,* pp. 49–116; *Harvard Law Review* 4, 5 (March 1891; April 1891), pp. 345–364; pp. 1–23.

65. Austin, *Lectures,* II, 668.

66. A. B. Schwarz, "John Austin and the German Jurisprudence of his Time," *Politica* 1 (Aug. 1934), 178–199.

67. Austin, *Lectures,* II, 701–702.

68. Ibid., p. 1065.

69. Holmes, *Collected Legal Papers,* p. 212; "Law in Science and Science in Law," *Harvard Law Review* 12 (Feb. 1899), 444.

70. Holmes, *Collected Legal Papers,* p. 225; "Law in Science and Science in Law," p. 452. See also *The Common Law,* pp. 32–33.

71. Holmes, *Collected Legal Papers,* p. 225; "Law in Science and Science in Law," p. 455. See also *Collected Legal Papers,* pp. 186–187.

72. Holmes, *Collected Legal Papers,* p. 225; "Law in Science and Science in Law," p. 452. See also *Collected Legal Papers,* pp. 225–229.

73. Holmes, *Collected Legal Papers,* p. 139; from a speech entitled "Law and Learning" given at a dinner in honor of C. C. Langdell, June 25, 1895. See also *Collected Legal Papers,* p. 211.

74. Holmes, *Collected Legal Papers,* p. 126; "Privilege, Malice, and Intent," *Harvard Law Review* 8 (April 1894), 7.

75. Holmes, *The Common Law,* p. 168. See also *Occasional Speeches,* ed. M. D. Howe (Cambridge: Harvard University Press, 1962), p. 156.

76. Holmes's skepticism also contributed to his position of judicial deference: "However I am so sceptical as to our knowledge about the goodness or badness of laws that I have no practical criterion except what the crowd wants. Personally I bet that the crowd if it knew more wouldn't want what it does—but that is immaterial." *Holmes-Pollock Letters,* I, 163.

77. Austin, *Lectures,* II, 1065.

78. Ibid., p. 666.

79. Holmes, *Collected Legal Papers,* p. 126; "Privilege, Malice, and Intent," p. 7.

80. Holmes, *Collected Legal Papers,* p. 129.

81. Lochner v. N.Y., 198 U.S. 45, 76 (1905). *Holmes-Laski Letters,* I, 243: "no case can be settled by general propositions . . . I will admit any general proposition you like and decide the case either way." See also Holmes, *Collected Legal Papers,* p. 184; "The Path of the Law," pp. 467–468.

82. Missouri, Kansas & Texas Ry. v. May, 194 U.S. 267, 269 (1903). See also *Holmes-Pollock Letters,* I, 216; II, 28.

83. Holmes, *The Common Law,* p. 101.

84. Holmes, *Collected Legal Papers,* p. 120; "Privilege, Malice, and Intent," p. 3.

85. Holmes, "Theory of Torts," *Harvard Law Review* 44 (March 1931),

775; reprinted from *American Law Review* 7 (1873). Also see Holmes, *The Common Law,* p. 101.

86. Holmes, *The Common Law,* p. 101.
87. International Harvester Co. v. Kentucky, 234 U.S. 216, 224 (1914).
88. Southern Pacific Co. v. Jensen, 244 U.S. 205, 221 (1917).
89. Austin, *Lectures,* II, 654.
90. Ibid., pp. 1031–1036.
91. Ibid., pp. 1039–1040. Also see p. 1031.
92. Austin, of course, thought that the difference between a close and a remote analogy was only one of degree. See Austin, *Province,* pp. 118–119.
93. Holmes, "Review of Langdell's *Contracts,*" p. 234. Also see *The Common Law,* p. 5.
94. Holmes, *Justice O. W. Holmes: His Book Notices,* p. 188; letter to Dr. Wu, August 26, 1926.
95. Haddock v. Haddock, 201 U.S. 562, 631–632 (1905).
96. Austin, *Lectures,* II, 1065.
97. Ibid., p. 1042.
98. Holmes, *The Common Law,* p. 32.

5. REALITY, IDEAS, AND LANGUAGE

1. Jeremy Bentham, *A Fragment on Government* (Oxford: Oxford University Press, 1951), chap. 5, par. VI, n. 7.
2. Ibid., n. 6.
3. Bentham, *Works,* ed. J. Bowring, 11 vols. (Edinburgh: William Tait, 1843), VIII, 246–247.
4. Ibid., p. 247. Another archetypal image for the term obligation was that of a man bound with cord. See *Works,* VIII, p. 126, note.
5. See C. K. Ogden's Introduction to his *Bentham's Theory of Fictions* (London: Keegan Paul, Trench, Trubner, 1932); H. L. A. Hart's "Bentham," in *Jeremy Bentham,* ed. B. Parekh (London: Frank Cass, 1974).
6. Bentham, *Works,* VIII, 323. Also see pp. 186–187, 227–228, 230, 242, 188.
7. Ibid., p. 126, note.
8. Bentham was aware that we experience only our perceptions and that the class of real entities, strictly speaking, included only our ideas and impressions. We did not experience rocks and trees, but inferred their existence from our perceptions of them. But nonetheless Bentham thought it paradoxical to call the permanent objects of the world "inferential objects," while labeling our momentary impressions perceptible ones. Therefore Bentham deferred to ordinary language and thought and reserved the term "inferential" only for God, soul, and matter.

9. See Bentham, *Works,* VIII, 195–196.
10. See George Berkeley, *The Principles of Human Knowledge* (New York: Liberal Arts, 1957); Hume, *Treatise on Human Nature,* ed. L. A. Selby-Bigge (Oxford: Clarendon Press, 1928), I, 1.7.
11. Bentham, *Works,* VIII, p. 198.
12. For Tooke's influence on the utilitarians, see Hans Aarsleff, *The Study of Language in England* (Princeton: Princeton University Press, 1967), pp. 73, 92, 95, 96; Elie Halevy, *The Growth of Philosophic Radicalism* (New York: Augustus M. Kelley, 1949), pp. 434, 445–448; Leslie Stephen, *The English Utilitarians,* 3 vols. (New York: Peter Smith, 1950), I, 137–142. For Bentham's appreciative citations of Tooke, see his *Works,* VIII, 185, 188. James Mill also had kind words for Tooke. See his *Analysis of the Phenomena of the Human Mind,* 2 vols. (New York: Augustus M. Kelley, 1967), I, 201.
13. Tooke, *Diversions of Purley,* 2nd ed., 2 vols. (London: J. Johnson, 1798; rpt., Roanoke: The Scholar Press, 1968), I, 27.
14. Ibid., p. 29.
15. Ibid., II, 17.
16. Ibid., I, 341–347; 320–323; 334–338.
17. Ibid., II, 7–9.
18. Ibid., 8, 14.
19. Bentham, *Works,* VIII, 187.
20. Ibid., p. 126, note. Also see pp. 187, 327ff. We must take special care to distinguish Bentham's linguistic fictions from legal (or political) fictions and from fallacies generally. Fallacies were fallacious arguments, and legal and political fictions were more or less deliberate misrepresentations of fact. All of these were avoidable and were accordingly condemned by Bentham. (See Bentham's *Handbook of Political Fallacies.*) On the other hand, linguistic fictions were the inevitable and indispensable abbreviations of language that facilitated the communication of ideas. For Bentham's distinctions of these matters, see *Works,* VIII, 199.
21. Ibid.
22. Ibid., p. 246.
23. Ibid.
24. Ibid., p. 329.
25. Ibid., p. 94, note.
26. John Austin, *Province of Jurisprudence Determined* (New York: Noonday Press, 1954), p. 18. For the connection of "superiority" with these other three terms, see p. 25.
27. Ibid., p. 18.
28. Bentham, *Works,* VIII, 247. For the family characteristics of this group of fictitious entities, see p. 206.
29. Austin, *Province,* p. 16.
30. Ibid., p. 43.

31. Austin, *Lectures on Jurisprudence,* ed. R. Campbell, 4th ed. 2 vols. (London: John Murray, 1873), I, 424.
32. Bentham, *Works,* VIII, p. 224.
33. Ibid., p. 279.
34. Austin, *Lectures,* I, 441.
35. Bentham, *The Principles of Morals and Legislation* (Darien: Hafner, 1970), pp. 95-96.
36. It is important to remember that the utilitarians assessed the beliefs and expectations of an agent by the objective tendency of the act. Though beliefs are real entities, we cannot peer into the agent's mind to examine them; we can only infer the relevant states of consciousness from the objective circumstances of the act.
37. Though Bentham adopted John Horne Tooke's philosophical method, he rejected his psychological epistemology. Tooke went beyond the conclusions of Hume and Berkeley. Not only abstract ideas were denied existence, but complex ideas were rejected as fictions. Just as it was improper to call a constellation a complex star, Tooke reasoned that it was misleading to describe a set of sensations or their traces (simple ideas) as a complex idea; see his *Diversions of Purley,* I, 37. Bentham, on the other hand, thought it absurd to deny abstract ideas since proof of their existence was a matter of simple perception. Bentham advised the nominalists that "if this position of theirs were true, nothing that they say in proof of it would have so much as the least chance of being productive of the effect they aim at." (*Works,* VIII, 123, note.) Arguments consist of general propositions containing names of general ideas. Hence, the nominalist argument was meaningless upon its own admission. But the most convincing proof was simple perception. Each individual "need but ask himself—whether, after, and by thus reading the word *plant,* his mind is not put in a state more or less different from that which it was in, before this word was read by him." Moreover, Bentham argued, any general proposition, like "Plants have a property which minerals have not," carries "three perfectly distinct *ideas,* each of which is of that sort which is termed a *general* or *abstract* one." (Ibid.) In Bentham's opinion, we need only attend to what goes on in our minds to prove the existence of general ideas. General terms were the "names of these real entities." (See also ibid., pp. 121-126; 225; 256-258; 264-270; 326-329.)
38. James Mill, *Analysis of the Phenomena of the Human Mind* (New York: Augustus M. Kelley, 1967), chaps. 3-4.
39. Ibid., chaps. 7, 11.
40. Ibid., I, p. 93.
41. Ibid., I, p. 91.
42. Ibid., p. 265.

43. Ibid. This does not mean that either James Mill or Bentham believed that classes of things exist or that classes of things were real entities. It all depended upon the intention of the speaker. If one used the general term to identify a particular object in the world, then it was a name of a real entity for Bentham, but not for James Mill; if one used it to communicate a general idea in one's mind, then both Bentham and Mill agreed it was a name of a real entity; but if one used it to identify a species or genus that supposedly existed apart from individuals, then the word was the name of a fictitious entity. The class name would designate also individuals of the past and future that obviously did not exist. Hence, when used in this manner, the general term was a name of a fictitious entity. See ibid., chaps. 9–10; Bentham, *Works*, VIII, 123, note.

44. J. S. Mill, *Collected Works of John Stuart Mill*, ed. J. M. Robson; vol. 9: *An Examination of Sir William Hamilton's Philosophy* (Toronto: University of Toronto Press, 1979), p. 305.

45. Ibid., p. 309.

46. Ibid., p. 310.

47. J. S. Mill, *Collected Works of John Stuart Mill*, ed. J. M. Robson; vol 7: *A System of Logic Ratiocinative and Inductive* (Toronto: University of Toronto Press, 1973), pp. 24–25.

48. Hume, *Treatise of Human Nature*, I.1.1 and note. Bentham agreed with Hume's criticism of Locke's vague use of the term "idea" to cover all types of mental phenomena (*Works*, VIII, 320).

49. Hume anticipated all of this. Indeed, much of the development of the utilitarian philosophical method consists of a return to Hume. Since ideas and impressions were of the same kind, differing only in the force and liveliness with which they strike upon the mind, Hume claimed that impressions (since stronger) could play a vital role in clarifying and rejecting vague concepts: "When we entertain, therefore, any suspicion, that a philosophical term is employed without any meaning or idea (as is but too frequent), we need but inquire, *from what impression is that supposed idea derived?* And if it be impossible to assign any, this will serve to confirm our suspicion." See D. Hume, *An Enquiry Concerning Human Understanding* (Indianapolis: Hackett Publishing Co., 1977), p. 13. For a fine analysis of Hume's theory of meaning, see Farhanz Zabeeh's *Hume: Precursor of Modern Empiricism*, 2nd ed. (The Hague: Martinus Nijhoff, 1973), chaps. 1–2. But there is an important difference between Mill and Hume. While Hume thought that an analysis of the impression specified by the word would help to clarify the idea behind the word, Mill directly linked the meanings of words to sensations. Ideas had no essential role in Mill's theory of meaning.

50. J. S. Mill, *A System of Logic*, p. 179, note. For Mill's general theory of meaning, see bk. I, chap. 2.

51. Ibid., p. 65. See generally chap. 3; J. S. Mill, *An Examination of Sir William Hamilton's Philosophy*, chaps. 7–12.

52. See ibid., II, chap. 2, especially section 2.

53. See ibid., chaps. 1, 3.

54. Ibid., I, chap. 5, especially section 4.

55. Ibid., I, chap. 4.

56. Ibid., II, 157.

57. Ibid., I, chap. 4, especially sections 5 and 6.

58. Ibid., II, 117

59. Ibid., p. 181.

60. Ibid., p. 193.

61. Ibid., p. 186.

62. Ibid., p. 195.

63. Ibid., p. 186.

64. Ibid., p. 186. See also pp. 196–199.

65. Ibid., p. 196.

66. Ibid., p. 187.

67. Ibid., p. 200.

68. See Mill's *Autobiography*, chap. 3, and see quote below, p. 228.

69. See James Mill's *Analysis of the Phenomena of the Human Mind* and Brown's *Lectures on the Philosophy of the Human Mind* (Boston: T.H. Carder, 1826). Both were critical of deductive logic.

70. Austin, *Lectures*, II, 1036–1053.

71. Ibid., p. 1047. Sarah Austin has told us that in Austin's class J. S. Mill questioned the value of the syllogism. Austin responded: "It may be gathered . . . that the conclusion of every syllogism lies implicitly in the premises; or that what is asserted by that, is asserted implicitly by these. In the process, therefore, of syllogizing, there is not really an illation or inference." Ibid., p. 1053; for Sarah Austin's claim, see p. 1050, note.

72. Ibid., p. 1048.

73. See chapter 4 above.

74. O. W. Holmes to William James, cited by R. B. Perry, *The Thought and Character of William James*, 2nd ed. (Boston: Little, Brown, and Co., 1948), I, 300; *Holmes-Pollock Letters*, ed. M. D. Howe, 2 vols. (Cambridge: Harvard University Press, 1961), I, 122, 126.

75. Holmes, *Collected Legal Papers* (New York: Peter Smith, 1952), p. 304; "Ideals and Doubts," *Illinois Law Review* 10 (May 1915), 2.

76. *Holmes-Laski Letters*, ed. M. D. Howe, 2 vols. (Cambridge: Harvard University Press, 1953), I, 139, 541, 565, 634.

77. Holmes, *Collected Legal Papers*, p. 311; "Natural Law," *Harvard Law Review* 32 (Nov. 1918), 40. See also *Holmes-Einstein Letters* (London: St. Martin's Press, 1964), p. 49.

78. Holmes, cited by R. B. Perry, *The Thought and Character of William James*, I, 300–301. See also *Holmes-Einstein Letters*, p. 16.

79. Holmes, *Collected Legal Papers*, p. 311; "Natural Law," p. 41. See also *Holmes-Laski Letters*, I, 580; II, 1146; *Holmes-Einstein Letters*, pp. 82, 213.

80. Holmes, *Collected Legal Papers*, p. 199; "The Path of the Law," *Harvard Law Review* 10 (March 1897), 477.

81. Holmes, *Collected Legal Papers*, pp. 304–305; "Ideals and Doubts," p. 2. See also *Collected Legal Papers*, p. 310; *Holmes-Laski Letters*, II, 1124; *Holmes-Einstein Letters*, pp. 16, 51, 82; *Justice O. W. Holmes: His Book Notices and Uncollected Letters and Papers* (New York: Central Book Co., 1936), pp. 165, 187; *Holmes-Pollock Letters*, I, 122, 126.

82. *Holmes-Laski Letters*, II, 955. See also *Justice O. W. Holmes: His Book Notices*, p. 165.

83. *Holmes-Laski Letters*, II, 955.

84. According to Holmes, Malthus especially had smashed many a humbug that still thrived in Holmes's day. See *Holmes-Laski Letters*, I, 122, 165, 272, 385, 431, 658–659, 762; II, 950; *Holmes-Pollock Letters*, I, 219.

85. Holmes criticized William James's "Will-to-believe" because he thought it encouraged us to believe what we want. See *Holmes-Laski Letters*, I, 69–70; *Holmes-Pollock Letters*, I, 78, 139–140, 191–192; *Holmes-Einstein Letters*, pp. 35–36, 52–53.

86. *Holmes-Laski Letters*, I, 210; II, 1124–1125; *Holmes-Pollock Letters*, II, 254.

87. *Justice O. W. Holmes: His Book Notices*, p. 165; a letter to Dr. Wu, June 16, 1923. See also *Holmes-Laski Letters*, I, 634; II, 1071, 1169.

88. *Holmes-Pollock Letters*, II, 22, 252; *Holmes-Laski Letters*, I, 131; II, pp. 1314–1315.

89. J. S. Mill, *A System of Logic*, III, 325. See generally chap. 5.

90. Holmes, *Collected Legal Papers*, p. 180; "The Path of the Law," p. 465. See also *Holmes-Einstein Letters*, p. 4; *Holmes-Laski Letters*, I, 122; *Holmes-Pollock Letters*, II, 252.

91. Holmes, *Collected Legal Papers*, p. 159; "The Bar as a Profession," *The Youth's Companion* 70 (Feb. 20, 1896), 92.

92. J. S. Mill, *A System of Logic*, III, 327.

93. Holmes, *Collected Legal Papers*, p. 37; from a speech before the Harvard Law School Association, November 5, 1886, on the 250th anniversary of Harvard University.

94. *Holmes-Laski Letters*, I, 129. See also pp. 810, 835; Holmes, *Occasional Speeches*, ed. M. D. Howe (Cambridge: Belknap Press of Harvard University Press, 1962), p. 161.

95. *Justice O. W. Holmes: His Book Notices*, p. 141; O. W. Holmes's Introduction to *Rational Basis of Legal Institutions*, ed. John H. Wigmore and Albert Kocourek (New York: MacMillan, 1923). See also *Holmes-Laski Letters*, I, 810.

96. *Holmes-Pollock Letters,* II, 158, 163.

97. *Justice O. W. Holmes: His Book Notices,* p. 140; O. W. Holmes's Introduction to *Rational Basis of Legal Institutions.*

98. Holmes, *Collected Legal Papers,* p. 238; "Law in Science and Science in Law," *Harvard Law Review* 12 (Feb. 1899), 460. See also *Occasional Speeches,* pp. 102–103.

99. Towne v. Eisner, 245 U.S. 418, 425 (1918). For Holmes's opinion of the dangerousness of language, see *Holmes-Laski Letters,* I, 704, 706.

100. *Justice O. W. Holmes: His Book Notices,* p. 164; letter to Dr. Wu, May 14, 1923. See also *Holmes-Laski Letters,* II, 1110.

101. *Holmes-Pollock Letters,* II, 213.

102. Holmes, *Collected Legal Papers,* pp. 293–294; from a speech at a dinner of the Harvard Law School Association of New York on February 15, 1913.

103. Ibid., p. 240; "Law in Science and Science in Law," p. 461.

104. *Holmes-Pollock Letters,* I, 118.

105. Ibid., II, 13.

106. *Justice O. W. Holmes: His Book Notices,* p. 175; letter to Dr. Wu, March 6, 1924.

107. *Holmes-Pollock Letters,* II, 212. Also see p. 200.

108. Holmes, *Collected Legal Papers,* p. 240; "Law in Science and Science in Law," p. 461.

109. Holmes, *Collected Legal Papers,* p. 203; "The Theory of Legal Interpretation," *Harvard Law Review* 12 (Jan. 1899), 417.

110. Bentham, *Principles,* p. 1. The moral-sense school claimed that man has an innate faculty that discerned immorality, while the natural law school insisted that reason could separate right from wrong.

111. *Holmes-Laski Letters,* II, 948. See also I, 8, 762; II, 1183.

112. *Holmes-Einstein Letters,* p. 93. See also *Collected Legal Papers,* p. 306.

113. "But it seems to me clear that the *ultima ratio,* not only *regum,* but of private persons, is force, and that at the bottom of all social feelings, is a justifiable self-preference." See Holmes, *The Common Law* (Cambridge: Belknap Press of Harvard University Press, 1963), p. 38.

114. *Holmes-Laski Letters,* II, p. 1035. See also I, pp. 762, 837.

115. Holmes, *The Common Law,* p. 167.

116. *Holmes-Laski Letters,* I, 21.

117. Holmes, "Codes, and the Arrangement of the Law," *Harvard Law Review* 44 (March 1931), 728; reprinted from *American Law Review* 5 (1870).

118. Southern Pacific Co. v. Jensen, 244 U.S. 205, 222 (1917). See also *Holmes-Laski Letters,* II, 896–897.

119. Holmes, *Collected Legal Papers,* p. 173; "The Path of the Law," p. 461.

120. Holmes always considered judges as the subordinate element of the sovereign power: "There is a tendency to think of judges as if they were independent mouthpieces of the infinite, and not simply directors of a force that comes from the source that gives them their authority. I think our court has fallen into the error at times and it is that that I have aimed at when I have said that the Common Law is not a brooding omnipresence in the sky." (*Holmes-Laski Letters*, II, 822.)

121. Holmes, *The Common Law*, p. 169. Also see p. 92.

122. Ibid., p. 170.

123. O. W. Holmes, A Book Notice, *American Law Review* 7 (1873), 318.

124. Holmes, *Collected Legal Papers*, p. 169; "The Path of the Law," p. 458. See also *Collected Legal Papers*, p. 313; *Holmes-Pollock Letters* II, 64, 200.

125. Holmes, "Review of Pollock's 'Law and Command'," *Harvard Law Review* 44 (March 1931), 788; reprinted from *American Law Review* 6 (1872).

126. Carino v. Insular Government, 212 U.S. 449, 458 (1908). See also *Holmes-Laski Letters*, I, 183.

127. Ibid., p. 115.

128. "It is true that if the will of the majority is unmistakable, and the majority is strong enough to have a clear power to enforce its will, and intends to do so, the courts must yield . . . because the foundation of sovereignty is power,—real or supposed." See O. W. Holmes, A Book Notice, *American Law Review* 6 (1871), 141.

129. Holmes thought no theory could explain every case. See *The Common Law*, p. 63; *Collected Legal Papers*, p. 190; Chapter 2 above.

130. *Holmes-Laski Letters*, I, 806.

131. *Touched With Fire: Civil War Letters and Diary of O. W. Holmes, Jr., 1861–1864*, ed. M. D. Howe (New York: De Capo Press, 1969), p. 28. Also *Holmes-Laski Letters*, I, 469.

132. Holmes, *The Common Law*, p. 45.

133. Holmes, "Trespass and Negligence," *American Law Review* 1 (Jan. 1880), 21. See also *The Common Law*, p. 86.

134. Holmes, *The Common Law*, p. 47.

135. Ibid., p. 49.

136. Ibid.

137. Ibid., p. 90. See also pp. 91–92.

138. Ibid., pp. 73–77.

139. Ibid., p. 119.

140. Ibid., pp. 107–108: "the tendency of the law everywhere is to transcend moral and reach external standards." See also pp. 89–97.

141. Ibid., pp. 123–124. See also pp. 121–122.

142. Ibid., p. 119.

143. But Holmes limited the legislative role of the jury for the same rea-

son that he granted one to it. The jury's role was "a temporary surrender of a judicial function which may be resumed at any moment in any case when the court feels competent to do so. Were this not so," it could "leave all our rights and duties throughout a great part of the law to the necessarily more or less accidental feelings of a jury." (Ibid., pp. 100–101.) Facts are rather stable creatures. Once they are ascertained, they demand respect. Therefore, if a number of jury decisions have established a specific concrete rule that separates dangerous acts from nondangerous acts, the jury's legislative role is over. The judge has only to apply the rule to the case (pp. 119–120).

144. Holmes, *Collected Legal Papers,* p. 42.
145. Mill, *A System of Logic,* II, 190.
146. Holmes, "Codes, and the Arrangement of the Law," p. 725.
147. Holmes, "The Theory of Torts," *Harvard Law Review* 44 (March 1931), 775; reprinted from *American Law Review* 7 (1873).
148. Holmes, *Collected Legal Papers,* p. 181; "The Path of the Law," p. 466.
149. Holmes, *Collected Legal Papers,* p. 184; "The Path of the Law," pp. 467–468.
150. Holmes, *Collected Legal Papers,* pp. 129–130; "Privilege, Malice, and Intent," *Harvard Law Review* 8 (April 1894), 9.
151. Holmes, *The Common Law,* p. 5.
152. *Occasional Speeches,* p. 66; from Holmes's answer to resolutions of the Bar, September 15, 1891.
153. See Chapter 4 above.

6. CONCLUSIONS AND COMMENTARY

1. Grant Gilmore, *Ages of American Law* (New Haven: Yale University Press, 1977), pp. 48–56.
2. Ibid., p. 56.
3. Ibid., p. 66.
4. Ibid., p. 53.
5. See above, Chapter 2.
6. See Morton Horwitz's review of Gilmore's *The Death of Contract* in *University of Chicago Law Review* 42 (Summer 1975), 787–797.
7. Ibid., pp. 790–791.
8. Ibid., pp. 790, 794.
9. See generally, Holmes, *The Common Law* (Cambridge: Belknap Press of Harvard University Press, 1963), chaps. 2–4.
10. Horwitz agrees that the effect of Holme's theory upon capitalists' liability was unintended. See his book review of Gilmore's *Death of Contract,* p. 796.

11. Grant Gilmore, *The Death of Contract* (Columbus: Ohio State University Press, 1974), pp. 16, 17. See also *The Ages of American Law* (Yale University Press), pp. 55–56.
12. Robert Gordon, "Holmes's *Common Law* as Legal and Social Science," *Hofstra Law Review* 10 (Spring 1982), 720.
13. Ibid., p. 727.
14. Ibid., p. 728.
15. Ibid., pp. 729–734.
16. Ibid., pp. 734–736.
17. Ibid., pp. 736–738.
18. Ibid., pp. 738–742.
19. Ibid., p. 742.
20. Ibid., pp. 720–721.
21. G. Edward White, "The Integrity of Holmes' Jurisprudence," *Hofstra Law Review* 10 (Spring 1982), 634.
22. Ibid., p. 635.
23. Saul Touster, "Holmes a Hundred Years Ago: *The Common Law* and Legal Theory," *Hofstra Law Review* 10 (Spring 1982), 696.
24. Ibid., p. 697.
25. Ibid., p. 694, n90.
26. White, "The Integrity of Holmes' Jurisprudence," pp. 649–652.
27. O. W. Holmes, "The Theory of Torts," 44 (March 1931), 775; reprinted from *American Law Review* 7 (July 1873).
28. O. W. Holmes, book review, *American Law Review* 14 (March 1880), 234. Saul Touster has appended this review to his article in *Hofstra Law Review* 10 (Spring 1982), 709–711. Another passage from one of Holmes's early articles is also relevant: "The very considerations which the courts most rarely mention, and always with an apology, are the secret root from which the law draws all the juices of life. We mean, of course, considerations of what is expedient for the community concerned. Every important principle which is developed by litigation is . . . the unconscious result of instinctive preferences and inarticulate convictions, but none the less traceable to public policy in the last analysis." O. W. Holmes, "Common Carriers and the Common Law," *American Law Review* 13 (July 1879), 630–631.
29. O. W. Holmes, "Primitive Notions in the Modern Law: Parts I and II," *American Law Review* 10 (April 1876) and 11 (July 1877). For further evidence of Holmes's early sensitivity to the anomalous survivals found in modern law, see "Misunderstandings of the Civil Law," *American Law Review* 6 (Oct. 1871).
30. O. W. Holmes, "Common Carriers and the Common Law," p. 630.
31. O. W. Holmes, "The Gas-Stokers' Strike," *Harvard Law Review* 44 (March 1931), 796; reprinted from *American Law Review* 7 (April 1873).
32. O. W. Holmes, book review, *American Law Review* 6 (Oct. 1871),

140–141. For a discussion of this event and Holmes's position, see M. D. Howe, *The Proving Years* (Cambridge: Harvard University Press, 1963), pp. 38–42.

33. White, "The Integrity of Holmes' Jurisprudence," p. 664.

34. O. W. Holmes, *Collected Legal Papers* (New York: Peter Smith, 1952), p. 245; from a speech at a dinner in honor of Chief Justice Holmes by the Bar Association of Boston, March 7, 1900.

35. For A. V. Dicey's description of Holmes as "a legal theologian," see his book review of Holmes's *The Common Law* in *The Spectator: Literary Supplement* 55 (June 3, 1882), 745–746.

36. *Holmes-Pollock Letters* (Cambridge: Harvard University Press, 1961), I, 17.

37. M. D. Howe, *The Proving Years,* pp. 250–251.

38. Dicey, book review of *The Common Law,* p. 746.

39. Touster, "Holmes a Hundred Years Ago: *The Common Law* and Legal Theory," p. 703.

40. Ibid.

41. Ibid., p. 692. Also see p. 694, n90 and p. 703.

42. Ibid., p. 693.

43. Ibid., pp. 701–702.

44. Dicey, book review of *The Common Law,* p. 745.

45. I can only suggest to the reader that he page through *The Common Law.* These references and more are there and are not difficult to find.

46. Touster is wrong when he says that Holmes never referred to feelings. The "felt necessities" which in Holmes's opinion were the seeds of every new growth of law were feelings. Moreover, Touster's claim in his article "Holmes a Hundred Years Ago" (p. 702) that Holmes appealed to justice only once—to criticize public accident insurance—is false. For example, in his theory of legal liability, Holmes explicitly refers to justice to explain why liability requires an act: "an act implies a choice, and that it is felt to be impolitic and unjust to make a man answerable for harm, unless he might have chosen otherwise." *The Common Law,* p. 46.

47. Again, I can only refer the reader to the book. To many, the first page—where Holmes insists that "the life of the law has not been logic; it has been experience"—will suffice to prove that Holmes was aware of the extralegal factors that bore upon the law's development and that he did not treat law as a closed system.

48. Holmes, *The Common Law,* p. 173.

49. Touster, "Holmes a Hundred Years Ago: *The Common Law* and Legal Theory," p. 702.

50. Howe, *The Proving Years,* pp. 199–200.

51. O. W. Holmes, "Common Carriers and Common Law," p. 631.

52. O. W. Holmes, *Collected Legal Papers,* p. 181; "The Path of the Law," *Harvard Law Review* 10 (March 1897), 466.
53. Truax v. Corrigan, 257 U.S. 312, 342 (1921).
54. Yosal Rogat, "The Judge as Spectator," *University of Chicago Law Review* 31 (Winter 1964), 213–256.
55. Holmes, *The Common Law,* p. 42.
56. Ibid.
57. H. L. A. Hart, *Punishment and Responsibility* (Oxford: Oxford University Press, 1968), p. 244.
58. See H. L. A. Hart's "Prolegomenon to the Principles of Punishment," in *Punishment and Responsibility,* pp. 1–27.
59. M. H. Fisch, "Justice Holmes and the Predictive Theory of Law," *Journal of Philosophy* 39 (Feb. 1942), pp. 85–97; Phillip Wiener, *Evolution and Founders of Pragmatism* (Cambridge: Harvard University Press, 1949), chap. 8; Morton White, *Social Thought in America: The Revolt Against Formalism* (Boston: Beacon Press, 1970), chap. 5.
60. *Holmes-Laski Letters,* ed. M. D. Howe, 2 vols. (Cambridge: Harvard University Press, 1953), I, 20.
61. Ibid., p. 725.
62. Ibid., p. 575. Also see *Holmes-Pollock Letters,* ed. M. D. Howe, 2 vols. (Cambridge: Harvard University Press, 1941), I, 139.
63. Ibid., I, 565.
64. Ibid., p. 541.
65. M. White, *Social Thought in America,* p. 62.
66. Those who try to prove a pragmatic orientation to Holmes's legal philosophy usually base very strong conclusions upon very diffuse premises. For example, James Millar has argued that at a fundamental level Holmes was a legal pragmatist because he treated all legal rules as necessarily communal (objective), and because he believed that a community's values played an important role in legal development. See James Millar, "Holmes, Peirce, and Legal Pragmatism," *Yale Law Journal* 84 (April 1975), 1123–1140. But clearly the notions that law is communal and that community values affect legal development are hardly new with Holmes. It would be hard to find anyone who doubts these propositions. But does that make us all pragmatists? Similar objections are applicable to Wiener's, White's, and Fisch's pragmatic interpretations of Holmes's legal philosophy. For citations, see above note 62.
67. Those who have followed Gilmore's interpretation of Holmes (discussed above) are the ones who, knowingly or not, object to the orthodox understanding of Holmes as the founder of American legal realism.
68. Very recently, after the bulk of this study was completed, I came across an exception to the rule that American legal philosophers,

and especially legal realists, have treated the utilitarian jurists somewhat disparagingly. Wilfred E. Rumble has uncovered important similarities between the legal philosophy of John Austin and the tenets of American legal realism. Moreover, in a footnote, Rumble speculates that there is a "possibility" that Austin had an "indirect" impact on legal realism through Holmes: W. E. Rumble, "The Legal Positivism of John Austin and the Realist Movement in American Jurisprudence," *Cornell Law Review* 66 (June 1981), 986–1031, especially p. 988, n13. Though I came to my conclusions independently of his article, I now understand my study as a confirmation of Rumble's hypothesis.

69. H. L. A. Hart, *The Concept of Law* (Oxford: Clarendon Press, 1961), p. 113.

70. Ibid., pp. 99–101.

71. Ibid., pp. 27–33.

72. Ibid., p. 33.

73. Ibid., p. 98.

74. See Article 126 of the Constitution of the U.S.S.R.

75. Hart, *The Concept of Law*, p. 112.

76. Herbert Wechsler, *Principles, Politics, and Fundamental Law* (Cambridge: Harvard University Press, 1961), p. 21.

77. Ibid., p. 27.

78. Herbert Wechsler, "The Nature of Judicial Reasoning," in *Law and Philosophy*, ed. S. Hook (New York: New York University Press, 1964), p. 295.

79. Eugene Rostow, *The Sovereign Prerogative—The Supreme Court and the Quest for Law* (New Haven: Yale University Press, 1962); Paul Freund, "Rationality in Judicial Decisions," in *Nomos VIII: Rational Decision*, ed. C. Friedrich (New York: Atherton Press, 1964); Edward H. Levi, *An Introduction to Legal Reasoning* (Chicago: University of Chicago Press, 1949).

80. Ronald Dworkin, *Taking Rights Seriously* (Cambridge: Harvard University Press, 1978); John Hart Ely, *Democracy and Distrust* (Cambridge: Harvard University Press, 1980); Bruce A. Ackerman, *Social Justice in the Liberal State* (Yale University Press, 1980); Michael J. Perry, *The Constitution, The Courts, and Human Rights* (New Haven: Yale University Press, 1982).

81. For a fine discussion of Wechsler's approach, see Kent Greenawalt, "The Enduring Significance of Neutral Principles," *Columbia Law Review* 78 (June 1978), pp. 981–1021.

82. Dworkin, *Taking Rights Seriously*, p. 105.

83. O. W. Holmes, "Codes and the Arrangement of the Law," *Harvard Law Review* 44 (March 1931), 725; reprinted from *American Law Review* 5 (1870).

84. O. W. Holmes's book review of *A Digest of the Decisions of the Federal Courts,* by F. Brightly, in *American Law Review* 5 (April 1871), 539; *Justice O. W. Holmes: His Book Notices,* p. 121.
85. O. W. Holmes, "Codes, and the Arrangement of the Law," p. 725.

PRIMARY SOURCES

In addition to the works listed below, I must mention two secondary sources that were invaluable to me throughout the preparation of this book: Felix Frankfurter's bibliography of Holmes's writings found in *Harvard Law Review* 44 (March 1931), 797–798; and Eleanor N. Little, "The Early Reading of Justice Oliver Wendell Holmes," *Harvard Library Bulletin* 8 (Spring 1954), 163–203.

AUSTIN, JOHN. *Lectures on Jurisprudence.* Edited by R. Campbell. 4th ed. 2 vols. London: John Murray, 1873.
——— *Plea for the Constitution.* 2nd ed. London: John Murray, 1859.
BENTHAM, JEREMY. *Works.* Edited by J. Bowring. 11 vols. Edinburgh: William Tait, 1843.
BRYCE, JAMES. *The Academical Study of the Civil Law.* London: MacMillan, 1871.
——— *Legal Studies in the University of Oxford.* London: MacMillan, 1893.
——— *Studies in History and Jurisprudence.* New York: Oxford University Press, 1901.
CLARK, E. C. *An Analysis of Criminal Liability.* Cambridge: Cambridge University Press, 1880.
——— *Practical Jurisprudence.* Cambridge: University Press, 1883.
DICEY, A. V. *Lectures Introductory to the Study of the Law of the Constitution.* London: MacMillan, 1885.
——— *Lectures on the Relation Between Law and Public Opinion in England.* London: MacMillan, 1905.
GRAY, JOHN CHIPMAN. *The Nature and Sources of Law.* New York: Columbia University Press, 1909; Boston: Beacon Press, 1963.
——— "Some Definitions and Questions on Jurisprudence." *Harvard Law Review* 6 (April 1892), 21–35.

HARRISON, FREDERIC. *On Jurisprudence and the Conflict of Laws.* Oxford: Clarendon Press, 1919.

HASTIE, WILLIAM, ed. *Outlines of the Science of Jurisprudence.* Edinburgh: T. and T. Clark, 1887.

HEARN, WILLIAM E. *The Theory of Legal Duties and Rights.* London: Trubner, 1883.

HERON, D. CAULFIELD. *An Introduction to the History of Jurisprudence.* London: John W. Parker and Son, 1860.

HOLLAND, SIR THOMAS E. *Elements of Jurisprudence.* 2nd ed. Oxford: Clarendon Press, 1882.

———— *Essays Upon the Form of Law.* London: Butterworth, 1870.

JAMESON, JOHN A. "National Sovereignty." *Political Science Quarterly* 5 (June 1890), 193–213.

LIGHTWOOD, JOHN M. *The Nature of Positive Law.* London: MacMillan, 1883.

LORIMER, JAMES. *The Institutes of Law.* 2nd ed. London: William Blackwood and Sons, 1880.

MAINE, SIR HENRY. *Ancient Law: Its Connection with the Early History of Society and its Relation to Modern Ideas.* London: J. Murray, 1885; Gloucester: Peter Smith, 1970.

———— "The Conception of Sovereignty, and its Importance in International Law." *Papers Read Before the Juridical Society of London* 1 (April 1855), 26–45.

———— *Lectures on the Early History of Institutions.* London: J. Murray, 1875; 7th ed. Port Washington: Kennikat Press, 1966.

———— *Popular Government.* 3rd ed. London: John Murray, 1886.

———— *Village Communities in the East and West.* New York: Holt, 1880.

MARKBY, SIR WILLIAM. *Elements of Law.* Oxford: University Press, 1871.

MILL, JAMES. *Analysis of the Phenomena of the Human Mind.* London: Longmans, Green, Reader, and Dyer, 1869; 2nd ed. New York: Augustus M. Kelley, 1967.

———— *Essays on Government, Jurisprudence, etc.* London: Encyclopedia Britannica, 1816–1823; New York: Augustus M. Kelley, 1967.

———— *A Fragment on Mackintosh.* London: Longmans, Green, Reader, and Dyer, 1870.

MILL, JOHN S. *Collected Works of John Stuart Mill.* Edited by J. M. Robson. 19 vols. Toronto: University of Toronto Press, 1963–1979.

PHILLIMORE, JOHN G. *Introduction to the Study of Roman Law.* London: William Benning, 1848.

———— *Letter to the Lord Chancellor.* London: James Ridgway, 1846.

———— *Principles and Maxims of Jurisprudence.* London: John W. Parker and Son, 1856.

POLLOCK, SIR FREDERIC. *Essays in Jurisprudence and Ethics.* London: MacMillan, 1882.

———— *Essays in the Law.* London: Macmillan, 1922.

———— *A First Book of Jurisprudence.* London: MacMillan, 1923.

———— *An Introduction to the History of the Science of Politics.* Rev. ed. London: MacMillan, 1920.

———— "Law and Command." *Law Magazine and Review.* n.s. 1 (February 1872), 189–205.

RAM, JAMES. *The Science of Legal Judgment.* New York: Baker, Voorhis, 1871.

REDDIE, JAMES. *Inquiries in the Science of Law.* 2nd ed. London: Stevens and Norton, 1847.

RICHMAN, IRVING B. "Law and Political Fact in the United States." *Atlantic Monthly* 64 (August 1889), 205–219.

RITCHIE, DAVID G. "On the Conception of Sovereignty." *Annals of the American Academy of Political and Social Science* 1 (January 1891), 385–411.

ROMILLY, SIR SAMUEL. "Review of Bentham's Papers Relative to Codification." *Edinburgh Review* 29 (November 1817), 217–237.

SALMOND, JOHN. *Jurisprudence on the Theory of the Law.* 2nd ed. London: Steven and Haynes, 1907.

SAVIGNY, FRIEDRICH KARL VON. *The History of the Roman Law During the Middle Ages.* Translated by E. Cathcart. Edinburgh: A. Black, 1829.

————*Jural Relations.* Translated by W. H. Rattimore. London: Wildy and Sons, 1884.

———— *Of the Vocation of Our Age for Legislation and Jurisprudence.* Translated by Abraham Haymand. London: Littlewood and Co., 1831.

———— *Treatise on Possession.* 6th ed. Translated by Sir Erskine Perry. London: S. Sweet, 1848.

STEPHEN, JAMES F. "English Jurisprudence." *Edinburgh Review* 114 (October 1861), 456–486.

———— *Essays by a Barrister.* London: Smith, Elder, 1862.

———— *A General View of the Criminal Law.* London: MacMillan, 1863.

———— *History of the Criminal Law of England.* 3 vols. London: MacMillan, 1883.

———— *Horae Sabbaticae.* 3 vols. London: MacMillan, 1892.

———— *Liberty, Equality, Fraternity.* London: Smith, Elder, 1873; Cambridge: Cambridge University Press, 1967.

STEPHEN, LESLIE. *The English Utilitarians.* 3 vols. London: Duckworth, 1900; New York: Peter Smith, 1950.

THIBAUT, A. F. J. *An Introduction to the Study of Jurisprudence.* Translated by N. Lindley. Philadelphia: T. and J. W. Johnson, 1855.

TOOKE, JOHN HORNE. *Diversions of Purley.* 2nd ed. London: J. Johnson, 1798; rpt., Roanoke: The Scholar Press, 1968.

INDEX

Absolutism, *see* Legal absolutism
Association of ideas, 13, 127–128
Austin, John, 2, 4, 5, 7; rights and universal jurisprudence, 8–9; nature of morality, 13; separation of law from morality, 15; unity of civil and criminal liability, 23–24, 39–40; unity of law and equity, 24–25; procedural structure of the common law, 25; external and general standard of liability, 29, 30, 31–39, 113–115, 162–163; negligence, 31–39; ignorance of law, 36–39, 40; role of knowledge in liability, 41–42; strict liability, 44–45; theory of liability different from Holmes's, 45–47; theory of law and obligation, 49–56, 69–70, 112–113; sovereignty, absolutism, and indivisibility, 50–56, 112; critique of democracy, 61–65; judicial deference, 80–83, 96–97; statutory interpretation, 82–83; precedent, 84–88; judicial legislation, 88–92, 94, 96, 99–105, 124–126; role of history, 94–95; legal development, 101–102; philosophical method, 106, 112–116; influence on American thought, 164–165

Bentham, Jeremy, 4, 7; science in law, 12; nature of morality, 13, 132; separation of law and morality, 15; unity of criminal and civil liability, 23–24, 39–40; unity of law and equity, 24–25; procedural structure of common law, 25; external and general standard of liability, 29–31, 32, 38, 40, 113–115, 162–163; role of knowledge in liability, 40–42; strict liability, 44, 45; theory of liability different from Holmes's, 45–47; sovereignty, absolutism, and indivisibility, 52–54; law and obligation, 69–70, 112–113; judicial legislation,

88–90; role of history, 95; the paraphrastic method, 106–109, 110–111; influence upon American thought, 164–165
Berkeley, George, 108, 118
Blackstone, William, 18, 24, 53, 77–78, 79, 80, 82, 84, 104
Brown, Thomas, 124
Bryce, James, 67

Case method, 157, 158, 159; Holmes's preference for, 160
Clark, E. C., 25, 26
Codification: Holmes's attitude toward, 5–7, 36; Bentham's and Austin's opinions of, 82, 90, 91
Criminal liability, 19–23; Austin and Bentham on, 23–24, 39–40
Custom, 57–59, 66, 67, 72–73, 133

D'Alembert, Jean, 110
Democracy: Maine on, 61–63, 65, 67; Austin on, 61–65
Dicey, A. V., 52, 60, 67, 153, 156, 157, 158, 159
Dworkin, Ronald, 175

Gilmore, Grant, 152–153, 158, 160
Golding, Martin, 3
Gordon, Robert, 152–153
Gray, John Chipman, 4

Hart, H. L. A.: on the utilitarian theory of law and sovereignty, 52–54; theory of legal obligation, 74–75; on Bentham's paraphrastic method, 108; on distributive principles of punishment and Holmes's theory of liability, 162–163; theory of a legal system evaluated, 166–173
Hearn, William E., 66–67
History: Holmes on its role in law, 94, 95–96; Austin on, 94–95; Bentham on, 95

221